My Mosaic

Discovering Each Spiritual Piece—One at a Time

A Spiritual Memoir

DR. WILLIAM E. WARD

ISBN 978-1-64492-977-3 (paperback)
ISBN 978-1-64492-978-0 (digital)

Christian Faith Publishing, Inc.
832 Park Avenue
Meadville, PA 16335
www.christianfaithpublishing.com

Printed in the United States of America

The Mosaic that Shows Us the Face of God

A mosaic consists of thousands of little stones. Some are blue, some are green, some are yellow, some are gold. When we bring our faces close to the mosaic, we can admire the beauty of each stone. But as we step back from it, we can see that all these little stones reveal to us a beautiful picture, telling a story none of these stones can tell by itself.

That is what our life in community is all about. Each of us is like a little stone, but together we reveal the face of God to the world. Nobody can say, "I make God visible." But others who see us together can say, "They make God visible." Community is where humility and glory touch.

—Henri Nouwen, *Bread for the Journey* (New York, Harper Collins Publishers, 1985)

Where do I begin
to tell the story of how great a love can be.
The sweet love story
that is older than the sea.
The simple truth about the love she brings to me.
Where do I start?

—Theme from *Love Story*

Part 1

My Old Testament The Road to the Priesthood

PROLOGUE

In any good memoir, the writer tries to meet the reader where she
is by offering information in a way it is felt—to reflect the writer's
inner values and cares in clever linguistic form or dramatic scene.
—Mary Karr, *The Art of Memoir*

Since I was a young child, I have been significantly involved in and
influenced by formal religion and later, in a broader sense, the entire
spectrum of spirituality. In my early years, the Catholic Church was
my home away from home, including the adoption of priests to act
as my surrogate parents. Until my midtwenties and while initially
living the life of a seminarian, I accepted every edict and proclamation of the church as pure fact. For numerous reasons, many of
which will be explained in the following pages, I began to question
the operational value of the formal church; I started to seek a wider
perspective of my faith and my system of beliefs. By no means was
there a sudden conversion to a new way of thinking. It involved years
of studying the works of theologians, getting immersed into psychological thinking as a therapist, and the reading of dozens and dozens
of books written by spiritual thinkers from all walks of life and faiths.
Finally, I have spent these last years writing this book. Sometimes it
was a painful process, but it was always rewarding as I revised each
page to accurately and clearly express my individual experiences of
what it means to live the spiritual life.

Throughout this spiritual evolution (I love the term "to evolve,"
for it implies it is ongoing), a new concern slowly came to the forefront of my thinking. I was observing my clients, close friends, and
people I did not even know leaving the formal church in droves.

I understood. I did not necessarily disagree with their decision. However, in making this accumulative exit, many entered a spiritual desert. For many, once formal participation in church activities ceased, an interest in spirituality never replaced it.

An analogy could be made between how we experienced the formal educational system and how we practiced our religion. In the first instance, many of us attended school where we learned how to memorize, do term papers, and take tests. What was often missing was the art of learning, the enthusiasm for learning, and the ability to work from an introspective posture where we searched for our gifts and abilities. A similar outcome occurred from many who went to church on a weekly basis, received the sacraments, and attended catechism classes. Our participation leaned toward a passive acceptance of all that was taught and preached. We allowed the church to tell us what was important, never considering our own point of view. What was missing was the internal experience of what it meant to be a Christian. In the first case, we did not learn the true art of learning, and in the second case we never learned the skill of becoming more spiritual.

My concern, therefore, for those who have left the church, and even those still actively participating, is that once they made the decision to leave, they also made the decision, at least indirectly, to turn away from the spiritual life. In other words, based on my conversations with so many people, they threw the baby out with the dirty bath water. My second concern, in this case more of a trepidation, is what did and what will happen to the children of these adults growing up in a spiritual vacuum.

The spiritual life, my own and that of others, has grown to be my top priority and the foundation of everything I do. I enjoy the incredible and remarkable rewards of being a psychologist, but as you will read later in this book, even after the therapy experience came to an end, I was left with the question of "what else is there?" when it comes to enhancing the meaning and purpose of our lives. The primary purpose of the book is an attempt to respond to this gap in my life and share with others how I am in the process of fulfilling it.

I chose the genre of memoir realizing it would be a huge challenge. It is perhaps more difficult than writing and contributing with another spiritual book. I wanted to make it personal so that the average person could come into my life and see how certain events and experiences contributed to my spiritual voyage. My personal memoir acts as a voice to express both my intrinsic and extrinsic experiences regarding who I was at one time, what I have become, and what I am in the process of becoming. I want those who pick up this book to see, hear, touch, and even taste these experiences with the hope they will often say "Me too." The book is not just about my feelings and thoughts, but includes the thoughts and feelings of many great thinkers and writers and how they directly affected me.

Hurts, conflicts, and worry drove me to write a memoir. It all involves the state of spirituality in my life, where it is thriving and where it is lacking. Throughout the writing of the book there were ongoing encounters with cognitive dissonance. I never wanted to sound ungrateful for all the formal church did for me, but at the same time I did not want to be deterred by guilt in expressing what I believe to be the truth. I am fully aware that I do not speak at all times with objective authority and I do not want to pretend to be impartial. I write, for the most part, of my subjective experience of spirituality; I hope the readers can identify with this and apply it their lives. My goal is to achieve the definition of a memoir presented by Mary Karr, the author of a number of successful memoirs. She explained, "In any good memoir, the writer tries to meet the reader where she is by offering information in the way it is felt—to reflect the writer's inner values and cares in clever linguistic form or dramatic scene."[1] I am not sure about the term clever, but my goal, most certainly, even while dealing with intrinsic schisms, is to share with the reader new spiritual information and how it felt to experience this innovative material.

There is never the intention to bash the formal church. The intention is to enliven it for those who still remain active and to urge those who have left to recapture their spiritual lives that exist within them. Thomas Moore, the bestselling author of psychological and spiritual books, underscores the importance of taking this spiritual passage. He emphasizes, "The disappearance of religious feeling goes hand in hand with the loss of the soul. Traditional religion may well need an overhaul from top to bottom, but personal religion is a requirement. It is the indispensable foundation of an intelligent, openhearted approach to life."[2] I wrote this memoir knowing full well of this mandate for us all.

PREFACE

The path to our destination is not always a straight one.
We go down the wrong road, we get lost, we turn back.
Maybe it doesn't matter what road we embark on. Maybe
what matters is that we embark.

—Barbara Hall

GRAND ENTRANCES ARE FEW and far between, but once witnessed, they often create a fixed image of opulence and success. The one I was nearing had iron gates attached to brick columns that seemed to announce you are about to enter a place of mystery and lore. As I would experience what I considered a sudden chill, it evoked throughout my body excitement and anticipation parallel with a sense of being overwhelmed and smallness of stature. The long and narrow pathway from the gates acted as birth canal through which I was about to enter a new and exclusive way of life. In this introduction to a novel-like world, I was thrust (without the slap on the fanny) toward a new horizon where anxiety-producing questions had yet to be formulated.

The world I was entering was not my omega point, but more of one step to a life-long aspiration. The final objection was saved for ordination to the priesthood. This first day was somewhat of a nativity. I was getting a second chance—a rebirth—to the belief I could, at last, have a tangible and meaningful place in life. The life I was living up until now, in marked passivity and detachment, was on a stage where I was habitually confused about my role. I was oblivious to life's theme or design. The majority of my thoughts and feelings had yet to find a consistent script, making dialogue with others superficial if not completely disengaged. Walking, and more often than not sloshing, I trekked through an unchartered, darkened maze with left and right turns leading to nowhere. Dead ends were not uncommon. The direction imposed trade-offs between frustration and confusion, anxiety and depression, all snowballing to a sense of being a frozen soul. I was physically present in each activity but only in the sense of getting through, barely surviving each event and each encounter. I became an enigma to others as I took on various and diverse characters with each interaction. Worse, I was becoming an enigma to myself.

A few, very few, verbalized their confusion about my persona. The majority simply linked to one of the many cast of characters I portrayed, silently giving little credence to the others. The choices of which mask to wear were as diverse as they were contradictory. The class clown attending class as if it was a three-ring circus (which much of the time it was); the jock overly obsessed with the need to win (losing led to depression city); the kid endlessly searching for "homes" outside the home (a friend's Italian mother with hugs of love and a home perfumed with red sauce and sausage); the young teenager saying he wanted to be a priest (my only place of comfort and association); and, perhaps most tragically, the empty soul wandering through events and interactions as if I were a ghost. I was a stick in a stream, going along with the flow whether I wanted to or not. Mind, body, and spirit stood in isolation from each other.

Approaching my first day at the seminary, even with its foreboding entrance, I felt I needed to force myself into a new beginning. I was coming from a place that was primarily dark and dismal, empty and hallow. It was a place that played havoc on my inferiority, vulnerability, and search for meaning. I imagined the dawn of a new day where I could initiate the start of being someone. The belief that this day would somehow, someway arrive, gave me the fortitude to get through dark phases of depression, periods of loneliness and separation, and painful beatings and encounters with demeaning people. Most of all, I could end the fear and dread that I would end up a failure. From this point on I would dress in my black cassock and know I was a seminarian studying to be a priest. I could separate myself from the outside world without guilt or discouragement. It would be a place I could call home.

The fifteen mile an hour speed limit mimicked my mental state functioning in slow motion. Speed would have blurred the experience, both externally and intrinsically. It needed to be taken in one frame at a time, slowly tolerating comprehension and absorbing the moment. I was arriving at a Gatsby-like world, like a character wishing, desperately needing, to become part of a higher and more significant calling. As the gray Chrysler (the one I washed with steel pads to the dismay of its owner) was maneuvered across the threshold, I sat rigidly in the back seat with my emotions frozen like sunken glaciers, hidden and petrified from awareness. They were equally balanced with shooting thoughts briefly felt but then involuntarily repressed, a habit perfected by years of practice. It was as if I was on automatic pilot and not responsible for the direction I was taking.

The back-seat ride was a familiar position. It was not a Rosa Park's dilemma, for much of the time the position was one I chose. Yet if I had to conjecture how she might have felt about her experience of the back seat, I believe our feelings would be similar. There were the long rides to Brooklyn to visit my father's sisters squeezed in the back seat between my four siblings. The ride was like a repetitive and tedious movie that we all forced to watch, like it or not. One might call it a family tradition. All the rides were similar. We had tickets to twelve-round bouts between two adults, people I rarely called Mom or Dad. To try to figure out what they were fighting about would have been a futile exercise and one that had no significance anyway. It happened so often it seemed more like an addictive need they were fulfilling. The addiction was filled with hate and anger. They would have severe withdrawal symptoms if they attempted to replace it with anything else.

There was also the back seat of the team bus escorting me to another game. I would sit horrified at the possibility of an embarrassing loss and then dealing with the wrath of my coach. I would be in the back seat of a friend's father's car as he stopped to get a dozen Dunkin Donuts, an entire dozen! I was left to wonder, actually amazed, how rich he must be to make such a purchase. Then there was the proverbial back seat of the classroom, the furthest I could be from the teacher's desk, hoping she would treat me as if I were absent for the day or at least to go unnoticed.

There was one exception and a time I will forever, forever cherish. It was when my fourth grade teacher had me sit all the way upfront and next to the right side of her desk. She somehow understood there was something I needed and knew I lacked emotionally but could not find the words for. Holding my hand, she would sing to me a personal song, giving me a sense of being unique and cared for. "You got the whole world in yours hands; you got the whole world in your hands." Her touch, her smile, her eyes riveted to mine, generated my first love. There was no doubt that I felt special, and it came without having to earn it. She died a few years later at a young age of cancer. I was too young to be there for her, to at least say thank you, which I internally regretted when I heard the news. Even at a young age, I wished I could have held her hand. I lived for that love to repeat, to show its face, to appear once again. I kept my expectations low as I knowingly was aware of a far different reality. For the most part, I kept opting for back seat. Experience commanded this choice. Holding, feeling the touch of another hand, became something just to dream about. Dreaming and fantasizing became a comforting habit as I got older.

The choice I was making to enter the seminary was more based on "freedom from" rather than "freedom to." Isn't that how most people make decisions? The bride who knows the clock is ticking and feels forced to take the first opportunity to walk up the aisle. The young adult in fear there will be no other takers and opts for the first job that is offered. Those who stay with unfulfilling friends as opposed to risking loneliness or, even worse, rejection from someone new. Then there is the multitude of people who opt for their sea of boredom and monotonous beach, while dreading the challenge of seeking new horizons. The seminary became a magnet that pulled me out of a cistern and pledged a relief from loneliness and a life without purpose.

As we approached the iron gates, an eerie silence clouded the two images in the front seat, not from vision but from emotion.

The lack of poignant content confirmed my position of isolation (man, when I get to heaven I hope God will not put me in the back seat.) The stoic two figures, my mother and surrogate father, a priest, lacked the ability to imagine, and more likely cared not to ask what was going through my mind in this ride toward this immeasurable change. It was not so much by choice but more in habit to repress all my vulnerable thoughts. The mood in the car, uninterrupted by any conversation or any musical sound from the radio, cooperated and reinforced the innate act of shutting down. There were no walls between the front and back seat, only a hollow vacuum lacking identification that kept us apart. They had their motives for helping me continue on this crossing and, therefore, never questioned or analyzed the purpose for my personal decision. My resolution to seek the priesthood would always be private. Their encouragement to continue on this path was dissimilar, coming from their own vantage point and need, only common in their foresight. If I made it to ordination, both could claim me as their possession. A son and an adopted son they could forever own without competition from others.

Only moments before, a mile or two from entering a domain like no other, I had broken the silence with a volcanic eruption of tears. I gasped for air as the tears flowed, and a numbing fear had me in its grasp. There was no warning to this wave of discharge. I presume it stunned my estranged passengers as much as it startled me. My high school spiritual advisor, a priest who intently took on the role of my earthly father, confidently pulled the car over and motioned for me to come to the back of the car. Standing next to him with my eyes lowered and fixated on the white-lined rode as if I was seeing it for the first time, I felt an awkwardness that was familiar but lacked words of explanation. I was baffled by the sudden downpour of tears, and the sounds of sobbing seemed to echo off the car, as if I was experiencing them twice. I was at a loss to find labels for any of the emotions pulsating, pounding, through my veins. The habit of repression and denial created a state of ignorance when any emotion, rare as it was, found its way to the surface. My solution to life's chaos and inaccessibility had left me sterile and in a state of emotional illiteracy. Yet I continued to cry. Most of it was visceral, with brief moments of standing outside myself and watching me cry.

The priest seemed calm as if he had taken this road many times before, perhaps with a previously adopted son. I somehow felt safe with him but, vaguely, steely aware there was always a price. I was his only child, where full obedience and compliance in our relationship were expected and therefore, assuming I had no other choice, required. The consequence of parental abandonment was that I was unknowingly left on the adoption block. With seemingly no other options available, I sensed being open to possession was inferred if I was ever to survive. I had no way of knowing how to move forward on my own. Fulfilling his personal needs that were usurped by the vow of celibacy, this particular priest yearned to adopt. There were those who came before me and those, most likely as needy as me, who would be deceived by him into a similar unorthodox relationship. For him any exclusive adoption was temporary. The length of time was dictated by the adoptee's usefulness. Little did I know that my time of acceptance would be shortly coming to an end and be replaced by a more committed and available son. Years later, at his wake I saw my latest replacement. I wondered if this most recent step-brother had a clue.

For now, we were a perfectly formed symbiotic fit. We both needed each other. Standing at the back of the car, partially slumped over and fully shaken, just moments from my commitment to the seminary life, fate and more than a smattering of luck must be considered. Even though I always knew I wanted to be a priest, the path to it was anything but a straight line. So few of my decisions, or more precisely the lack of decision-making, suggested a priestly vocation. The present moment of confusion, enveloped in a perplexity of tears, revealed a signpost of how much fate and luck directed my life. (I would later refer to this as grace.) For the time being, full comprehension and awareness were never part of the equation.

I continued to gawk at the road as if expecting a message written in white chalk that would inform me of my next move. I was left with one choice, which was to trust this priest who had been my safeguard for the past three years. Calmly, seemingly without hesitation, he pronounced, "You don't have to go through with this. You can change your mind and go home."

It was a thought that never occurred to me. The decision to become a priest was made a long time ago. It was formulated at a young age with such assuredness and presumption that it erased all other possibilities that might come up for consideration. This unwavering belief was my anchor in the waters of turmoil and threat. It was as if I bought a ticket on a public ferry that would sail me forward on a current with only one destination. I was a passenger submissively allowing my fate to carry me to this day. So often fueled by loneliness and despair, I was now about to dock at a harbor filled with promises. I was convinced my new family, those who would bring clarity to my life, were living just beyond those iron gates. Turning back was not an option.

Perhaps the vocational goal I was making should not be considered a choice by definition, since a choice presumes there are other options. My destiny, based on a rational I would only discover much later, was that at this time and place I would arrive, without much self-examination, at the next leg of my journey. The seminary, the arena responsible for preparing men for the priesthood, is where I intended to spend the next six years. It would be a respite from a world where I was lost, confused, and felt I did not belong. It would be a relief from the self-imposed sense of being inferior, which eliminated, always at first thought, all other options. It allowed an escape from environments that were for me empty of meaning and purpose. I would join a group filled with ideals of encouragement and support. Higher principles, diverse from the ones I was accustomed to, would be put into action. Leaving a world I often viewed as cruel and demeaning was not a sacrifice, as some tend to define this choice, for it simply held the promise of emancipation. As neither my adopted father nor my mother may have described it, it was my time to unite with a group of men who wanted to make a difference. It was my time to feel real.

My adopted father and I returned to the car, and I returned to my customary position, the back seat. Emotionally exhausted and more than a bit dazed, I was still unsure on how to interpret this last bout of unannounced tears. I did not have to wait for the other passenger to ask for an explanation or, at the very least, to inquire how I was doing. Some sons might expect, even look forward to the question, "Are you okay?" Some may even anticipate the slightest interest in how one was feeling about beginning the first day in the seminary. Or, God forbid, that my mother would assure me that things would be okay. I expected none of the above. Expectation, a foolhardy thought for this relationship, would have only led to more discontent. My father was absent, which was basically the norm for our relationship. My guess is he was unaware that this day had arrived.

My mother sat there motionless as if deleting the last ten minutes from time. I stared at the back of her head and momentarily questioned, as I had done so many times before, who is this woman who spouts attention on and off as if a broken faucet? Unreliable and unpredictable as she was, there was no possibility for cleansing. She was my mother, yet a mysterious riddle that someone concocted in a way that there would be no answer, no solving. As if surgically implanted at birth, she was more often than not a painful thorn in my side, sending intermittent reminders of our affiliation, often packaged with a subtle aching. At eighteen years old, I rarely called her Mother or Mom, for the classification was empty of reference. I wish I could say I had a love-hate relationship with her, for what I felt was worse. She created mental and emotional infections of the worst kind, ones for which, as a child, an antibiotic had no power. When close enough to her to experience her virus, mostly filled with anger and the aspiration to cause physical pain, I always knew my mind and heart would be bedridden for weeks at a time. Recovery from her wrath and physical abuse became a natural family pastime, as I was to find out much later from one of my siblings. The physical wounds healed in due time, while the emotional scars, reopened at whim, were deep enough that no scab had the time to hide its effects. Ignorant of psychology, I was unaware that the choice I was making was dictated not simply by a spiritual calling but in reaction to layers of pain, abuse, and depression. Unwittingly, I was also searching for an identity and for a place to belong. For the time being, the seminary would be an answer to all the agony, or so I thought.

Two people I referred to as mother and father, the first literal and the second by informal adoption, were escorting me past the iron gates to the building I would call home for the next six years, two people who in some deranged way found a purpose in having me as their son. Their common and only interest in me was that I wanted to be a priest. If I left the seminary, my relevance would fade almost immediately to the point of disengagement. Their bond with me was that I was going to be a priest. My bond with them was a ticket to the seminary.

From childhood experiences I was inheriting a distorted view of what relationships were meant to be. Gradually but deliberately they came to be perceived as harmful and painful and most certainly not long lasting. Open to vulnerability and a want for truthful expression became dangerous acts of self-violation. My physical growth in size was matched by the magnitude of barriers I formed between the outside world and myself. The process of socialization made my persona conflicted, a paradox between who I was intrinsically versus the self I revealed to others. If anyone dared to notice, which was few and far between, they saw me as a mystery filled with contradictions. For the majority, however, the blockades I built around myself were interpreted and accepted as my true self while my intrinsic self was either ignored or too unbelievable if ever expressed. Finding my true self would come much later in life when I discovered the importance of intrinsic examination. In my younger years, I was not only ignorant of this dynamic, but I also lived in an environment that never would have allowed it.

The seminary, I so fervently believed, would give me the foundation I so desperately needed to grow and develop, intellectually and spiritually. I could be real for the first time and resolve the contradictions. I could stop the movie, even leave the theater, and connect with a totally different cast of characters. In the seminary, I could rewrite my life and put the past on a shelf hidden in some locked closet. As we passed through the gates and drove along a serene tree-lined path, passing other seminarians out for a walk, each waved and I timidly waved back. The warmhearted hellos from these men seemed to melt away a frozen block of nerves. Thawing, I began to feel welcomed.

1

See, I think there are roads that lead us to each other.
But in my family, there were no roads—just underground
tunnels. I think we all got lost in those underground
tunnels. No, not lost. We just lived there.
—Benjamin Alire Saenz, *Last Night I Sang to the Monster*

Since I was eight years old, I wanted to be a priest. To the non-Catholic, this may seem hard to fathom or, at the very least, something to question. For the person who is Catholic, performed altar boy duties, or was deeply influenced by priests, this consideration was often part of one's childhood religious experience. What might have been different for me was that I never contemplated anything else. I never had the boyhood fascination of being a fireman, driving a huge truck, or being a cowboy. Even as I grew older, becoming a doctor, teacher, or maybe president of some company never competed with the desire and drive to be a priest. I not only wanted to be a priest, I simply believed I would be. For valid reasons, my friends, teachers, coaches, and even my family and relatives would never have believed it, especially based on my unpredictable and certainly non-priestly behavior. So as not to be a walking, talking contradiction, I kept this goal to myself.

Some may believe it was not necessarily healthy to be fixated on just one career choice, but I never heard this said or would have ignored it if it was expressed. I needed to believe I was going to be a priest. In the dismal darkness in which I was living and barely surviving, I was often lost in despair. The only hope was the belief there would be an end to this darkness ignited by the light of the priesthood. Looking back on this time of my life, given my experiences or the lack thereof, and the key people I was influenced by as a youth, it is not such a mystery that this goal remained a burning and singular desire from such a young age. The church became my family early on, filling a gap that was begging to be filled. Overly involved with the main actors in church activities, primarily priests and nuns, was the one place where I felt most accepted. Participating in church rituals gave me an identity and a purpose, something I truly lacked in every other area. It was also the only place where I felt a sense of peace as opposed to the tension and turmoil faced outside its walls. The church acted as a health center to heal mental and emotional wounds. It was a place I could land after a fall. It acted in opposition to the demeaning messages I was receiving and reacting to from the other primary figures in my life. It defied gloom and doom and carried with it the possibility for hope. Outside the church, it was a routine of flip-flops between survival and recovery. The church environment offered a life that seemed worth living. It was always agonizing to leave this conclave and return to its disparaging competitor. I desperately wanted to stop this revolving door—taking me in and pushing me out—and have the church environment be permanent. I did not know it was a long shot. I was riding on a wave solo and blind.

I was raised in a house filled with strangers. My parents, three sisters, and a brother lived dispersed lives with a minimal amount of interaction with each other. I felt no need to reflect on the situation nor considered it odd for us to be living like this as a family. It was all that I knew. There were hints that other families were different, but I chose to give it a mere glimpse of recognition. I did not want to feel more atypical than I already did.

It is hard to grasp that seven people could live together, pass each other in the hallway, at times eat together, sleep under the same roof, come and go to our personal affairs, and still not have a clue about each other. My two older sisters lived on the third floor, working through, I imagine, their own personal conflicts and traumas. Rarely crossing this threshold, the third floor might as well be in another building. My younger sister had her own room, but more often than not she was displaced by my mother who decided sleeping in my father's room was a contradiction to their contemptible and often violent relationship. My younger sister, pushed aside without concern, became an unwilling volunteer left to sleep with her father's snoring and stench of alcohol. My brother and I shared the same room, and it was with him that I had some degree of interaction. It lacked depth not only for the fact we did not know how to swim in deeper waters, but also neither of us wanted to openly recognize the realities of the household we found ourselves in at this young age. For the most part, when we left the bedroom he went his way and I went mine. For all of us, it was a dreadful loss of possibilities.

We were close to each other only in terms of it being the same house, where we spent our days as displaced individuals adrift in our own self-contained bubbles. Fragile and at the mercy of volatile outbursts and vile moods, we lived in a vacuum void of warmth and attention. Not having the ability to analyze or self-reflect, wordless impressions were being formulated in all our developing percep-tions, both of ourselves and others. All our experiences became the deeply-rooted foundations for future anxieties and depressions. We were being molded and fed on a daily diet of conflict and animosity. Through it all, each one of us was on our own. We were left to fend for ourselves, most especially in establishing some sort of direction.

Then there were the beatings. My parents' generation had no problem with physical punishment. It was accepted, and as a group, they pledged allegiance to the dictum do not spare the rod and most definitely do not spoil the child. This order of the day extended itself to teachers, coaches, and anyone who had a position of authority over children. They truly believed that the dispensing of physical punish-ment on young children taught valuable lessons and was effective in turning around any lost or misbehaved child. A sometimes slap on the fanny is one thing, but my mother certainly took it to another level.

When I was about five years old the physical beatings began and lasted until I was about eleven years old. I assumed at the time I was the only one in the family who was the target of my mother's out of control rage and undiagnosed madness. I would learn later that at least my eldest sister received her share of floggings also. There might have been others, but none of them shared this information. I would not have known even if it did occur since, as siblings, we were rarely in the same room together or home at the same time. There was so little in terms of conversation and nothing in terms of sharing personal thoughts or feelings. It never crossed my mind to ask my sisters or brother what they thought after I incurred another physical attack from my mother. In truth, I never talked about them to anyone and accepted it was just another thing I had to deal with. When the beatings did take place, the response was to lick my wounds and move on.

When the actual beatings did take place, there was no reaction from anyone in the family to the sudden and unpredictable eruption of violence or the manner in which it was so viciously delivered. It was as if our house had its own self-contained volcano. We all knew it was active and that it could erupt at any time and without any reasonable cause. It was never a question of will the eruption occur, only when. If any of my sisters or brother were around when the volcano decided to spew her lunacy, or if they heard the desperate screams and shouts that had to echo throughout the house, they were probably too terrified to react and forced into a muted silence. As I underwent each well-aimed strike from a woman crazed within her sadistic world, no one dared to interfere with her mission. We all inherently knew, including myself as her target, that trying to put a lid on an active volcano would be a frivolous activity and might be personally dangerous as well. I had a built-in terror button, and my mother had total control over its use. I sensed this power gave her some kind of satanic pleasure and most certainly a sense of importance, as deranged as this may seem. If she felt unlovable, at least she could be feared. What my mother's intent for us was I cannot imagine. Most likely it was absent of any purpose, other than to use her own children as a way to release her amassed anger that was constantly fermenting toward an explosive rage. Whatever the situation was, the reckless damage my mother had the power of creating would take a lifetime to repair. Maybe two lifetimes.

Many years later, when I was in my fifties, my younger sister, dying with her second bout of cancer, called me at my office. It was unusual for her to call me at my office, and I immediately knew something would be different about this particular call. But even knowing this did not prepare me for what she had to say. It was a brief call since her energy level was extremely low after months of chemotherapy. She said, "I called to apologize for never doing anything when Mom was beating you." I immediately interjected, "Come on. What could you have done? You were only four or five at the time." She continued, "I know, I know, but I would just sit on the floor in my room and close my eyes as you just kept screaming and screaming. I couldn't stand it and felt so horrible I did nothing about it." I again told her there was nothing to apologize for and told her we were all helpless when it came to mother. We said good night and she hung up.

I sat for some time at my desk, wishing I had the words to bring my sister some peace. Her words were a sorrowful hint to what all of us were forced to carry around with us and then transport into adulthood. As I sat there trying to put the phone call in some place of acceptance, my thoughts extended to all my sisters and brother and about the types of horror and guilt all of us are carrying around in the hope we can someday attain some form of peace of mind. The beatings were one thing and they did their damage, but the emotional abuse we all experienced extended far beyond physical pain. Emotionally, we were damaged goods, and it seemed only some sort of divine intervention could begin the healing.

My younger sister died the next day. I wish, with my sister as with any of my siblings, that we could have shared our childhood experiences as they occurred or at least when we got older. For the most part, we kept the traumas to ourselves, perhaps fearing the repercussions of facing them openly. The solution of repression seemed easier and safer. We all followed that same formula: don't think about it, don't talk about it, and most certainly don't analyze the effects. Our past was always the elephant in the room as we tried to make it through the tasks and challenges of our adult lives. We knew the elephant was there and hoped others did not. That was our primary challenge.

All of the angry outbursts and surprise attacks taking place within our household had their origins with my mother. She was physically intimidating in size alone, and a quick glance of her patrolling the house imitated a prison guard wheeling her ever-threatening baton. The only difference being that my mother's choice of a weapon was either a wooden hanger or a thick leather belt. She also liked the closed fist. No slap on the fanny for her. She used all of her weapons as a trained professional, while seemingly enjoying the supremacy she had over her innocent victims. The purpose of her giving birth to five children has no reasonable or lucid explanation, especially her sense of the responsibilities of motherhood. Most likely incapable of introspection, her sense of righteousness expected nothing less than admiration, honor, and obedience.

One of the main dilemmas I had to face was there was no logic to when my mother decided to initiate one of her attacks. With some of my behavior, I just presumed a hanger was on its way. I was most certainly not the perfectly behaved child. I can easily think of several, actually numerous, occasions where I was in the wrong and needed to receive some form of correction. It was during these times where I thought a whipping was seconds away, yet so often there was nothing. Like the time I went up to the attic where all the Halloween candy was kept and I proceeded to drop about ten candy bars out the window with the intention I would retrieve them momentarily and enjoy a feast. Not being an astute thief at seven years old, I did not case the situation enough to realize our neighbor had a perfect view point to observe from her kitchen window these tiny missiles falling through the air. I descended the two floors and exited the back door, all the while making sure I showed no sign of my most recent caper. I was excited knowing I was only seconds away from its successful completion. I walked around the house to retrieve my treasure only to discover my mother had left by the front door with enough time to arrive at the crime scene at the same time.

I froze, surprisingly not pissing in my pants, and was forced to focus on a sneering face, almost like a smile, projecting victory over the criminal caught in the act. I was terrified; a brain freeze took over any rational thought. She reclaimed her possessions and walked away. When I went back into the house, I was dumbfounded there was not a strap whirling through the air and heading in my direction. Her intermittent manner in doling out punishment led to a subtle but persistent nervousness. Her inconsistency and lack of rationale for the beatings had enough effect to keep us unswervingly on edge not knowing when or if another assault was coming. It was not intentional on my mother's part, for I believed, at least some of the time, that she had no command of her own eruptions. That reality made it even scarier.

Around the same age, I stole five Rollo bars from my mother's top drawer and handed them out to my friends at the local outdoor skating rink. Once again, the novice crook that I was, I did not realize one of my sisters was observing my acts of generosity and reported this gift-giving to my mother back home. As evening approached, I returned home to find my mother waiting in the living room for my return. I went through a brief interrogation and wisely confessed to my latest miscue. Her response was once again shocking. She said, with an odd calmness, "As long as you tell the truth that is what is most important." I went to my room in disbelief. Did the patrolling guard experience a sudden conversion? I doubted this as a possibility, but was totally confused about her customary wrath was not ignited. The beating, although totally overkill, would have made more sense. Maybe she knew more than I did. Not knowing when the next assault was coming kept me on alert, and I was emotionally weakened by hours and hours of anticipation.

While I remember many of my so-called transgressions as a young child, I never considered none of them predicted a road to the priesthood. Like the time my friends and I threw rocks at windows of newly constructed homes and then relished in the sounds of broken glass. With no control at home, I was often out of control when out of the house. By all means, I knew this and other childhood pranks were wrong, but I often could not resist the rush these indiscretions created. Delinquent behavior seemed more appealing and real than ordinary life. Perhaps drained from any sense of self at home, these selected offenses left me with a feeling of having an inherent ability and power. Having my friends as co-offenders made it even better as we urged each other to try another toss. This for sure, if my mother found out, deserved maybe not a prolonged beating, but least some consequence of her choice. I was never able to figure her out.

When the time arrived for a real beating, they never seemed to be connected to any justifiable act that I can remember. There is a chance that I blocked out what might be the cause for such beatings since the punishment far exceeded anything I could have done. There was no logic to what my mother thought was a reasonable and therefore matching consequence to whatever I did that day. Somehow, she did make a connection and thought it was her warranted right to proceed with her vicious onslaught. I did not know at the time that insanity is never reasonable nor can be explained by logic.

Forgetting what misdeed the beating might be allied with was most likely a reaction to the overwhelmingly violent nature of what could be called a scourging. A few of these beatings do stand out without much effort of recall. They all seemed to follow a pattern as if both assailant and victim had play-practiced it before. When I saw her coming with her weapon of choice, a hanger or belt, I would fall to the ground, curl up to a wall, a bed, or a corner of a room like a kitten getting ready for a nap. There was going to be no nap for sure, but it was a wide-awake nightmare. Defense was never a consideration. I would submissively take on the swift and powerful blows, never considering to stop her or to retaliate in some way. I did not try to defend myself because I did not know I had an option. Given the power she physically displayed and acted out with unrelenting bashes, there was no other solution than to accept my fate. I clearly recall one occasion when the wooden hanger cracked and I was told to go get another one. For reasons I cannot explain, I did so, and the beating started up once again as easily as if a pause button was used. I knew of the David and Goliath story, but never believed for a second that I could pull off another David. Physical confrontation in any form would terrify me for the rest of my life.

I learned early on to deal with the pain of each blow by trying to concentrate on something else. Dealing with pain became one of my well-developed assets, having no choice in trying to survive in this insanely volatile residence I called home. The more common mental defense was counting of the hits. Counting took my mind off what was actually taking place. It sounds not only outrageous but also unbelievable that there were times when the number reached well beyond fifty. Whether these numbered hits were true or not, this reaction of counting became like a game, guessing how long she could last this time. There was no rhyme or reason for why the beatings began, how long they continued, and why they stopped when they did. There certainly was not a sounding bell noting the end of the round. When she finally did stop, I presume she walked away exhausted, for why else would she have ceased her onslaught at the moment she did? Where she went or what she did after each brutal mugging I cannot imagine. One thing for sure: there was no guilt or a sense on her part that what she had just done was animalistic at best. There was no time or any place for remorse since she knew, as well as I did, that there would be another assault sometime in the near future.

What seemed to highlight her perspective of the beatings was a deranged sort of pride, as in look what I can do. If rewards of praise were being given out for what she deemed as worthy accomplishments, my mother would be first in line to receive hers. She truly believed she was in the right. This perverted attitude toward the beatings was confirmed years later when I was sitting in her living room with my most recent girlfriend. There is no way I can explain how the topic came about, but I do know out of nowhere my childhood beatings became a momentary focus of the conversation. My mother turned to my girlfriend and coolly explained her opinion on the beatings, while presuming my girlfriend would be most interested in what she had to say. She went on to explain that it was because of her that I would be able to have children. What came next was derived from that deranged sense of self-importance that my mother seemed to experience at the strangest of moments. Not blinking an eye, she specified what she meant by my ability to have children when she explained, "Bill used to curl up in a little ball when I was hitting him with a hanger. Sometimes he would expose himself, you know where, but I would never hit him there." The look on my girlfriend's face was as if my mother had just taken a shit on the floor. As usual I had no reaction but to stand up and refresh our drinks. My mother was as proud as a peacock. I was numb. Who knows what my girlfriend thought and I made sure never to ask.

After each beating, my mother would be out of breath and panting as she exited her latest scene of butchery. I was left to do whatever I felt I had to do or could do. Concern for my well-being was never one of my mother's priorities, which I am sure my siblings experienced this palpable omission as well. The majority of time, I returned to my room and spread out on the bed and waited for the pain to subside. It was recovery time, more mental and emotional than physical, although there were times when the physical throbbing demanded attention before any emotion could be given a consideration. In one instance, and this occurred only once, my mother came into my room a half hour or so later and began to rub witch hazel on my back. It felt wonderful and as contradictory as this sounds and is, I was thankful for her doing this act I labeled as kindness. It created the classic case of cognitive dissonance. Do I hate her for her brutality or do I love her for her thoughtful gesture? I was left to live with both. I presume all my siblings had to figure out these repetitive contradictions.

No one in my family spoke of these beatings, or any other forms of madness, outside of the home. I was fully aware that I was living in two separate worlds that had nothing to do with each other. I never spoke to the outside world about what was taking place in my home environment. Embarrassment in telling my story outweighed any calls for help. Who would have believed me anyway? The air of stability my parents were able to portray outside the home was deserving of an Oscar. For their children, pretending everything was satisfactory as we faced our outside world became an art form, and also deserving of a similar award. There is no question I repeated this routine of passive acceptance in my adult life as I dealt with massive depression in the seminary and later with a marriage that died long before it was finalized in a divorce. In all three situations, the childhood home life, the seminary time period, and my marriage, people were in shock when some of the truths were exposed. I watched some of my siblings in their adult lives implement a similar talent by presenting to the outside world all is well and even joyous within the confines of their home, when the reality was just the opposite. We all had our rationale for doing so and maybe considered it normal, for it was all that we really knew. What is crucial in all of this is that we all had the ability to do so as if it was the expected way to live life. We all could write a book!

2

There is no greater agony than bearing an untold story inside you.
—Maya Angelou

Whether it was the experience of the pathological nature of our parents or some other acts of insanity acted out by others, none of us knew what the others were going through or had the ability to think we should. Over years of reinforced experiences, I became emotionally numb and mentally blind to the vicissitudes of daily life, never feeling as if I fit in and always feeling different internally. I became emotionally inept due to a severe lack of nourishment. I sailed through life in a rudderless boat, always waiting, with alarm, for the next storm. I, along with my sisters and brother, lived with two adults living in their private world of selfishness and indifference, permeating the atmosphere with anger and negativity. Most pathetic, there was no interest on their part in correcting the situation or even a sense they should.

How they got to be this way I will never fully comprehend. It would take years for any psychologist to work through their individual complexities. So much was hidden about their lives, or the details were rearranged to make everything look respectable. As far as I know, my father grew up with three older sisters, an elder brother, and his mother. I never met my uncle for he reportedly died in the war. I never knew my grandfather either; he was the mystery man. No one spoke of him nor referred to him, almost as if he never existed. Years later my brother attempted to formulate a family tree, but his questioning of my aunts fell on deaf ears. They ignored my brother's queries, as simple in format as I am sure they were. Did he split from the family and take off with another woman? Was he in prison for some hideous crime or was he institutionalized after several break-downs? Whatever and wherever he ended up, it had to be something that was worth the silence to my two aunts.

One of my father's sisters became an extremely important figure in my life. As a child and entering early adulthood, she was one of the few people who believed in me, even though I did not give a long list of reasons for having this faith. She was one of those old-time Catholics, but different in the sense she put her faith into action right up to the day she had her stroke. Her spirituality was consistent and strong, including daily Mass, financial support of her parish church, volunteering at hospitals, and tutoring the less fortunate. She truly believed I was going to be a priest, and we both enjoyed the times we attended Mass together. I cherished her emotional support, especially since there were so few people in my corner like her. I took on a subtle guilt for this reality since my childhood behavior did not call for much cheering. My aunt, most thankfully, was different right up to the end. I visited her the day before she died, and she was hardly able to speak due to the stroke. Before I got up to leave she said to me in a matter-of-fact fashion, "You know how so many people thought you were at the bottom of the ladder? It makes me feel so good and proud that you are now at the top." I could not have asked for a better aunt.

My father was close to his sisters, and we often took drives to Brooklyn or they came out to see us. I do know that my father went to Brooklyn Prep and then onto Fordham University. I once saw his picture in his yearbook and would stare back at him looking for a clue as to who this man was and how he came to be the person he was now. My eyes would meet his with the hope it would reflect back a readable message, some sign that would help me understand. As steely vibrations bounced back and forth between our stares, I was left with only conjectures as to what he was thinking. His face was thin and slightly drawn that produced a forced smile, which I assume was requested by the photographer. He seemed serene enough, but I detected the slightest air of sadness. This, however, might have been a biased projection on my part. Then again, maybe it wasn't.

I heard rumors that many thought he was going to be a priest, based on his mild and friendly nature. At some point after college he joined the FBI and was involved in espionage during World War II. This career forced him to move around a great deal, which was the plight of all agents at the time. I was not yet born, but my mother asked him to leave the agency either due to an extremely low salary or because of the constant relocations. I would later view this as a major turning point in my father's life. Years later, I read correspondences between him and the FBI, most of it blacked out with a black magic marker. He loved the agency as if it were his entire life and identity. He went on to be in sales, at one point selling coffee to restaurants throughout New York City. I am sure there are many reasons for his alcoholism, but who would not drink with this thankless and meaningless employment, especially after the significance he felt in being an agent in the FBI? He tried to get back into the FBI, but it seems once you turned on Hoover, the director at the time, it was taken personally and he was unforgiving to anyone who left the agency. My father never found a suitable career as he floundered from one job to another. He married my mother when he was around thirty, and she was ten years younger. Those early pictures of their marriage, revealing wide smiles of joy, totally contradict the relationship they had for most of their marriage. Among a plethora of emotions that I experience when I think of my father's life, the one that stands out the most is one of melancholy. This makes me experience sadness for him, overriding the fact he was never what a father should be. The last years of his life, when viewed objectively, were one long extended tragedy. Sad does not begin to define it.

My mother's background was the opposite of what my father's seemed to be. The only similarity is that both came out on the short end of the stick compared to how their siblings lived and ended up, most especially monetarily. My mother had two brothers and three sisters. My grandfather was financially successful; he was able to retire at a very young age. I am guessing he was a robber baron of some sort. As a family, they lived in the upper and wealthier part of town and were able to hire help that most could not afford. When my mother chose to boast and make herself above those she was speaking with, she turned to this time of her life to express her explicit sense of importance. At fifty or sixty years old, she would bypass her years of marriage, not worth an ounce of bragging from her perspective, and return to the glorious years of being a member of the upper class. The way she boasted, one would think she had something to do with attaining this elite posture. It was embarrassing, a common emotion I felt when with her, to stand silently as she stood on her pedestal expecting everyone to be impressed.

She married my father at a young age and immediately, as prescribed by Catholic tradition and even the slightest of Irish descent, to have five children separated by only two or three years. Not knowing what her childhood was like in terms of interacting with her siblings, as an adult it seemed to be often contentious, permeated mostly by financial jealousy. We were the poor ones among the relatives and made do with their hand-me-downs. This never sat well with my mother, who might have grown accustom, even expected, to have a butler and maid. If they ever had a happy and loving time in their marriage, I for sure never saw it. Divorce was not socially acceptable at the time, especially if one was Catholic. As with many Catholics at the time, their faith left them in a constant state of purgatory, with the hell's fire thrown in from time to time.

Five children were born to two adults with lost souls, or at least souls that lacked any meaningful content or nourishment. There was nothing of sustenance to offer as painful as this reality is to face. The construction of a house of strangers was inevitable.

This image of a house of strangers gained clarity and further confirmation years later in one of the classes I was attending in graduate school. We had an art therapist visit our class, and one of the exercises she asked us to do was to draw our home and put our family members in the house as if it were a typical Sunday afternoon. As a novice to this form of therapy, I initially gave the assignment little in terms of credibility. I went along with the exercise and did as she instructed, thinking not much would come out of it. Once I was done, I shared my drawing with the professor and the rest of the class. Drawing a thinly outlined house, a typical A-frame, I put my father in the second floor den, my two older sisters up on the third floor, which was their bedroom. My brother and younger sister I placed in their separate bedrooms and my mother in the living room. Once I had a chance to view my drawing more objectively and with the help of the professor, the interpretation jumped from the page. There was not only no interaction among family members, but I unintentionally made all the walls separating them extremely thick, as if they were stockades keeping them fixed in isolation. Finally, the professor asked me, "Where are you?" Inadvertently my perspective clearly manifested that I did not see myself as part of the home or family. So much for an exercise I gave little credence to.

There were some minor interactions among all of us, some of them bizarre and most of them lacking depth. Four years younger and perhaps six years old at the time, my little brother and I would have made-up contests with each other before falling asleep. One was where we would each sing a short song and then vote who had the better voice. I would say to him, "You go first and vote for me and then I will vote for you." He repeatedly went along with it even though I voted for myself. I would announce, making the contest sound important, "I won, two to zero." There would be a similar sequence when we would take turns tucking each other in with sheets and blankets tightly bound to our bodies. I always volunteered to go first and then he would have to get out of bed to do my blankets. I hope there were not many of these instances and certainly hope that I did not create a pattern for my brother. At this age, I remember him as always having a cute and innocent smile on his face. That sadly would change.

There would be nights when one or two of us would watch TV in the den, which was off the three bedrooms on the second floor. My father would have already passed out for the night. One night my younger sister and I, along with my mother, stretched out on a couch, were watching *I Love Lucy*. It was one of those rare times that I would see my mother laughing hysterically. It was the opposite of the way I usually pictured her, and I therefore experienced these isolated moments with a sense of wonderment. I most certainly did not trust it. On one occasion, she handed my sister and I each one-half of the orange she had completed peeling. She would then proceed to eat the orange rinds. I was never really surprised by anything my mother did, especially what seemed to be spontaneous performance acted out as if they were a routine part of everyday living. Like blowing her nose in her bed sheets as if it was her private Kleenex or biting into chocolate candy and if she did not like it would leave the remaining bit for any child desperate enough for some sweets. For one reason or another, I questioned her on this one about the orange peels and she unassumingly replied, "It is good for your skin." Desperately wanting to cleanse myself of teenage acne I tried a rind only to be immediately repulsed. Lacking common sense myself, I did believe for years the rinds were a medical solution, along with dozens of other suggested worldly solutions she offered. Thankfully, these family scenes were a rarity, for how many other fabrications from my mother would I have heard and believed?

The majority of my time, if I was not in school, was spent outside the house. Throughout my preteen years, I would often go next door to watch the Yankee game with Mr. Skiff. He was a grandfather type, living alone and retired. Unannounced, I would appear at his door and we would go into his den where two lounge chairs and a TV barely fit. He never questioned my arrival. Midway through the game, he always served a glass of milk and chocolate chip cookies. On other nights, it would not be unusual for me to walk around the corner to visit Mrs. MulDoven, an elderly grandmother in her eighties. We would watch *The Lawrence Welk Show*, a half hour of monotonous music and singing meant for a much older audience. It was by no means the same as watching the Yankee game, but I was achieving the same end. This is what a normal life might be like. The cookies and milk, as small a token as it might seem, carried with it an immense sense of warmth and comfort. As my stomach was being satisfied with the sweetness of sugar, I always returned home from both visits with a heart that felt massaged and comforted. Without formal planning, I made these visits part of my regular routine.

These times of feeling complete acceptance and warmth were matched by the times I would visit my local church or the chapel on the school campus. Even before I entered the church, a sense of peace would overcome me. I felt I was visiting a good friend and that I could do so without fear or repudiation. At first, I would often just sit in a pew and take in what I felt was an atmosphere like no other. If it was my local church, I would choose the pew where I attended daily Mass, like a season ticket holder. The difference being I was not rooting for a team; a team was pulling for me. When I was in grammar school, there would be the typical childhood requests. Please let me pass tomorrow's test or let win me the game this coming Tuesday. I would always say a prayer for my parents, sisters, and brother and mention something specific if one of them needed a particular request. On these visits, I would not stay long, unlike the Holy Hours I planned ahead of time. I always left feeling I had an identity and I belonged to someone. The sense of connection never failed, which made these visits not only something I wanted to do but also desperately needed to do. Even more so, it seemed by comparison nothing else mattered. This sensation never faded but increased with assuredness as I grew in age.

I do not remember the topics of conversation with Mr. Skiff or Mrs. MulDoven, with one exception. On one particular evening during one of the commercials, Mrs. MulDoven asked me out of the blue, "How did you break your front tooth?" I was not surprised by the question, for it had been asked before, and even if it were not asked, I knew it was easily recognizable to anyone looking at me. My memorized lines flew out with ease. "Oh, I was playing in the woods last year with some friends. I fell while running, and my teeth hit into a rock. The dentist tried repairing it, but the crack was too big."

I was always too embarrassed to tell the truth about this episode or any other family situation for that matter. The tooth incident did happen the year before but most surely not in the woods. When I was about eight or nine, my father and I became embroiled in one of our very few physical pushes and shoves. Our conflicts were rare, and for the most part we just ignored each other, even when we were the only two in the room. There were a few times when I would enter the den where he sat reading the newspaper, isolated from us all once again. There was no intention on having conversation, for neither of us would have had a clue of where to start. I entered as if I wanted to get a closer examination of this stranger, like approaching an unfamiliar caged pet at a zoo. I was curious about who this man was and tried to fill in the gaps with wide-ranging speculation. I once walked around the back of his chair and he had the newspaper opened wide and held high, close to his face. I read the headline in enlarged black letters: "WARD THROWS A TWO-HITTER." I left the room as confused as I entered. Who did this man of mystery think I was?

Any physical clash, mild and quick skirmishes at best, happened out of context as in a misplaced paragraph suddenly appearing in a flowing novel. The one of two conflicts that I do remember immediately followed a verbal fight he had with my mother. I once followed him into the den to confront him, feeling the need to defend my mother, as contradictory as it was. I do not remember much of a conversation, most likely because there probably was not much of one. I know it ended in total mental and emotion exasperation, a not uncommon feeling existing in this household. He admitted to nothing about the fight with my mother and stared back at me with a scowling yet pitiful look. It is a look that is forever etched in my mind as if someone hung it there like a photo on a living room wall. I pushed him half-heartedly, and he fell back into the couch. I was immediately taken back by how light and frail he was. As I walked away from him and out of the room, instant guilt overcame me, along with the deepest of shame. He had major issues for sure, as both husband and father, but I still felt like shit. This household environment always brought out the worst side of me and had the power of eroding any positive sense of self.

The second clash that has been forever memorialized in my memory bank took place in the upstairs bathroom—an odd place to be with my father under any circumstances. This time he got the better of me. Taken by surprise, he pushed me down and my front teeth met the tiled floor, sending lightning rods throughout my upper gums. I knew my lip was bleeding. The taste was all too familiar thanks to the plentiful and violent confrontations with my mother. It took a few minutes to realize the damage done by the fall. I saw the majority of my front tooth rested on one of the tiles, as on a tray in a dentist's office. The tip of my tongue confirmed it belonged to me. My mother rushed me to the dentist but to no avail. My father did not say a word when we returned home nor did my mother think it was such a big deal. All I knew was that I was now left with an outward sign of what life was like in this household: broken and cracked.

Similar to my parents, I do not recall any remarkable reaction on my part to this damaging interaction with my father. One would assume there would be some screaming or crying in response to what just happened, or perhaps rage toward my assailant. Neither of these occurred. Even at this young age, reacting was not part of my persona. I recall so many events where there should have been a reaction, some recognition of the experience, but so often there was none. The time I was riding my bike on our neighborhood sidewalk and an older neighbor appeared out of nowhere and punched me full force in the stomach. Able to keep my balance on the bike, I just rode on. Another time the high school basketball coach, with a wad full of tobacco in his mouth, spit in my face for missing a layup. I just trotted to the other end of the court as if this was just another situation to accept, like it or not. I always found this lack of reaction to be an odd omission to my already damaged personality.

From that moment of the chipped tooth foray, it was as if I had been given my own personal scarlet letter. Just as Hester Prynne was forced by Puritan moralists to outwardly display her once-hidden actions, I too was now left with this permanent insignia throughout grammar school, high school and into college. The cracked tooth acted as a metaphor for the state of our broken family and symbolized how broken I intrinsically felt. It was an outward sign of how unrepairable our family would always be. With a simple movement of my tongue, I would be reminded of it on a daily basis. It prompted repeated feelings of embarrassment for the condition of my being and the reality of my deplorable way of life. Pretending to others that it happened in a harmless fashion was equivalent to my simulating I was like everyone else and was living a normal life. The repeated actions of covering my mouth in the hope no one would notice corresponded to the soulful urgency to conceal what was actually taking place inside our peeling front door. Without volunteering for the comparison, I could identify with Hester Prynne as being intrinsically mortified while trying desperately to fake an outward semblance of sanity. There was a constant fear someone would discover the truth, and then I could no longer live in repressed denial. I needed to live in denial. The times I was unable to rebuff our family's day-to-day existence, an internal dread would overcome me as I contemplated the consequences of such family brokenness. No future porcelain cap would do the trick.

3

Adults who were hurt as children inevitably exhibit a peculiar strength, a profound inner wisdom, and a remarkable creativity and insight. Deep within them—just beneath the wound— lies a profound spiritual vitality, a quiet knowing, a way of perceiving what is beautiful, right and true. Since their early experiences were so dark and painful, they have spent much of their lives in search of the gentleness, love, and peace they have only imagined in the privacy of their own hearts.

—Wayne Miller, *Legacy of the Heart*

IT WAS ONE OF those beautiful summer mornings, not too hot or humid. I had just completed sixth grade and felt relieved I would be free from the classroom madness for at least two months. I am sure the good nuns felt the same about me. Headed to my friend Gene's home, I rushed from the house early that morning looking forward to playing war games in the woods and then later some basketball or stick ball. In a search of some extra excitement, we might throw some mud balls from the top of a hill at cars passing below us. If one of us hit a target, it created instant excitement as we ran as fast as we could from the crime scene. For some reason, self-rationalization most likely, this was not on my list of sins to confess. The weekly sins I did confess, such as bad thoughts, were more dictated by church leadership and their perspective of what was sinful. At the time, I never questioned their logic and the conclusions they reached. I could not have foreseen at this young age that in my later years I would be obsessively questioning and doubting church authority.

My younger self, who viewed the church as indisputable, would have been appalled by the elder self.

I rounded the first corner from my house and approached Gene's home with the same enthusiasm I had dressing that morning. I went to Gene's side door, knocked, and waited. After a short wait, I knocked again and finally Gene slightly opened the door as if he only wanted me to see part of his face. I did not need to announce myself since this ritual had been played out so many times before. Before I had a chance to say anything, Gene initiated the conversation with a short but curt declaration, "I can't play today. Sorry." Not allowing me time to speak, he shut the door without further explanation. He left enough time for me to hear my other friend call from upstairs. My other friend's voice hit me as if the door was not shut but slammed in my face. It was not the first time I experienced utter rejection, but this one took me by total surprise. Overall, I was usually more careful about risking any form of denunciation. Gene completely caught me off guard, making the pain more formidable and potent.

I returned to the corner once again, much slower and certainly less animated than I had just moments before. The tears rolled down my cheeks, absent at first of any correlating sound. The agony of being so easily dismissed crushed any sense I had of worthiness or value. My early morning balloon of happiness and excitement was unexpectedly popped, and I now hung like a useless and crinkled piece of thin rubber. I did not know where to turn.

I knew full well that home was not a welcome mat of comfort for such marked episodes of rejection. Based on previous experiences, I was convinced my tears would mean nothing to either parent. I knew too well the door leading to a possible connectedness to either of my parents was always shut. As I grew older, I became accustomed to it, as one grows accustom to a bitterly cold day. Therefore, I was rarely surprised by my parents or other authority figures treating me as a non-person without feelings or thoughts. This time, however, it was a friend who shut the door. As I grew older, I would slowly but most assuredly distrust all types of relationships, as I had done with so many other areas of my life. The option of being a lone ranger seemed like the optimum of choices. It was safer and certainly less painful. I would sit in church the next morning and be comforted.

As I walked from Gene's house, I slowed down by one of the huge and well-rounded maples that were lined up like soldiers along my street. My shoulder leaned up next to one tree, and a short while later my head rested on its bark creating a welcoming pillow. The tree felt alive and seemed to communicate comfort and reassurance by virtue of its strength and stability. I had the sense there was solidarity between us as if the tree, filled with an unfamiliar intensity, gave off a chemistry filled with solace. It was not the first time that trees, most especially those that expanded their arms wide in a dense forest, would give me the impression that I was part of something bigger and more powerful than I could ever be. Nature, in all its forms, was something I could trust. A running stream had a similar effect. The endless flow of water always held the promise of consistency and a renewal of purity in its freshness. Often alone in my self-created world of isolation, I would often turn to the experiences of nature and absorb all that it had to offer. The darkness that preceded a pending storm enveloped me as a blanket of warmth, just as the first part of a snowfall swallowed me up in its eerie silence. As I approached my teenage years, it was raw nature that I began to rely on, certainly more so than human nature. In due time, it would be always this way. It was a formation that made the solitary life of priesthood a real possibility. It most especially underscored my continuous need for God in my life and for the things he created that remained nourishing and never rejecting.

While living through these times, if one could call it living, I did not perceive myself as being an innocent youth partaking in a wretched life. Not in the habit of self-reflection, I was far from developing a perspective that life was not fair. These are words I would never have used. I was acting out, actually reacting, as if my life was directed by a puppeteer. I would move about, without questioning, when the strings of the puppeteer directed me it was time to go forward, jump, to move back, or to be still. Not conceiving or considering there might be other options, there was simply no expectation for life to be otherwise. I accepted my norm as being normal. I endured not knowing there were alternatives.

As I was making my way through grammar school I was beginning to feel that life was like leaning on the back of a chair waiting, not thinking I had the right to move, for one assailant or another to stop by and strike another blow to the back. The strike could be physical or verbal, whatever their personal whim would give them pleasure to impart. I was becoming convinced, due to the part I was playing in being socialized, that the demeaning blows might be deserved and well-earned by the nature of my juvenile behavior. Commentaries and targeted reactions from others were having their effect. Who was I and what was I becoming? For sure, Gene was not alone sending a definitive message.

The back of my report card throughout grammar school, which entailed comments on personality and behavior in the classroom, was always filled each month with the letter *M*, meaning must improve. It was not enough for my teachers to write it in the traditional blue ink. They deemed it more fitting to use red ink, lighting up the back of the card like a Christmas tree. Some of them were nice enough to remind me, from the early years of grammar school, I was nothing like my two older sisters, always elongating the word "nothing" to gain its full effect.

My father would receive, due to his days in the FBI, daily most wanted posters, like the ones stapled to the wall in post offices. One day, he was staring at one of the most recently sent posters and then glanced for a few seconds at me. Then he would go back to the mug shot, examining each facial feature, only to look back at me with the same speculating eye. At the end of his silent scrutiny, he decided to inform me of his conclusion. He stated, as the professional he thought he was, "You know, you have the face of a criminal." I must admit I spent more than a few minutes staring into the bathroom mirror to see if his spoken reflection was true. I never reached a conclusion, which left the indictment open for further review.

Not all condemnation came from others wishing to express their opinion of me as if they thought it was their rightful responsibility to do so. The building blocks that were slowly forming my self-image were often framed by my own actions and deeds. Some of these mounting blocks began leaving me with a sense of shame and guilt.

One in particular will always stand out among all the other labeled blocks and left me in fear of the person I might be or could become.

There was a small brook directly across the street from where we lived until I was six or seven. When bored, I would walk across to the brook and try to skip flat stones or drop a bigger rock in the deep end and listen to the thumping sound it amazingly made. It seemed I was always tossing or throwing something. On one occasion, I suddenly noticed a sitting duck not more than three feet from me. It took me aback that it just sat by the water's edge and had not flown away in fear of this rock-throwing kid. I stared at it for a few moments and wondered why it continued to sit quietly as if it were frozen on a throne. I made some loud noises, and it still did not move. I then picked up a stick and poked it on the back. Its head moved slightly, but nothing more. After a few more pokes, I hit the duck hard and it landed on its beak. It remained motionless and quiet as I saw a drop of blood form on the tip of its beak. I threw the stick in the water and began to walk back to the house. Halfway across the street, a thought struck me as if I had been hit by one of my own rocks. "My god, what if it was sitting on eggs and was bravely protecting its children?" In the darkest mode of emotion, I pondered in disgrace what I might have just done.

Shame immediately enveloped me. Saying I truly felt like a piece of shit would not even be close to describing the descending darkness that overcame me. How could I have been so thoughtless, so incredibly stupid, and so ruthless as I gave into the urge to challenge this helpless creature? Spending a few moments in the house, I returned to the brook to check on the duck. It was still sitting in the same position. There was no blood, which brought some relief. The impact of such cruelty, whenever recalled, would always act as a lance to the very depths of my soul. Later in life, it would become an important part of my prayer life as I would ask God to lead me not into temptation, especially knowing what I was capable of doing at any time.

If I was not demeaning myself, which was becoming a nasty habit, I was waiting for someone to do it for me. Days were defined by whether the emotional blows were active or not. I was moving toward the conviction, as I went through the process of dealing with everyday events, these blows were possibly earned as direct consequence of my abhorrent behavior. If I were a better person, I concluded, they simply would not occur. Any sense of peace was defined by the days the striker took a day off. A good day at school, as was the case with the nuns in grammar school, was delineated by the days when one was smacked or not. In addition, if on a Saturday my mother was out shopping with her mother, as she often was, it was a day when my built-in shield could somewhat be put at ease. Memories of the blows always outranked their absence. The shutting of Gene's door, a repetition of past experiences under different circumstances, formed an engrained hesitancy to ever knock again. I gave the Genes of the world and others like him a great deal of power over defining my worthiness and value as an individual. Slowly eliminating most of those I knew, it was only in God I could trust.

How inane are the behaviors of children labeled as grievous and mortal? I began to form this notion I was capable of committing serious offenses even as a naive third grader. Like the time I turned to my classmate to pretentiously ask her what the strongest letter in the alphabet was. "What, Bill?" she said with not much interest in what I thought to be not only interesting but insightful as well. "P," I proudly told her. "Even superman can't stop it." For reasons I am not sure of other that she agreed with the teaching this might be one of those mortal sins, she ran up to the nun as if she were performing her good deed for the day. As if turned on by a switch, the nun's face turned into a distorted rage, creating self-inflicted wrinkles making her seem much older than she was. She bellowed out my name, not once but twice, followed by the directive to come to the front of the room. My fellow classmates did not seem to flinch, most likely since they heard this thunderous pitch with my name on it many times before. I could tell immediately my classmate and the nun did not appreciate my humor.

I recall her slaps to the face primarily due to the way they were delivered. The corporal punishment was expected, for it was not the first time I stood in front of the class. As with previous physical punishments, the technique of delivery became more of the focal point.

I turned to my usual defense of disconnection, perfected via Mom, and began to count the number of times she would hit me. With precision and dedicated order, she delivered six back hands to the right cheek, six back hands to the center of my lips, and then six more with an open hand to my left cheek. Even though somewhat disorientated, I still wondered how odd this part of her performance was one of relevance and interest on my part. In an odd sort of way, I was giving her credit for her creativity. She proceeded to tell me to kneel before the cross and profess the act of contrition. I was not sure if I had committed a mortal or venial sin, but confessed nonetheless. Embarrassed with an added dose of shame, I returned to the back of the classroom with fully wet pants and the task of assimilating another bit of craziness.

Lying in bed that night, a phone call came from the nun who had hours before dealt slaps of precision to the most tender parts of my face. As my mother answered the phone, I could only deduce the nun's opening lines by virtue of my mother's seemingly reassuring response. With no hesitation and undoubtedly no concern for at least the embarrassment I underwent that day, my mother complacently said to her, "Hit him again tomorrow, Sister, if he does something again." I was not surprised. My mother was an expert in this area of physical conflict and seemed to enjoy the opportunities to exercise her talents. To hear that someone else was of like mind most likely reassured her role of mother in one of her most favorite activities. Maybe I should have been grateful that my mother did not suggest her typical armor of belts and hangers. I went back to listening to the Yankee game as if listening to the game was what really what mattered. Actually, it truly was one of the few things that did matter.

So walking home after Gene's harsh rebuke did not present the prospect for seeking comfort from home. It never was an option. The experience of loneliness that day set in as if it was a comrade who had been absent for a while. I did not welcome this companion of regularity back, but was not surprised at its sudden return. I was beginning to believe that loneliness was a given factor of life, almost like it was genetic. It was something I grew accustomed to accepting and therefore was rarely startled by its sudden reappearance. The sense of isolation from others I simply presumed was something that would come and go. They became memories that would dance back and forth in and out of consciousness. In my younger years I participated in the dance without much thought.

Due to these nagging periods of loneliness, I routinely turned to my one place of reliable comfort. While walking through the large front doors and inhaling the latent odors of incense, I knew immediately I entered a home where there was no question of acceptance and love. Confidently walking to the right side of the church, the regular site for my position at daily Mass, I knelt in preparation for what I knew would be a calming relief. I was assured, as I had been so many times before, that being in God's house meant unconditional love, no questions asked, no condemning judgments. There was no fear or trepidation of a door being shut. There was always a sense of dark oppression when loneliness appeared with its ugly face, but I seemed to accept it as part of the path to knowing how much I needed God. The door to Jesus was always open, and I entered it often. Every time I sat in my self-assigned pew, it could be any part of the day, I was confident I would be once again feeling complete and rejuvenated.

I cannot say I ever liked my childhood, for it offered little in terms of achieving a positive sense of who I was and what I was becoming. My real self was locked inside somewhere and surrounded by walls of protection. There was little in terms of self-reflection, and certainly there was no form of soul-searching. No one suggested that this is what I should be doing. The message, seemly, was to build more walls.

Sensing I had no intrinsic power of my own, I would sail through the day focusing primarily on trying to stay above water. The only closeness I expected was in the form of a slap, physical or verbal. It was as if my parents and a number of authority figures held a death grip on inner joy or a sense of pleasure. I learned to hide the hurts and fears but always aware of the intrinsic locations where they existed. With the exception of a respite at church rituals or my visits on my own, the pain of isolation often acted as boulder pulling me down in a sea of shame. Deterred from a proper growth and development, I remained entrenched in a debilitating stage of adolescence.

Put simply, I just did not get it. How maddening it is for anyone to be born into a loveless environment yet still aspire for something better. Frustrating as it might be, hope saved me from the depths of resignation. The lifesaver was that someday I would be a priest

My hours spent in church were only matched by hours on basketball courts and baseball fields. The strong appeal to be out of the house can be equated with someone rushing from a house on fire. Even on Sunday mornings, in order to enhance the speed of my exit, I would put my Sunday clothes over my play clothes and after Mass strip down in the car, grab my basketball, and be on my way. My bizarre actions were never questioned, for that would involve caring. To be fair, I also never wondered what my family members were doing for the day. All I could be assured of, without the words to express it, was the freedom I felt being away from the tension and turmoil.

One of my favorite destinations was known as the Community House. It became my home away from home. Somewhat like my church visits, it was welcoming, accepting, and familiar. Within the building were pool tables, ping pong tables, and TVs, along with the ball fields and courts surrounding the main building. It would not be unusual for me to arrive there on the weekends at nine in the morning and leave when the lights were dimmed at nine in the evening. I would steal a dollar or two from my mother or one of my elder sisters to get me through the day. I remember some days getting through on thirty-five cents, allowing two popsicles from the Good Humor ice cream truck. The special of the day was fifteen cents and the regular ten cents. Stealing became a necessity for survival, for food that is. I actually became rather good at it. My mother kept a small tin bank in her dresser drawer, a few inches in width and height, which she fed with dimes. When it reached ten dollars, the back lid would unlock and she could retrieve the savings. In my budding criminal mind, I was able to figure out how to open the back of the can ever so slightly and shake ten times out on a regular basis. There was an ice cream store in the middle of our town, and I became addicted to a sundae known as the Dusty Road. Sitting at counter, sometimes with a friend, I would indulge in coffee ice cream, covered with chocolate syrup and topped with a malt powder. I must admit that I experienced no guilt, for the delight of the sundae was well worth the crime. My mother, for reasons I could not comprehend, never questioned as to why the bank never reached ten dollars. For me, it was kind of a childhood high to pull off such a caper, which led me to seek other rewarding scenarios similar in nature. Years later I saw the movie *Goodfellas*, depicting the making of a mafia figure. I totally identified and understood searching for a place to fit in. For him and for me, anywhere would be fine as long as there was acceptance. His place of comfort was with the mafia and gangsters, while mine became the church and the priests. I would later question if that was part luck or grace.

After spending weeks on end at the Community House, I was offered a job. It was run by a young couple who saw me there constantly and had to wonder about this life I was living, always there, never home. I was relieved they never asked where I spent my night time hours, thinking they may have thought I slept with a bunch of hoboes under the nearby train tracks only to return the next morning. So much of my life was one long stretch of possible embarrassments, both in the way I was living and the environment I came from. I could hide only so much.

At the Community House, I liked both the husband and wife and, to my amazement, they seemed to really like each other. It left me with a sense that maybe there were couples in existence that actually liked, even loved, each other. They had no children of their own, and I would sometimes fantasize how it might be living with them. The father was a strong figure for me, and the mother was gentle and kind. When I was around them, I always felt a sense of warmth, but most especially acceptance. I did my chores, and they seemed pleased. I was proud.

Returning home would be like pulling down a shade to the outer world. I was literally stepping from one stage to another as if a curtain was lowered behind the one and raised to the other. I became a professional at switching roles, perhaps deserving of an actor's award, or at least participate in the lifetime services of a good therapist. On returning to the family stage, there would be no expectation of personal interaction and I rarely had any idea how my brother or sisters spent their day. If I did not go to the Community House, my brother and I would spend hours in the back yard playing whiffle ball games. Some summers we would reach well over a hundred games. Sometimes the neighbors would join in. Sports filled and fulfilled my life and who knows what kind of trouble I would be getting into without this passion. I recall many times Mr. Skiff leaned on his iron fence watching our games. It felt good knowing someone was watching, noticing our existence, even if it was only playing with a plastic ball. I knew I would spend the evening with him if there was a Yankee game that night. It was something to look forward to and another chance for escape.

There would be late nights when I would crawl into my father's darkened bedroom and pilfer his wallet. Eventually, he was forced to keep it under his pillow as he slept off another nightly stupor. I cannot imagine what this poor man was feeling, living in his own house of strangers who steal from him. At the age I was, what he was thinking was never a concern. His need to hide his wallet just raised the challenge. The entire second floor reeked of Ben Gay, a heating lotion my father rubbed on his temples every night to ward off what I assumed was another vile headache. Sometimes, I would take my younger brother with me as if I was teaching him a new trade. The excitement on those nights was addictive. Opening the bedroom door, crawling on all fours in the pitch dark, I would move ever so slowly to the other side of the room where my father slept. I would reach my destination, peak my head up to assess the situation, reach ever so slowly under the pillow, and bingo. I felt the prize. Emptying it, I returned the leather to its place of origin. Crawling from the room, my heart would pound. I would give most of the stolen bills to my mother and keep a few dollars for my ice cream treats or maybe get a hot dog. Nutrition was never part of the family menu.

Passing on my stolen goods to my mother became a way of getting her briefly felt acceptance and approval. I never confessed this activity to a priest, for at the time it seemed the right thing to do. I knew it was wrong, but perhaps not sinful. I interpreted it almost as a son's duty. Such thinking was part of my distorted and underdeveloped conscience, simply responding to what I thought the situation called for. Stealing, whether it was from department stores or candy stores, became a form of entertainment. I was on my way to producing my own *Goodfellas*. My mother, of course, was happy to get the money no matter its origin. She not only never reprimanded me for it, but made it seem, in her silence, as if I was performing a good deed. Her perspective on being a mother was frightening. Even scarier was the effect she was having on her children.

Living within the confines of two worlds, the church and my home life required two completely different responses. Not quite the making of a schizophrenic, but it certainly required duel personalities. During my childhood it was a toss-up which persona would win out. I most certainly preferred one over the other, but as a teenager I did not have the capacity to comprehend the immense contradiction between the two worlds. The numerous defenses I had to shed as an adult is still a work in progress. It is a painful process at times, but cathartic even as I type away reliving a past that still hammers away within me. Pulsates might be a better description.

I compensated for the emptiness and meaningless behavior of the one world by having the church as my place of stability. I was not consciously aware of the underlying reasons for this daily transition into this other world, but I most certainly pursued it diligently on a regular basis. All I knew, or more correctly felt, was that a specific priest, at various stages in my life, became the surrogate father I so desperately needed. I more than willingly became his son. The adoption process was mutual on both our parts. We were both living lives of estrangement and disengagement from the real world, permeated with hours of loneliness. Our environments were very different, but we nevertheless shared the mutual need to belong to something and to experience a sense of connectedness with someone, appropriate or not. We crossed paths starving for a sense of recognition and identity. It was only later in life that I recognized the relationships I developed, especially with one priest, were obsessive, overly demanding and often ill-chosen. Coming from a house of strangers, I was starving for some sense of connectedness and acceptance. Coming from the loneliness of the rectory, many of the priests were forced to partake in their own personal search for a more personal sense of purpose. I am so grateful that none of it was sexual in nature, as I was later to find out was not an uncommon practice between many of the priests and their psychologically captive victims. Later in life, some of my adult friends said I probably repressed it. Shit.

4

Home is where you go when you run out of homes.
—John le Carre

THE CHURCH, THE BUILDING itself along with its participants, most definitely gave me a place to be a part of something apart from having to deal with the insanity of home and school life. It was an oasis from places that generated lasting hurt and pain. Even at a young age, I was attracted to ideals which gave me hope, comraderies which gave me a sense of belonging, and a prestige which gave me a purpose and that I was someone worth considering. In grammar school, I was the main altar boy in my class and, therefore, was often called upon to serve funerals and weddings. It gave me a special feeling as I was often called out of class to be a part of another ritual. My weekends were not exactly busy with family activities, creating a huge gap in terms of what to do with my time. The parish priests may have known this, for they scheduled me for many of the Saturday weddings, sometimes two or three in a day. With a parish full of the elderly, it would not be unusual for me to be pulled from class two or three times a week to be part of the somber funeral proceedings. At an early age, I was already good at being somber.

I am sure the nuns who taught me were happy to see me go. If Ritalin were in vogue at the time, they would have bypassed the pills and fed it to me intravenously. Just as I had not a clue as to what my role was at home, I did not have even the slightest trace of understanding regarding what it meant to be a student. My mind and body reacted to class confinement as if someone had floored my internal engine. Even when idling in neutral, I was racing to nowhere. There is no question I must have caused more than one nun to reevaluate her teaching position, perhaps her entire vocation.

The stage for having a sense of significance was the church building and all the rituals that took place within its walls. I considered being an altar boy was my first step to the priesthood. As a man I would be a priest, someone who was sought out, dignified, and routinely respected. As an altar boy, I felt unique in this precursor to the priesthood. My separateness from others was given a place of honor by donning the cassock and surplus. My friends may wear a shirt of a basketball star as they made layups in their driveway, pretending to be the star that bore the shirt's number. They may wear an army uniform while playing in the woods, projecting the bravery of real soldiers. I did those things, but my uniform of choice was that of an altar boy. The black cassock and white surplus portrayed the essence and substance of the role I was to play somewhere down the road. I would reach high to light the candles before the service began, sensing all eyes were upon me from those sitting in the pews. I always had an underlying fear that I could screw up and thus experience that embarrassment button again. My fear of failure was a disease I acquired from home and from school, especially the repercussions of failing. The power of embarrassment was one of my strongest suits. Yet preparing the altar for Mass led me to experience a sense of dedicated commitment to something that had immediate impact. Standing in the sacristy as the priest donned his robes and then leading him out to the altar made me part of a team. It was not about holiness; it was about belonging.

The Mass was still recited in Latin and therefore required Latin responses. I was always grateful no individual priest chastised me for the responses I muddled through. With some of the more difficult responses, I would make sounds to resonate a foreign language as much as possible and somehow it worked. In any other environment, I would be most likely called out for my simulated portrayal of the Latin language, or at least stared at as if I was from another country. It was just one more reason for being grateful for priests. From a totally different analysis, it was just the beginning of the many free passes I received on the path to the priesthood.

As I walked out of the sacristy leading the priest to the altar and the rite of Mass began, my thoughts experienced a sense of fulfillment like no other. The smell of incense reminded me I was in an extraordinary place, so different from the smell of Ben Gay. The ringing of the bells formed an angelic tone carrying my thoughts to a realm of peace. The kneelers clanging, the blasting of the organ, the choir musically creating an atmosphere of holiness, and the echoing of the priest's words all created a distinctive mood of specialness. I was where I wanted to be. Times spent away from this hallowed building only generated the urge to return. My friends, after spending time in school or playing in the fields, returned to their home. I often briefly stopped by the church building knowing full well it was a place I preferred to call home.

There were those who encouraged this dream and those who were angry at the special treatment they thought I received. I recall one of my mother's friends announcing to me after I left the seminary, "Now, you are one of us." Her anger at years of having to accept the pompous credit my mother was taking for my so-called esteemed position must have nauseated her. Yet there was some truth in what she was saying. In order to endure a sense of nothingness, I sought an arena where I had a sense of uniqueness. Where she was misled was to think it was arrogance and superiority that directed this choice. In truth it was an act of desperateness and the only place I discovered a peace of mind.

The brilliant poet and author, Maya Angelou, expressed it so well in her memoir.[1] She explained that so many of us experience pain and hurt in childhood, which eventually takes on a life of its own. Overly self-conscious about the true reality of my existence at home, I was too embarrassed to let anyone know the truth about my home life. I learned, as Maya described, a manner of hiding my throbbing aches with thickening pieces of scab. Following this surgical-like procedure of emotional repression, a mask would be formed to cover them over. Others would observe this disguise and presume it was real. In unambiguous ways, unbeknown at the time, the white colored surplus and black cassock became part of the disguise.

The separation of my church activities from the other areas of my life created a huge abyss. The gap between my church life and school performance could not have been wider. Although no one mentioned it, it must have caused some confusion to any one observing the contradictory life I was living. It began in the early years of grammar school. My classmates' day ended at the normal three o'clock hour when mine was closer to four thirty. For sure it was not that the nuns wanted to spend more time with me but must have believed that in punishing me I would change my ways. At this age in grammar school, I had nothing else better to do and certainly had no urgency to return home. So their intended punishment was more of a reprieve from not having to go home. I think I broke a record in seventh grade by sitting with a nun every school day of the year. The mother who picked up my sister and brother along with her children would come back at four thirty to get me, never telling my mother of her good deed. I should have remembered to thank her.

Attending daily Mass began somewhere around third or fourth grade. It became a routine to get up around five thirty, boil two eggs and maybe grab some bread, then set out for church. It was about a three-mile walk that I took with conviction and a sense of purpose. Later in life I wondered how my parents permitted a ten-year-old to leave the house so early in the morning, especially during the dark wintery days. It was just another example of how both of them were so tied up with their own lives that their children were essentially overlooked.

Their discounting our existence was not a conscious concern of mine at the time. All I cared about was that I was headed toward the one place where I felt totally accepted. I was always early for Mass and entered a church that was for the most part empty. I consistently sat on the right side, near the front. A nun would walk in and take her place in the middle of the pews, while an older man always sat in the last pew. As I left the church he would greet me with a smile and handshake. We never introduced ourselves, but perhaps he did not have to. He was there for his particular reason, and I was there for mine. A half dozen or so more people would come in as Mass was about to start.

I would open my missal written in Latin on the left side of the page and the English translation on the right. The familiarity of the

Mass and the routine of the ritual created for me an atmosphere of familiarity and the comfort of consistency. No other place did I feel so comfortable without an ounce of reservation. The classroom, the basketball court, the baseball field, or even at friends' homes there was always a sense of not fitting in or of being different. Most certainly at home there was no sense of being a son or brother. I cannot blame my siblings for this, for I am sure they were going through the same form of detachment. No matter where I was outside of church, it was as if an imaginary wall surrounded my body leaving me with a sense of separateness, distance, and the conviction of disparity. The distinction of being different only fed into a powerful sense of inferiority and the strongest sense of vulnerability.

It was only in the church where acceptance was never an issue. When I was performing the duties of an altar boy, I never worried about being judged or worse being excluded. I was mostly confident in the role I was to perform, and the main participants, the priests, accepted me without question. I felt we were truly a team going through distinctive acts of worship, and therefore had a sense of higher importance. Entering the church for early Mass was as if I was coming home from days of indifference. I slept somewhere else, but this was my residence of comfort and identity. The numerous Holy Hours I made had the same effect. Special occasions, such as Good Friday, would be spent in silence in the church from noon to three o'clock in preparation for the Stations of the Cross. The time frame, or so I was told, was when Jesus began his walk to eventual crucifixion. I identified more with the suffering Christ, or any kind of suffering for that matter, which gave me a rationale for my own suffering. Crazy as it sounds, there would be occasions when I would seek the suffering out. In my grammar school days, I would refuse Novocain at the dentist's office and take on the pain as if it put me in a place of distinct holiness. If Christ could do it and I was to follow him, then so could I.

5

At the innermost core of all loneliness is a deep and
powerful yearning for union with one's self.
—Brendan Behan

THE DAILY MASS CONTINUED into my high school days. I left the
house usually before dawn for my three-mile walk to the school
chapel. When I would later relate this walk to friends, I would get
the look expressing, "Oh, you walked up this long hill in the wet
snow and then had to later walk up a long hill in the wet snow back
home." It does sound incredulous, but the reality is that these daily
jaunts were true. My first rosary of the day would be prayed. Not
having a relationship with my mother, praying to the Blessed Mother
undoubtedly filled a void. The prayer emphasizes she is full of grace,
and I believed it. I identified with her in not having a home and
forced to find a place to give birth. I pictured her as being a loving
mother caring for the person I loved. I connected to her massive pain
in watching her son die. Most of all, she was the mother who walked
with me to school.

About midway through the walk up the main avenue, there
would be times when I would bother to look into the window of
Bunny's Bar and see my father sitting there for his first drink of the
day. It was like looking into a private world meant only for a few.
A few men were hunched over their liquid breakfast, but only one
character was recognizable. Objectively, he was my father, but absent
was any emotional response to this loathsome scene. I did not know
whether to consider him with disgust or pity. Other than that, I had
almost no reaction to it. These glimpses through the bar window

were more simply just an observation. There is this person, who just happens to be my father, having his first vitamin of the day. My lack of effect was becoming fine-tuned. Yet in some strange way, I shared with him, in what had to be, an immense loneliness.

There is one memorable exception to these long periods of separateness. It took place when I visited a close friend's home. His mother, in typical Italian fashion, would greet me with arms wide open and draw me into her body. It always included a positive word of encouragement or praise. I felt safe with her, and the atmosphere she created in the home only added to it being a shelter from maltreatment. The house always smelled good with the aroma from a heated cooking pot spreading smells throughout the home. My friend's father was also as welcoming and always showed a genuine interest in the sport I was playing at the time. Years later, when my friend's mother passed away, I wrote to him how the memories of his mom had such a lasting effect. She was such a contrast to the majority of other circumstances that lacked such security and warmth. Admittedly, however, by the time I was in high school, I was viewing my world with biased eyes and a predisposed mental outlook. Trusting others, either their actions or their words, was an option I more than often declined. It never seemed worth the risk. This was another gift of omission, with dire consequences, from Mom and Dad.

When in therapy many years later, I had to come to terms with this omission and see it as a major flaw in my development. It had numerous corollaries beyond the physical nature of a hug. My emotional growth took a hit as well. My personal issue with trusting physical and emotional closeness became evident when my therapist had me do an exercise that created a great deal of discomfort, fear, and anxiety. He had me imagine I was being hugged, but not hugging back. He instructed me not to think of any particular person but to focus on the hug itself. While doing so, he wanted me to verbalize any thoughts or feelings I was experiencing while I was imagining being hugged.

After a few minutes into the hug, I began to feel extremely uneasy. To my surprise, I imagined at one point that I was becoming smaller and smaller in size. Then, I thought I was in the palm of someone's hand and suddenly realized I could be crushed at any moment. For a brief moment, I had the passing thought I was in my mother's palm, but then it returned to being just someone with a great deal of power. I ended the exercise in trepidation of what might come next.

The interpretation was obvious to us both. The message was that closeness is something to fear and carries with it only the terror of pain. I was somewhat shocked at the intensity of my reaction, but it made sense when considering the damaging pieces of my past. The significance of the exercise showered a light of understanding for my defensive posture toward others and my unconscious willingness to prefer isolation. If I ever was to become healthier, my task was to learn to be close to others both in the giving and receiving sense. For the time being, as I went through my high school and college days, this stark omission in my personality and behavior would help me to endure the requirement of the priesthood for celibacy. In the ignorance of my youth, I did not consider that living the single life would be a sacrifice, as so many seemed to describe this vocation. I would later discover that this was true for many seminarians for one reason or another. It took years of hard work to be comfortable in my own skin and to trust the basic goodness of others. My guess is that my brother and sisters had to endure the same challenge.

During my high school years, I came to the full realization that each of my siblings was existing on their separate island, rarely knowing what each of us were doing throughout the day. Even though I was extremely active in sports, none of them came to one of my games to see me pitch a baseball or shoot a basketball. It never crossed my mind to ask them what they were up to and, therefore, did not witness any of their activities. I have numerous memories of coming up from the locker room after a basketball game and entering the gym where the game was just completed. Parents and friends would be gathered around to greet and congratulate each of my teammates. I would walk through the crowd pretending I did not mind. Playacting, putting on another face so as not to let on how awkward I felt, was an art I was slowly perfecting. In so many instances, I felt like I stuck out like I was wearing an orphan's clothes. Unless I faked a different persona, one that was self-assured and confident, I would reveal how different I and my world really were. On these particular nights, I would avoid all eyes as I exited the gym and reach a zone of safety outside. The walk home was done without thought. On Tuesday nights, when many of the games were played during the week, I would reach home around ten o'clock, plant myself on the couch with a textbook on my lap, and once again pretend, this time that I was studying. The group upstairs never knew I just played a game, and certainly gave no recognition I was home. Segregation was a substantial part of the family culture, creating hearts that beat to the tunes of loneliness. Each of us was entrenched in our own dark cloud of confusion and uncertainty, left to move on to the next day as if we knew what we were doing. The art of pretending would be put to good use.

There is one special memory that was worth celebration. It is a recollection that still brings tears to my eyes and a deep sense of gratefulness to my heart. It was a hot summer afternoon and I was standing on the pitcher's mound preparing to start another inning. Before I threw the first pitch, I glanced to my right more as a form of habit than expecting to see anything. An older-looking couple was walking, actually hobbling, along the fence toward the entrance to the field. Their form of dress was what really made them stand out. The older man wore a long overcoat and one of those classy rimed hats that many men of the previous generation tended to wear. The older woman, even though it was a warm afternoon, also wore a wintry-like coat and a hat surrounded by fur. They walked hand-in-hand and most assuredly with a purpose.

I froze with excitement. My grandparents had walked from their nearby apartment and had come to see me play. When the inning ended, I hugged them both and they hugged back. They were one of the few where I felt no threat. My grandfather, with his strong German chin, smiled with pride. He loved baseball and was getting the chance to cheer for his grandson. When I was not out on the mound I sat with them on the first row next to my teammates. Unbeknown to them, they were creating a memory of a lifetime for someone who was in short supply of such love. I would later view these extraordinary moments as sparks of grace that kept an undernourished soul from completely collapsing.

The experience of my immediate family was another story. The creation of positive memories is few and far between. The effects of living among my family members, as if each of us were in a state of quarantine, created a personality that left me almost totally inaccessible to others and, more significantly, unreachable even to myself. We all lived separate and disconnected lives from each other, left to fend for ourselves. None of us had a clue there might be another way. Secluded and left to survive on our own, we did not know we were supposed to care. Only later in life were a few of us able to reflect on how such dysfunction was pulled off. The reflecting is still a work in progress.

Living within a few feet of each other, passing each other innumerable times, sitting around a silent table at dinner, we were ghosts with no name. Insulated by layers of suspicion and distrust, our hidden emotions lay dormant, desperately craving an awakening. The atmosphere was born from the relationship my parents had with each other. Like the slow drip of Chinese torture, we were all being innocently poisoned by the hatred they had for each other. The message was clear even if not actually verbalized. We had to make it on our own, whatever "it" was.

6

A son or daughter in any human family is either born
or adopted by the parents. By definition, a child cannot
be both. But with God we're both born of him and adopted
by him.

—Jerry Bridges

DAILY MASS OR MY visits to church during the day had nothing to do with the rest of my day. Leaving this place of serenity in the early morning hours, I then proceeded into a domain of survival, barely conscious to whatever was taking place. As was the day before, it simply would be another day to get through. I viewed the classroom experience as a necessary requirement to play sports. My baseball coach, who happened to be my algebra teacher for two years, dismissed me from all tests once he found out I could pitch rather well. The discharge from taking any tests was not hidden. He would go up and down each row handing out the tests. When he reached my desk, he would pass it by with the instruction to head out to the gym. With a grin, revealing once again my participation in the circus-like atmosphere of school, I would wave to my classmates with a mischievous smile. They, absent of jealousy, confirmed back with various hand gestures indicating a particular pride we shared in this latest anecdote of school life. Even if I had the wherewithal to take school seriously, which I did not, there would rarely be a place for it among these cast of characters, teachers and students alike.

Most of my teachers did little to improve my impression of school life. One actually spent the good part of the class period standing behind me while rubbing my arm. One only has to have the slightest of an imagination the nickname he acquired. Then there was my science teacher who spent the entire class reading word for word from the text, never taking the time to look up. I often thought we could all leave and he would never know the difference. There was no possible way he had a degree in science, let alone education. I would often generously break the forced trance of my classmates by jumping out of the class window (it was on the first floor) only to immediately return with a polite "Good morning, sir" to my robotic lecturer. This act of compassion for my imprisoned brothers through the art of entertainment became one of my primary high school roles. I would repeat exiting the window two or three times in one class period, revealing only the comatose certainty of our exalted professor as he responded once again to my cheerful good morning as if it was the first time. My classmates took great joy in the free performances.

To further break the monotony and to bring some good cheer to my fellow incarcerated victims, I would on a regular basis raise my hand, coughing several times to get the attention of our esteemed science teacher. When he finally recognized me, I would proceed in a somber manner. "Sir, I am trying to take in all the gems of knowledge that you are passing our way, but my classmate next to me, who goes by the name Joe, keeps interrupting my concentration." To the uproar of my audience and compatriots in crime, the science teacher would proceed to kick my accused classmate out of the class. We all loved it. Of course, usually not waiting more than a day, Joe would return the favor and I would be thrown out of the class, once again to the delight of my peers. I never questioned how I went from kneeling in a pew a few hours before to jumping out a window. There were numerous other gems that I acted out unplanned, which over the years became part of my reputation as a so-called student.

As I learned so well in my home life, living in separate and contradictory worlds seemed to take on an acceptable pattern of being normal. It was like going to one movie for a brief period and then leaving this one theater to observe another movie. A period of time would be spent at this second showing and then I would return to the original movie. There would be days when several movies would be running, which often took a degree of creativity to get through. It was like having a part in *One Flew over the Cuckoo Nest*. There were times when I took on the role of Jack Nicholson, entertaining the gang who thought I was crazier than they were. I have to admit I was more than delighted to help my fellow patients get through the day. Of course, the staff felt otherwise and doled out what they considered to be appropriate punishments of consequence. They never seemed to realize how ineffective these responses were. For most of us, no lobotomy was necessary.

The higher-ranking sections in my class, those supposedly more intellectually astute, enjoyed hearing of the comical ways my lowly-minded peers of my class section went through the day. We had acquired a reputation. If there was a yearbook award for the least likely to succeed, it would be difficult to guess which of my classmates would receive this esteemed honor. I regrettably had to leave my fellow comrades of vaudeville and enter another academic section for my last two years in high school. It was a class section for those wanting to be a priest and was referred to as the Divinity Class. I was a parolee with mixed emotions. I would miss the comical interactions with my fellow inmates but knew I had to move on in order to fulfill the academic part of wanting to be a priest. Nonetheless, we would miss each other.

The day of this separation presented my classmates with one final performance worthy of the theater. The dean of academics informed us we would all be taking physics and chemistry in our final two years. The exception, he explained, would be if any of us were considering the priesthood. He declared these individuals would be taking Latin and Greek. He then inquired if anyone present was considering this as a vocation. There was a pause. Even the dean would think this a foolish question presented to this group of future criminals. I waited, wondering if I should make this the moment to go public. I raised my hand indicating they had a future priest among them. Never once concerned with order and discipline, the class erupted. It might have been more believable if I said I was going to be an astronaut, or perhaps my plan was to find a cure for cancer. Without intending it to be, I became the topic of the day as my classmates broke into a gleeful riot, some even shouting out and banging on desks. Most interpreted my raised hand only equal to the farcical act of jumping out the window. They presumed my announcement was another one of my daily gags. It only gained some semblance of acceptance as I started my junior year with the men wanting to be priests. Yet my behavior in school continued to be a paradox when anyone considered I was on a path to the priesthood. I never considered, as in lacking any form of introspection, the unresolvable contradiction.

High school was in so many detrimental ways a repeat of my preteen years, yet with a greater impact. As in grammar school, many of the rebukes and reprimands were deserved but not in the manner in which they were delivered. There was one primary advantage to the high school I attended: first and foremost, it was a preparatory school for college. By no means did I profit from the curriculum as the appreciation for learning still lay in a dormant stage. The school was an advantage because there was only one basic curriculum in each of the four years. The courses offered each semester were consistent and expected, and all taught in preparation for college academia. If I attended public school, this would not have been the case. If a student presented himself as being non-college material, as I most certainly did, he or she would have been delegated to less challenging courses. There would be courses such as auto repair shop and mechanics. Due to my dreadful outlook and approach to academics, my class assignments in public school would have been predictable and college would have been not an option. I might have become very proficient at making bird houses and fixing cars, which is not so terrible, but certainly this would have derailed me from the path to the priesthood. It is frightful for me to think of this dreadful reality had I not attended a prep school. The thought of being a priest is what kept me alive. How I was going to get there was another question. Obsessed in surviving in the moment, I never thought to question or develop a game plan. No one around me seemed to care about this stark omission.

It would be a real stretch to refer to those in charge as being legitimate teachers. It was a time in the school's history where so much was ignored. The teacher's role was closer to babysitting, something they were more qualified for and we, just shy of being lost puppies, required. Most of us went through high school waiting for the last bell to ring. For me it meant freedom from the dungeons of confinement, boredom, and acting in a reckless fashion. Freedom came in the form of the gym for basketball or the fields for baseball. Sports were the one area where I had some level of confidence and believed I could perform. I came to the school with a natural talent, most especially in basketball and baseball. Unfortunately, the majority of my coaches were on the same level in terms of coaching ability as my teachers were academically. The majority of us were treated as bodies meant to excel. This expectation was driven home with only the minimal amount of coaching or teaching. The amount of coaching that was done, if one stretched the meaning of the term, was done under the rages of belittlement and shouts of disparagement.

One coach was a severe alcoholic who left us to practice on our own the majority of the time. The school authorities were well-aware of his drinking habits, but similar to so many other injurious and pitiful issues, it was ignored. Even under these conditions that bordered on being a laughingstock to anyone aware of it, winning was everything and losing was simply not accepted. Regrettably, I was of the same frame of mind at the time. From early childhood, putting so much of my self-esteem into sports and the outcome of games, I would fall into a deep depression with any loss. The majority of my high school coaches confirmed this way of thinking by their reaction to when we did lose. The name-calling and words of degradation were endless and harsh. What they thought they would accomplish by demeaning us as a group or individually had to be based on some sort of demented thinking. As with other areas of my life, my self-image was situational in sports as well. It was all founded on winning or losing, success or failure.

The one thing my classmates and I had was the raw talent to achieve success, despite the lack of leadership. In baseball, we were state champs three out of the four years and state champs in basketball my senior year. Abuse, however, was always part of the atmosphere. Spitting in your face for not making a layup, or having a childlike fit when your opponent scored a goal, or yelling or screaming at halftime as if their position was equal and as important as winning a world war. They blatantly got away with their manner of coaching, and in cases they were rewarded by having a field or building named after them. What was unfortunate, to say the least, was their assaults were always effective.

The relationship I had with the one priest in high school was in one sense a reprieve from a corrupted and volatile home life. Rather than having to go home to a place of emptiness after practice in basketball or baseball, I could find solace and a sense of comfort by having his room to go to. The relationship gave me an anchor which rescued me from totally floating from place to place as if in a bottomless cavity. The one major drawback to the relationship was enough to almost sink what could have been a saving ship of grace. The relationship required, actually demanded, a full-time obligation for me to be available to him when and if he wanted. I would be judged as disloyal if I spoke or became friendly with another priest. It had to be totally exclusive without any outside influences.

I went along with these possessive demands because I thought I needed to and because he was extremely helpful in getting me though the day. Having a place to go to was like having my own private piece of heaven. Other than the time I spent in church, his room became a haven where I felt safe and accepted. I would watch television, maybe do a little bit of homework, and he would drive me home around ten or eleven. At some point, I began to refer to him as my number 2 pop, which in some odd way pleased us both. He had me sign a baseball stating, "To my #2 Pop" and hung it in a class case on his living room wall. I found it somewhat embarrassing but accepted it as the price for admission. There were so many good things he did for me that I considered the embarrassment worth it. It became my safe haven to go to at any time. It was distressing that the emotional rent was so high.

One Friday night, I had plans to play basketball under the lights at a friend's home. As I was about to leave, my priestly father showed up at the door and my mother let him in. They were sitting in the living room when I told them my plans for the night. Without a pause, my mother emphatically insisted I was going to go bowling with Father. I told her I had made these plans the week before and it was not fair if this is what I chose to do. As the priest just sat there self-righteously, my mother and I went back and forth for a few minutes before it erupted into a full-scale shouting match. I was called ungrateful and was repeatedly asked why I was not more appreciative for all the priest had done for me. I said I was very thankful for all he has done but that it did not mean I had to do everything with him. As the three of us sat in the living room, the screaming became more and more intense with the priest making small comments about all he had done for me and given to me.

My younger brother appeared out of nowhere. With a look I had not seen before, he turned to both of them yelling, "Leave my brother alone." I was happy to see him and that he cared for me in this way. Even though it had little effect on the two of them, it was good to have a sense of assurance from someone else. Priests had a great deal of power at the time, and this particular priest's dominance was magnified by the feelings my mother had for him. It was either that night or maybe another time that I accused my mother of being in love with him. The priest was taking full advantage of her feelings for priests and especially him, while feeding on my innocence and lack of influence. I knew full well that I was not the first that he controlled in this way and most certainly I would not be the last.

Yet without exaggerating, I feel this one particular priest, as controlling as he was, saved my life during these high school years. One afternoon, as I as roaming the hallways waiting for that last bell of freedom to ring, I was approached by my varsity coach and the athletic director who happened to be a priest. I said hello to them both with the expectation they would simply respond in a similar fashion. One would think I would have known better after four years of interaction with these people. The priest paused and the coach followed his lead. There was this terse moment of silence following my hello as if the priest was preparing to make one of his profound proclamations. Stated with the conviction and ease as if he was pointing out the colors on the wall, he announced for all who cared to hear, "Ward, you are the biggest waste ever to come to this school." The two continued down the hall without the slightest interest to my condition.

My reaction was a repeated response to the sucker punches I had endured before. I never saw them coming, but the results and intention of the deliverer were always a success. It was like my mind and heart were like silly-putty and at the mercy of manipulation. My sense of self was flattened and left to recover on its own. As so many times before the tears flowed down my cheeks at will as I climbed a set of stairs in search of a place to hide. I headed for number 2 pop's room. I sucked in air as if the blow had been physical. I once again recovered through the process of repression, each time with a more thickened and hard-edged resolve. If one leaves silly-putty out long enough to the impact of open air, the consequences are predictably certain. The process of hardening was well on its way.

By the time I finished high school, the layers of defense around my vulnerable and battered self became more formable. The majority of people I interacted with most likely presumed they were dealing with the real me and not with the defensive mechanisms they actually were. As I lived more and more within these rings of protection, I also came to believe they were part of my true self, one not necessarily developed out of necessity and fear. The goal became to avoid vulnerability as much as I could and to admit it even less. My true self, however that could be defined, disappeared behind the walls of discontent and disappointment.

The self I needed to become experienced minimal growth as it lay undernourished and unemployed. To replenish this starving part of myself, I began at a young age to look for God in everything I did and everything I saw. I was truly a child seeking a fatherly acceptance. In so doing, I had the chance of discovering some parts of my real self. It happened on my walks to and from school reciting the rosary. It happened at daily Mass and the messages contained in the readings of Scripture. A sense of peace arose from the weekly Holy Hours knowing this one person would never turn me away. In my pre-teen years, I began to practice saying Mass with my younger brother and sister as altar servers. A small table would be set, my church missile opened at the appropriate page, and white candy wafers used for communion. I was no longer on the outside looking in. During those moments of pretending to say Mass, I was someone. I was a priest.

7

I had come to a place where I was meant to be. I
don't mean anything so prosaic as a sense of coming
home. This was much different, very different. It was
like arriving at a place much safer than home.

—Pat Conroy

I DO NOT REMEMBER the goodbyes or the exchanging of hugs that one might expect as they left me off on the first day of life away from home. This was not due to a fractured memory on my part but more truly because there was nothing to remember. The only touch my mother knew was with a closed fist, an open-handed slap if you were lucky, or the use of her armor of extensions in the form of a belt or a hanger. Warmth and intimacy were not part of her character traits and certainly not part of her motherly agenda. I cannot say affection was something I missed since there were no expectations for this as being a part of the relationship I had with my mother or father, or any other member of the family.

A lack of expectation and the growing resistance for closeness was transferred on to most of the people I encountered. By the time I went to the seminary, any form of physical closeness made me uncomfortable, translating into a sense of awkwardness whenever any form of closeness seemed inevitable. Even the slightest touch of a hand on my arm made me recoil as if a snake was about to strike. Although not visible to the naked eye, I had created a space around me that was definitely a no-fly zone. In most cases, this was respected by others, not because of some fear on their part but more for my unavailability. The kiss of peace at Mass was the one exception for a brief exchange.

I sat in my room that first evening and tried to adjust to my new home. It was a monk-like room perhaps fifteen by ten feet. A desk, a sink, and a bed filled the space. One window opposite the door would soon enough become a place for long hours of staring out questioning where I fit in among this group of men. At the time I presumed we were all striving for the same thing. Only much later did I reach the conclusion that each individual's desire for being in this exclusive domain of study may not be based on logic or rational decision-making. Private agendas and personal intentions were more of the norm dictating the direction of each seminarian. Some of these intentions would be revealed in due time, while others would come to light only after I left the seminary.

I sat at the edge of my bed on that first night after I emptied a huge trunk containing more clothes than I ever possessed in my life. Growing up in the same room with my brother we simply shared a two-foot-wide closet hosting two or three pants and a few shirts. The clothes I unpacked acted as a reminder that I was not at your typical college, in case anyone thought differently. The trunk had been filled with the required attire for daily life in the seminary. It included a dozen black socks, a pair of black shoes, a black belt, and two black cassocks, along with one white surplus. It included a dozen shirts without collars to be worn under the cassock, leaving room for a white plastic strip attached to the neck of the cassock. The dress code was that of a priest. Not being a priest yet, I was always uncomfortable wearing the white collar. I was dressing in a uniform that was not yet earned. It was the reason I rarely put on the collar outside of the seminary as so many of my peers did. We were still so young to be playing priest. My pimples gave me away.

The cost of the clothes was incomprehensible to me. All these items in the trunk were gifts from my adopted father. He correctly knew there would be no other donor for the attire, along with the fact that I did not know what was needed for daily life the seminary. As with so many things in my life, being ignorant of such common knowledge was par for the course. It was one more task in my life where I approached each event so totally unprepared and so unaware of what was required. It became a natural exercise to just move on to the next step. Everything was learned as you go, sometimes without cost and sometimes coming very close to a catastrophe. On more occasions than I would like to admit, the price for being oblivious often left me in a state of confusion or startled by what was required. As a result, I became an artist at bluffing my way through things and quickly finding a way to get by. This way of living left me in a perpetual state of discomfort. Where were my parents? All of us, my three sisters and brother, were raised like a tree in the backyard. Hopefully there would be enough sun and water to get us by. Call it luck or grace, there seemed to be just enough to get us through each event. In a very real sense, there were mini miracles to save the day.

I awoke the next morning ready for a full week of orientation. Ready in the sense I was physically present, not in the sense of what to expect. I fell asleep the night before with one of those eruptions of tears. I was still very much in the psychological stage of experiencing wordless impressions and non-definable experiences. Other than the ongoing desire to join this exclusive group, I was still a stranger to myself. The lack of understanding for sudden outbursts of tears represented just one example of how self-awareness was repressed, along with any pain or hurt. For me, at least, it was a problem that self-awareness and pain could not be separated from each other. It was a packaged deal. Throughout my early years I had innocently built a solid shield to ward off sharply flung arrows and well-aimed bullets from others. The intense vulnerability I intrinsically felt only brought further embarrassment and shame for who I was. There was never a sense I had the capacity to change, only to survive. By necessity, I slowly became an expert at repressing all personal hurts and the suffering that followed.

Involvement in the Catholic Church was the one place—actually the only place—that consistently kept me from feeling totally isolated. The relationship I was developing with Jesus as a friend and regular companion, the church family, the priests, the nuns, and a few of the church members kept me from falling into an abyss of loneliness. It is this aspect of the church to which I will always be grateful. I was convinced that the seminary was the place where I could enhance these relationships, especially the one I believed I had with the Lord. Any sense I had of meaning and purpose was intertwined in this growing and deeply felt relationship. By coming to the seminary, I was on the path to making this my full commitment. Leaving a world where I felt misplaced and misdirected into a world that held the glorious invitation: "Come follow me."

The seminary orientation was typical in many ways to what the average college student goes through upon their initiation to college life. There were, however, some notable exceptions unique to seminary life. When the dean of students spoke, he had a few of the typical rules, but the one that set me back was when we were told we could not cross the threshold of anyone's room. The priest instructed us that we could stand at the door but not enter the room. He referenced the term "particular friendships" and that such relationships must be avoided at all times. As I sat listening to the dean, I tried to run through a list of possible reasons for such a rule. I kept wondering what could be possibly the translation and meaning of "particular." None of reasons I hypothesized seemed to justify why he was spending so much time on this specific directive and emphasizing it as if it was seminary by law. I buried the entire subject as I had with most things I did not immediately understand. Entering my third year of college, I was still plagued by an inferiority regarding my own level of intelligence. Any form of lingering with a confusing notion only led to more feelings of inadequacy. Getting rid of the issue was easier and certainly more comfortable.

As I sat next to one of my classmates who had spent five years in the Navy and thus five years older, I briefly looked to him to confirm my confusion. Not only did he not corroborate with my sentiment, but he seemed to get a kick out of my lack of understanding. That is when I decided to ignore this peculiar instruction and pretend I did comprehend the rule by remaining silent. It took a great deal of time, months into years, for me to grasp why friendships, "particular friendships" in this case, would be distinguished as something to be cautious about. It was just the beginning of my introduction of how different this place would be. If I was more insightful, mature it could easily be said, the orientation would have been a wake-up call to what was ahead.

My bewilderment was further heightened when the spiritual director focused our attention to rules he must have believed came under his jurisdiction. I cannot recall much of a spiritual direction being presented, but I was once again taken aback by what he thought needed extra emphasis. He leaned forward on the podium and scanned this new group of seminarians. He then pronounced directives as if it were a something we would most assuredly understand. As strange as the dean's commentary on friendships, one specific announcement stood out above the others. Leaning forward to give his next statement more emphasis, the spiritual director said, "I do not want to see any of you in the woods with your head on someone's lap while they strummed a guitar."

He might as well have said, "I don't want to see any of you taking a shit while walking in the woods." I turned once again to my older classmate, perhaps mistakenly, with the hope he would clarify this latest tutorial line spoken to us as newcomers. It was most disconcerting since it came under the category of spiritual lessons to be followed and adhered to. My friend leaned forward and whispered, "I'll talk to you about it later." My personal comprehension of the threshold directive and now the "no head on someone's lap" would take the full year to grasp in even the slightest form. By the end of my four-year stay, it made a great deal of sense, given the population and the environment of the seminary. Regrettably, due to the dire consequences seminary life gave birth to and fostered to, it was a rule that was regularly ignored.

My first summer in the seminary, which was actually entering my junior year in college, was like a summer camp. I was dumbfounded by some of the complaints by some of my classmates who seemed to think the day was too long and arduous. I was accustomed to working all summer and the hours spent earning money were always beyond an eight-hour day. I experienced this summer session as if I was on vacation. The previous summer I caddied at the local country club. I would leave my home around six in the morning, walk about five to six miles to the club, and wait for an opportunity for the caddy master to assign me to a club member. The round of golf would usually end around two, and I would line up for another round. Making a hundred dollars a day was certainly commendable back then, and I was proud of the daily achievement.

My work habits started rather early in life, certainly by the time I reached fifth grade. A prime example was on snow days. If a heavy snowfall was predicted, I would set my alarm every two hours throughout the night to see if it had stopped snowing. No matter what time of night it did stop snowing, I would get dressed and go out and do my seven or so regular jobs. I would do this so when the sun came out I could go out and knock on doors for more jobs. I would come home and change if I was sweating too much and then set out in search for more walks to shovel. This work habit continued into my adult life. Once I committed my mind to one direction, I became obsessed with it. Some might say it was because I did not have a life fulfilling me in appropriate ways or something of worth to participate in. I try not to think how correct they may be. The work ethic did not involve emotions, therefore helped to nullify all the pain and discontent around me.

Following the habit I developed with previous job earnings, I turned over every cent to my mother. I would like to say I did it knowing we did not have much money and this would help the family. When I was doing a particular job, the making of money was always secondary. I was simply trying to fill a major sense of emptiness and a lack of purpose. Giving the money to my mother was not my way of being altruistic. It was more due to an attempt to please this woman of importance in any way I could and then receive some sense of recognition. These attempts were never successful or perhaps temporary at best, forcing me to eventually pass on this desire for some sense of self-worth onto other significant figures in my life. This is how my attachment to priests transformed from a need to a prerequisite for my next stage of life.

I looked forward to returning to the seminary after the summer break. For the first time in my life, I felt I had direction and an objective. In a few short years, I would be a priest. Each day in the seminary seemed complete and fulfilling. A universal alarm would go off around five-thirty in the morning, calling us to Mass to start the day. Breakfast followed and I always considered this and every other meal a feast. Given the complaints from many of my peers this perspective is probably more of a reflection on the kind of food I was accustomed to eating. I would hear others complain about the food when I thought I was at the Ritz. Daily meals of this kind were certainly not part of my past life. Following breakfast, the mornings were spent in class, chapel prayers before lunch, and then onto a very acceptable lunch menu. In the afternoons we were free to do what we wanted and my time was filled with one sport or another. Many of the older men in the seminary were good athletes, which made the afternoon fun and challenging. Many of our repressed emotions, especially our four on four basketball games, were released during this time period. I actually saw the need to wear a mouthpiece as a protection against flying elbows. After dinner, there was a short break, night prayers, and then lights out shortly after.

Night prayers seemed special. It had to do with all six years of seminarians gathering at the end of the day with a spiritual intent. I was so proud and honored to be a part of this unique and committed group of men. It was a time period of innocence regarding seminary life. I did not know how much I did not know. As waves of awareness began to steadily pound forth, my utopian world began to crack. For now, my first year of seminary life, it was never a question that I was where I wanted to be.

I was in my glory as a seminarian intoned the final prayer of the day. One of the deacons, a seminarian in his final year and one step away from the priesthood, would sing out the Latin phrase, "Salve Regina." Then all three hundred of us would join in singing the rest of the prayer. Our voices echoed throughout the chapel. There was no organ playing or any other instruments, just our voices. I wondered why this type of singing had such an effect on me. Later in life when I listened to chant music, I realized the beautiful sound of these voices held the capacity to take me to another place unlike any other. Even now, I can bow my head, thrust my mind and soul into the synchronization of the monk's voices, and I am lifted to this special place once again. It was especially during these times in the seminary that I renewed the choice I had made to come to the seminary and to become a priest. I felt I most certainly made the right choice.

The majority of my classes involved areas in the various philosophies, such as epistemology and cosmetology, along with discussion
of the works of writers like Aristotle, Plato, and Kierkegaard. As a
student, I still took on the same attitude that I had in high school.
I was physically present in the classes, but mentally I was just putting in my time. I do not take any pride in this but see it more as a
reflection of how much the attaining of knowledge meant so little to
me at the time. I certainly did not have a self-image that I could put
into words, nor did I think such an examination was necessary. Most
assuredly I had yet to see the purpose or meaning of knowledge as a
key component to self-worth. Why I did not question it at the time
is once again an indication of how unplugged I was from reality and
my true responsibilities. With the exception of wanting to be a priest,
it also mirrored how lacking a direction seemed acceptable to me. As
was also the case in high school, it did not help that those in charge
were ineffective toward helping me make the necessary changes. One
of my seminary philosophy teachers did go as far as to write on one
of my tests, "You will never be another Aristotle." If he meant this to
be beneficial or to facilitate growth, I missed it.

Other than academics, the first two years in the seminary were
fulfilling and enjoyable. I was basically proud to be part of a group
that was taking part in a world of high ideals with the intention of
turning them into concrete actions. I formed this image of seminary
life mostly due to my association with the older group of men who
were in their final two years before ordination. As soon-to-be priests,
I respected them a great deal and knew in a few short years I would
be in their position. For the most part, they were better-rounded
than my classmates in terms of personality, their participation in various activities, their spirituality and, of course, I liked the fact that
many were athletic. In some ways, I was unknowingly repeating my
naïve idealization that took place in my grammar and high school
years. I presumed what I saw on the surface was also intrinsically
true. Awareness of the truth regarding seminary life came slowly, and
acceptance of this truth came even slower. However, there were certainly those seminarians I greatly admired at the time, especially how
they carried themselves and were responding to this distinctive call-

ing. I saw it as a comradeship to be treasured and presumed I would have these relationships for a lifetime.

Along with the positive feelings generated by being part of this unique team of men, I was also experiencing personal feelings and thoughts that seemed to contradict the path I seemingly was dedicated to. My sexual desires were alive and well and were often directed to one woman or another. More times than not I would deny the contradiction because the feelings were such a powerful pull, and while enjoying them I simply did not want them to stop. The feelings and thoughts were not new and were with me throughout my seminary life. Still swimming in my pool of naïveté, falling in love or experiencing love's vibrations was interpreted as being true love.

My first-year assignment outside the seminary was to teach religion classes to grammar school children at a local parish. One of my classmates and I would drive to the parish every Sunday morning looking forward not so much to the children but to spending time with two of the younger nuns, who were also at the initial stages of responding to their vocation. With limited experience with dating prior to my years in the seminary, my sexual understanding of myself was limited at best and at worse still in the infantile stage. I was constantly falling in love, feeling exhilarated and alive. This initial experience was repeated numerous times in other seminary assignments. I rarely ever questioned it. As with so many other areas of my life, I did not want to admit to anything that might contradict my desire to be a priest. I never considered the notion of how and why I ended up in the seminary, and I am sure my superiors preferred I not go there also. To be a priest was considered a calling, purely spiritual. The underlying psychological reasons for any of us being there were never discussed. If one happened to reflect on reasons other than the spiritual, it was responded to with a simple and ingenuous resolution. There were definitive consequences for this ongoing denunciation and for the shallow rebuttals to serious questions. Denial often led to serious problems. The effects of refuting all thoughts of opposition to our calling often led to perverse and indelible aftereffects for many.

At some point during this first year, I did approach my spiritual advisor to discuss the sexual thoughts and feelings I was having on a regular basis. The discussion I wanted to have with him was not limited to these cute nuns who were trying to fulfill their vocational demands of celibacy as well. I was aware the nature of my thoughts was becoming more obsessive and intense, especially when there was nothing strong enough to distract me. The spiritual advisor was an older man whom my adopted priest from my college days suggested I choose for guidance and as a confessor. At that time, we went to confession weekly, and during one of these sessions I expressed to him the sexually obsessive thoughts I was having not only toward this young nun but other women as well. His bowed head suddenly shot up from his pious position, and he stared at me as if he was greatly disappointed. He then said with not so subtle disdain, "And I thought you were doing so well!" Lucky for me, I suppose, he did forgive me my so-called sins, at least the ones he thought were sins. I thought it better to find another confessor, for his sake as well as mine. Just as I was in denial regarding the reality of my sexual drive, so it seemed the faculty of priests were as well. It was a subject that was basically ignored, leaving each seminarian to deal with it on his own. We all knew the priesthood required a celibate life but never genuinely considered how this would be accomplished. The cost for this denial becomes more than evident as the hidden lives of seminarians and priests came to the forefront.

During the next two years of my personal development as a human being, the sexual aspect did not mature in the slightest. Regression or deformity was closer to the truth. I was not sure if men outside the seminary were growing at a faster pace or were having similar difficulties, but most certainly the environment in the seminary was not conducive to any sort of healthy progress in this area. The seminary was a breeding ground for sexual pathology.

With each of my parish assignments, the "falling in love" experience would be repeated with various levels of intensity. My mind existed in two worlds: the extreme desire to be a priest and the natural instincts to be in love. I did not discuss this contradictory dilemma with any of the priests at the seminary for fear I would be judged as unfit for celibate life and be asked to leave. I also presumed it would just go away in time or perhaps foolishly thought it was something I would just have to learn to live with. I never considered the disastrous consequences for such a plan, and I am sure neither did my fellow seminarians. I am presuming the authority figures looked the other way most likely due to fact they were living this contradiction themselves. The ignoring and denial often led to tragic and dreadful consequences for many, both in the seminary and later as priests. Yet the root causes for these consequences while in the seminary remained unaddressed or disregarded as if inconsequential.

Those in authority, as I was to discover later, knew full well the appalling consequences for the denial of one's basic humanness and, more importantly, the costs in terms of behavior for this denial. Their awareness was clearly evident in their warnings regarding the theme of "particular friendships." It was, however, a caution that lacked any form of sincerity or authenticity. It was like giving a child a huge chocolate bunny at Easter time but telling him he cannot touch it or eat it. Somehow the child would have to satisfy their aroused need for chocolate either by sneaking a taste of the bunny itself or finding another questionable substitute. Their warnings put us all on a gang plank of inevitable failure. As the children we were, we were forced to unknowingly search for a problematic alternative. "Particular friendships" took center stage.

Friendships, and the desire for commitment on the part of another to a friendship, were an obsessive preoccupation in seminary life. To the point of being fanatical, open discussions about who were friends with whom and the degree of their loyalty were not only obsessive in nature but increasingly detrimental regarding our human growth. In my second year in the seminary, I went to a Yankee double-header that lasted over five hours. The older seminarian I was with spent at least four of those hours discussing specific seminarians and their lack of loyalty and trustworthiness regarding friendships. The entire topic was eating him alive, and he was by far not alone. He would ruminate with irrational thoughts of losing a friend to a rival. The entire conversation involved clues and examples of betrayal by one of his particular friends. In many respects, it was the number one topic of the day for a vast number of my classmates. Plagued by deep disappointments in relationships as a child, I was enticed to join this creepy and bizarre theater of desperation.

I was not as intense as this older seminarian, but it did become an issue for me during the last part of my second year in the seminary. While denying how desperately alone I felt, I became engulfed in the childish game of jealousy. Underlying the absurd need to have specific boyfriends (the seminary officials called it "particular friends") was the need for some sort of compensation for not having girlfriends or normal friendships. Our intrinsic need to belong and to be included was transferred onto the activity and dynamics of friendships. Although it made me feel sick and more like a degenerate, I began to focus on a few seminarians, older and younger, as potential friends. I started to analyze and rate their degree of allegiance to me. If and when one showed more attention to another seminarian, I would initially feel jealous, then crushed, and then follow it with an irrational anger toward him. I knew my mind was being contaminated with unreasonable and senseless thoughts, but the need to feel significant and the drive for acceptance often outweighed common sense. Enclosed and bounded in the environment of seminary life, the options for healthy choices were extremely limited. The authorities in charge were well-aware of this emotional Catch-22. There were times when I was literally driving myself crazy as I attempted to survive the seminary's amphitheater of "particular friendships."

On one occasion, I approached one targeted friend to test him on his loyalty and fidelity to me. Desperate for reassurance, I asked him if they transferred everyone, himself excluded, from the seminary to another place and brought it an entirely different group of seminarians, would he care. His answer of "No, it would not bother me," was quick and to the point. My disappointment and letdown were immediate. He would not want me to stay? Did he not place some value on our friendship? Was he this cold and indifferent as a human being? The questions were driving me into frenzy, followed by equal bouts of anger and depression.

If I was smarter and not so immensely naïve about the imposed consequences of seminary life, my anger would have been better directed to those in charge. It was truly a setup. We were all being framed into thinking we could live a celibate life if that what was required to be a priest. Those priests in charge knew full well how unlikely this was a possibility in any healthy manner and that the majority of seminarians would have to find a way to compensate for this irrational requirement. They also knew the compensation would be far from a healthy choice and would more than likely lead to abnormal if not deviant behavior. It was, one must be reminded, the life they were trying to live themselves. The costs for doing so were often devastating to them and to all those closely involved.

We were putting on a show to the outside world. What was taking place within the walls of the seminary was hidden in dark secrecy. There would be times when one seminarian or another would profess out loud that we might very well be taking the vow of celibacy, but certainly not the vow of chastity. It was said as a joke but also with a non-verbal sense of relief. The willingness to live out this lie, hidden to those outside seminary life, would continue after ordination for most. Those with inside knowledge knew of the deception and became more than proficient in carrying it out. Decades later, it would blow up in their faces in the form of a major crisis within the church's priesthood. Only the lay people would experience shock.

8

I've written more about my parents than any writer in the history of the world, and I still return to their mysterious effigies as I try to figure out what it all means—some kind of annunciation or maybe even a summing-up. They still exert tremendous control over me even though they have been dead for so long. But I can conjure up their images without exerting a thimbleful of effort.
—Pat Conroy, *A Lowcountry Heart: Reflections on a Writing Life*

I HAD TO RECEIVE special permission from the rector to obtain a regular paying job between the summer of my first and second theology years. Most of my classmates would be assigned to a local parish, hospital, school, or orphanage. The purpose of this type of work was noteworthy but came with one major deterrent for me: no money. I went through my years at the seminary basically penniless or living on the bare minimum. I had a morning ritual of mooching cigarettes from my classmates until I had enough to fill a pack. The pack was filled with all different brands, but at this point in my life one could not be choosy. At the end of each meal, I would follow what was referred to as the "slop wagon" and pack as many left over apples, bananas, and oranges I could to carry to my room for food during the evening. I did not consider myself poor or deprived, for it was just a continuation of a lifestyle lived as a child. My siblings and I somehow made it through each day and learned the techniques of financial survival, which for me often involved many hours working to make money. When this was not enough, I would turn to mooching and, at times of desperation, stealing.

It seemed many of my peers at the seminary did not have to agonize over the lack of money. I was one of the few people that had no choice on whether to work or not. During the school year, their individual rooms were filled with snacks and a range of items that brought them additional comfort. Most of them had their personal stereos, which I interpreted as they must be rich, since that was not in the realm of being possible for me and a few others like me. Their clothing was a vast variety and always store-bought, while a friend and I paid a dollar for our pants and shirts from the mission box. When the rules became less rigid at the seminary, they were able to afford on a regular basis lunch or dinner out at some fancy restaurant. When we returned to the seminary from winter break, there would be stories of their skiing vacations or basking in sun on some island. Rarely did any of this actually bother me because I was accustomed to this discernable difference growing up as a child in my neighborhood. Nothing was ever new in our house; items were always passed down from a wealthier relative or obtained at a recent garage sale. There was no complaining by me or my siblings; and we just assumed this is the way it is and will continue to be. It was a lifestyle, financially speaking, that commanded an intense work ethic.

What began to bother me by the end of my second year in the seminary was all the talk of money and the need to be around it. When conversations centered on future parish assignments, the desire to be placed in one of the wealthier parishes seemed to be a prerequisite for becoming a priest. Some outwardly detested the possibility for being assigned to a poor parish, which often led to a degree of politicking with the appropriate pastor of choice. As time went on and my experiences in the seminary began to take on common denominators, I was becoming wiser to the intentions of many of my seminary peers. During one summer, I had finished reading Graham Greene's *The Power and the Glory* and recalled a portrayal of the main character, a priest. In refection of his life, the author clarified the basic intent of the priest. He explained, "It had been a happy childhood, except that he had been afraid of too many things, and had hated poverty, like a crime: he had believed that when he was a priest he would be rich and proud—that was called having a vocation."[1] Too many of my fellow seminarians were repulsively following this intention.

The rector needed some convincing about my financial dilemma and need to work. He told me he grew up without much materially and seemed proud to say he did have a car until he was in his thirties. In an attempt to bring some logic to his reasoning, I silently wondered if he grew up in the horse and buggy era. As he went on countering each one my causes, I began to think I had lost the argument. Losing my case was not a consideration, and I knew while sitting before him that I would never comply with his directive to work in a parish. I needed to earn money one way or another and deal with the consequences at a later time.

This form of thinking was consistent with my entire path to the priesthood. I certainly always wanted and presumed I would be a priest. Yet my behavior and some of the choices I made along the way often seemed to contradict this goal, and sometimes ruthlessly risk negating it. There were many times throughout my journey to the priesthood, if observed by an outsider, that they would never presume I had the priesthood as a goal. I personally never considered the incongruity of my actions nor considered there may be a price to pay.

In truth, it probably had nothing to do with my goal of being a priest. During preteen and teenage years, goals were rarely established due to my presumption they would only bring disappointment. Life during those years was unreliable and unpredictable. Looking forward to something or making plans would often be an exercise in futility. Survival was more of the manner of operation. At this time, I desperately needed a summer job and any consequences to this momentary decision were not part of my thought process.

At the end of our meeting I was relieved to receive his permission to work, as reluctant as he was to do so. I lucked out and was able to get one of the highest-paying summer jobs in the area. It was in a brewery a few towns from where I lived. The hours were three to eleven and was referred to as the alcoholic shift. It did not take me long to learn how it acquired this infamous distinction. Even though the beer was free, the majority of the elder adults preferred to bring their own libations of vodka or gin. I immediately found the beer prior to pasteurization especially delicious. The first week, I was like a kid in an ice cream shop where each item seemed to beckon you to grab it off the rack. The consequences of such excess during the first few nights cured me of such intemperance, and I turned to drinking soda the rest of the summer.

The job itself required me to arrive at the brewery and shape-up, meaning to wait until there would be an opening for that day. The person in charge of choosing who would work that day turned out to be an older, conservative Catholic, and he somehow found out I was a seminarian studying for the priesthood. It made his day and therefore it made mine. His only requirement for giving me a job each day was that I promise to say my second Mass for him and his intentions. He presumed I would be saying my first Mass for my family. Of course, I willingly agreed yet felt some degree of shame for selling my future in such a manner. It was my first dealing with what extra favors could be obtained just by being a priest. It almost seemed like the old days of selling indulgences to the naïve Catholics promising to get poor souls out of purgatory. In this case, I was selling my second Mass to earn a summer job. Unbeknown to me at the time, it was just the beginning of charade that would continuously take place between the faithful seeking an advantage on their path to the heavenly gates and the priest who fabricated his ability to offer a guaranteed benefit. It was an offer that few lay Catholics could refuse. The so-called benefits, of course, were always attached to some financial donation.

The working hours of three to eleven basically killed any opportunity to do much during the off-hours. After morning Mass, I would stop at the bakery for my favorite cherry crumb buns and share them with my mother over a pot or two of coffee. To those aware of the contentious relationship I had with my mother, this breakfast ritual would seem paradoxical. I think using the label of "momma's boy" would be stretching the definition of our relationship, but certainly there was the underlying need to get her approval. I learned in my psychology class about the power of the intermittent reward system. Skinner's pigeon would be in a constant state of tranquility as long as it could tap the food box and receive its pellet on first request. The pigeon's calmness turned into a crazed frenzy when Skinner repeatedly changed the number of times the pigeon would have to tap the box for the reward. Even though it might tap fifteen or twenty times before the food was delivered, it never wavered from trying, even to the point of causing self-destruction. I was not a momma's boy, but certainly close to being a dumb pigeon with the motherly rewards being few and far between.

For many of the other seminarians and many of the priests, there was another scenario taking place with the relationship they had with their mothers. This was pointed out to be by an older seminarian when he brought up the timing of when priests or seminarians decided to leave the seminary or priesthood and go in another direction. It seemed more than a coincidence it often occurred not long after the death of their mother. We briefly went down a list of names of those who left and discovered how uncanny it was the case for more than just a few of them. This theoretical proposition could not be discussed openly since the priesthood was regarded as a divine calling and therefore had to be absent of any psychological undercurrents or influences. The extended numbers involved in this motherly scenario, no matter how much they were denied or ignored, suggested other motivations for a vocation other than a heavenly calling.

Statistically untested, this one insinuation for what might be part of a priestly vocation was never a topic given any serious reflection. It did not seem to matter as to the underlying reasons for a man, at a very young age, to choose the celibate and chaste life of the priesthood. The motherly relationship was just one of many possibilities. There was, however, a psychological test prior to entering the seminary and one which I was prepped for by my then high school spiritual advisor. Among many of his directives, one of the ones he emphasized was to make sure I drew the full body of a woman when asked to do so on this supposedly all-inclusive exam. He stressed to be sure I included all of the woman's parts. He also advocated I not reveal the feelings I had about my parents or any of the personal troubles I might be struggling with at the time. I never understood how all of this was part of my desire to be a priest, especially the appropriate drawing of a woman. Understanding something was not at the time a requirement for my decision-making. As a mindless and mechanical puppy on a leash, I dutifully followed his directives.

To those in authority, the most vital test was the personal interview with the rector. It was an extremely short interaction with the primary concern being if I had an index finger and thumb. I only learned later that this was a huge requirement, for these would be the fingers that would handle the host. No thumb, no priesthood. Thankfully, I suppose, mine were intact. I also must have passed the drawing of the woman, as primitive as I am sure it was. I was accepted, along with most of the candidates. It most certainly was not a difficult process for admission when it most assuredly should have been.

Six of my classmates were notably rejected. The rumor spread quickly that they had gone to a topless bar the week before. This incident was treated as a scandal of the highest level and definitively demonstrated to those in charge the unworthiness of these individuals to become priests. Aside from the poor timeliness of their excursion, no other factors were contemplated regarding their worthiness for seminary admission. The six went to another seminary run by another diocese. Could it be these seminary officials judged the bar incident as not being abnormal? I felt for my peers to have been judged by one single incident, for each of them were good and decent people. I was well-aware, but for a bit of luck there go I.

Following Mass, I got through the summer mornings by listening endlessly to the music written by Burt Bacharach. With his tunes as a backdrop, I would go through the hours fantasizing about one theme or another. At times, I would be a parish priest performing my priestly duties and successfully bonding with people in a meaningful way. There would be times when I would be a successful author or have a highlighted athletic experience. Scoring over sixty points in a game or pitching a no-hitter was not unusual. A good portion of the daydreaming would involve a relationship with a woman, sometimes known personally or some celebrity I was attracted to via her latest movie. Not that I hold them entirely responsible, but none of the seminary spiritual advisors, or one priest for that matter, were able to offer a way to stop what would become obsessive thoughts about women over my years in the seminary.

Fantasy kept the reality of having a possible relationship alive. Even though there was a major gap and a sense of loneliness throughout the days and weeks, daydreaming acted as a partial compensation. It also shielded me from the harsh reality that I was willingly giving up an intimate life with a woman and the joys of having children. It was a pretend drug that temporarily cured a life of predictable deprivation. As I imagine most seminarians and priests do, I presumed that I could successfully pull off a life of celibacy. Part of that thinking was based on my past and present experiences with close relationships. For the most part they were hurtful and painful, especially with the encounters I had with my parents. The same was true with the significant authority figures in my life. The majority of experiences were demeaning and left me feeling degraded and humiliated. Therefore, relationships were not so much something I was giving up but more something I wanted to avoid.

This had to be true for my three sisters and brother as well. The reality of the dysfunction we were reluctantly participating in was most evident with the death of my father. I was home from the seminary for Thanksgiving, and the tension and fighting between my parents was reaching a new high. I can still picture their face-to-face confrontations, always leaving me in the fear of the possibilities with another round of battle to begin. The fear, however, was overshadowed by the woeful nature of the situation. It was pathetic but certainly more sad than scary to watch two adults spray their self-created venom on each other. It once again galvanized the gloom of the household.

Home from the seminary on this first evening, I intervened in their most recent verbal and nearly physical battle. As by custom and a distorted sense of allegiance, I took the side of my mother. I did this not because I was close to her or thought she was the wounded one. She was simply more of a physical presence, both in frame and spirit. She demanded loyalty from the minors she was in charge of. I knew well the price to pay for taking another position. My biased perspective could not have been more evident and more painfully acted upon as I once again made the decision to be on her side in this latest confrontation. She was a much stronger force than my father, more prominent in every way and therefore demanded my attention. A son so wanting to please took the bait.

Up to this point my father continued to be a non-entity in my life. We rarely spoke to each other since the time I was ten years old. There is no pride or satisfaction in this stance, even when I recall the rare occasions we did speak. The worse sides of me came out where I felt I was swimming in a gutter of filth and obscenity. We would often pass each other as he entered the stairwell to go upstairs. His cheek would be protruding, filled with another shot of liquor. Our eyes would meet and I would utter in disgust, "Don't choke on that, now." Was I meant to be his accuser? Who was this angry and pompous child who dared to lack the compassion for the weak and the miserable? Both my parents filled all of us with a less than subtle remorse for not being better children. Self-reproach would become a way of life, permeated with a sense of endless adult guilt.

My father's family role was not always passive. He consistently committed acts as if he were on a trail of revenge. He carried out acts of retaliation as if to say "fuck you" to us all. With five hungry children in the house, he would return home from the deli on Saturdays with six slices of baloney. Was he concerned that any of his five children may want lunch also? If I was home, rare for me on a Saturday afternoon, I would watch him hunched over the kitchen table biting into white bread filled with six measly slices. With his thinly lined back to me, I would repugnantly approach him with loathing, perhaps thinking I was standing in for my siblings. I would sit by his side as he bit into a morsel of baloney and, as his bold and self-righteous son, whisper in his ear, "I hope you choke on it." Immersed in an atmosphere meant for the malevolent, I allowed myself to become as equally malicious. If he only yelled back or slapped me across the face, then I could say there was some link between the two of us. He would rise up and leave for the backyard. His chaise lounge, a coffin without a lid, would be the place to sleep off another intoxicated body. His ongoing silence and isolation from us all made his fatherhood a deceptive delusion.

My relationship with him was not unique just to me, for he was absent from all my siblings as well. There certainly was not a favorite daughter or son. He seemed to live his life in seclusion, walking around the house like an uninvited guest. It was one thing to have a disparaging marriage, but he seemed to consciously elect to detach so forcibly and so noticeably from his children. How many times did I take in his frail and saddened face? We would just stare at each other, digesting the other's scowl. A father and a son both filled with torment and tortured by the others existence. If nothing else, it was bizarre more incidences of violence did not take place.

I saw him as a frail man. Depression is not a word I would have known to use at the time. His face always seemed filled with sorrow and dejection. My parents continued to sleep in separate bedrooms, and my younger sister still had the honor of sleeping in the other single bed in his room. Although much fewer in number, I still crawled into his bedroom in the middle of the night to empty his wallet. A poor soul that his son steals from, passes him endless times in the hallway, sometimes with a grunt and sometimes with a "fuck you." His facial reaction was tragic and at the same time heart-wrenching. The engrained guilt is still firmly implanted like an unrequested pacemaker hidden under my chest. The emotionally charged impulses are a constant reminder of the pain that permeated this relationship. The only self-forgiveness I can muster in order to gain even a slight relief is that I was young and ignorant. I am positive some of the deeply-sealed scars in my heart and mind were carved out by him. I would continue to look to the church for healing. It is no wonder that I was such open prey for that priest searching for a son to adopt.

Do I now feel miserable about the entire relationship with my father? That would be an understatement. The pre-Thanksgiving fight between my mother and father was bringing this part of our family history to a climax, an ending none of us would have predicted. Having taken my mother's bait, I once again became the untested mediator in their face-to-face combat. I confronted my father as if I were an adult. I pulled him aside and told him I was sick and tired of the destructive atmosphere he and my mother were routinely creating, slowly decaying the minds of their children. I told him, as if I had the power to do so, that he had two options: either go live with your sisters in Brooklyn or find a hotel. I demanded he leave by the time I would go back to the seminary, which was a few days after Thanksgiving.

That night, or it might have been the following evening, my mother received a phone call from a hospital in Newark that my father was in a car accident and was required to stay overnight. I went with my mother to the hospital, repeating my role of escort and involuntary bodyguard. We found him in a single room with a huge bump on his head. The visit was brief as my parents began fighting immediately. Round one was vicious, and I did not let it get to round two. I told my mother to leave the room and turned to my father and said, "This has to stop! This shit has to stop! Shit, why don't you just kill yourself!"

I left the room, totally disconnected mentally, and never thought to question the car accident. I cannot bear to think what his thoughts might have been as he lay in that bed alone in darkness. I do know we were his children and he was responsible for the life he created for himself and for us. I know he left us all with a lifetime of incurable welts that would disfigure the perspective we started out life with. Nonetheless, he did not deserve this isolation. No human does.

The next day, somewhere around noon, I was upstairs with some friends in the den. The doorbell rang and I went down to answer it. In the middle of the stairway I witnessed two police detectives speaking with my mother and aunt and uncle. My aunt and uncle were there to discuss the situation with my father being in the hospital. Suddenly, I saw my mother pass out and my uncle break her fall. As I joined them I can only remember someone saying my father was dead. He had killed himself. I went back upstairs, traumatized I presume, and reported to my friends what I just heard. My immediate reaction was no reaction, for I already, at twenty-one, have been well-trained in defensive maneuvering. My efficiency in shutting down all unwanted thoughts and feelings was nurtured early and had reached maturity by this time. I would be motivated further by future events to expand my capacity for repression. It is a button I can still turn on and off.

The newspapers reported he landed with a thud! The word itself is planted in the depths of my subconscious, rising to awareness with the slightest provocation. Eyeing the sixth-floor window of a tall building is enough to bring the horror back. The suicide was something a priest friend tried to keep from the papers, but I would later realize this is something the press, and perhaps their readers, thrive on. I went with my uncle to the police station to pick up my father's belongings. It was there I was told there were no skid marks on the road where the car accident took place the night before. It was my father's first attempt at suicide. For the longest time I wondered how I could have been so ignorant that night in the hospital. Then, there were my last words to him! Hindsight is often brilliant, but can also carry with it an ongoing shame.

Priests from the parish came to the house. I distinctly recall one of them saying matter-of-factly, "If I had to pick the number one family in the parish, it most certainly is yours." I should not have been as surprised as I was. The life my siblings and I were living was hidden from view to the outside world. In the majority of interactions with others we painted a different picture, one impressed upon them by our lack of emotional affect to repulsive behavior taking place behind closed doors. It was not that any of us were consciously faking it. What was probably more the truth is that we did not know we could talk about it, or too embarrassed to do so. Like the rape victim who feels dirty and ugly, and wonders if they did anything to deserve the carnage. If there were an opportunity to discuss our situation, it would sound more unbelievable than true. Who would believe us? Who would care? Certainly, we fooled this priest. There was no doubt our manner of surviving left so many others with a different image of us as a family. I think I can speak for all us when I wish if only it were true.

The events that followed all seemed to take place in the midst of a dark overhanging cloud. I went through the following days like a robot, moving from place to place fully zoned out, as if someone else was monitoring each movement. The morning after his death I took a bath rather than the normal shower, perhaps thinking it would offer a more potent cleansing. Since the newspapers made the event public, I knew I had to prepare for telling my mother how my father died. Passing out, she never heard the policeman's words. I walked into the room with my eldest sister at her side. Both watched me with glazed eyes and mouths open as if still in shock. I sat on the side of the bed, reported the incident as it was written in the newspaper, and left as detached as I had come in. Comprehension was beyond my capacity. Intrinsically I was about to explode.

I went to the funeral home the next morning to see if my father's physical condition was something my family could take seeing. The bump on his head was taken care of by a capable professional staff. It is something funeral people do very well and perhaps more often than we realize. I was more worried about what the fall might have done to his body. Everything seemed normal as he lay dressed in a suit and tie. He seemed at peace, adding another contradiction between what seemed to be and what really was before his death.

At the wake, I did my sibling duty and greeted all the people who came. Still mentally and emotionally frozen, there were no tears or remorse. People filled the funeral home, and a long line formed outside. Following the tradition at the time, the wake went on for three afternoons and three evenings. Our friends and parents came, along with teachers and coaches. One coach inanely said to me, "I thought your father was already dead." It made me think that maybe people did notice my absentee father at the games. Seminarians and priests filled the room, most likely as bewildered as we were. Our family image forever fractured. A fate, perhaps, that could not be avoided. Each member of the family was on a path without a map to show us the way or give a hint to where we were headed. We were most certainly ignorant of the after-effect. Personal pieces of cognitive despair would take years to find their suitable and somewhat acceptable place.

I still had not processed the painful enormity of what was taking place. A bishop came to the wake. He had witnessed the fall and its consequence. He sat by my mother and I greeted him. I praised him for his courage for the prayers he said over my father. I was told he was tightly holding a medal of the Blessed Mother in his hand. I took solace my father was not alone. I returned to my place at the coffin, still not grasping the melancholy darkness of the day. Then again, there were no rehearsals for this role I was designated to play.

I never thought to wonder where my brother and sisters were in the room. We were acting out our own parts as perfect students taught to suffer alone.

The funeral was packed with priests and seminarians, along with relatives and friends. Any detail of the service has been mentally negated. I am assured, but cannot visualize, that I sat with my mother, two married sisters, and my younger sister and brother, who were nineteen and seventeen at the time. The burial scene is absent from my memory. A day or two later we did have Thanksgiving dinner at my aunt and uncle's, the same people present at the dire pronouncement of my father's death. They promised us we would recover.

As a family, we had yet to discuss the tragedy of the days before. It would be years before we would do so. As individuals still dangling in isolation, we might as well be dining with strangers from a foreign land, each speaking in varied tongues. It was not a conscious act of rejection or malice toward each other, since there was never a connection to enable such actions. To this day, it still staggers my mind that we did not reach out to each other. More astounding is that we did not know how. We would end the day with a return to our reclusive rooms of isolation, as if each one of us were an only child. Our mother was nowhere emotionally to be found, not that we would know what to do with it if she were. The Pompeii-like covering of all sensitivities had begun, the excavation of which would takes years to uncover.

Prior to returning to the seminary, I took the responsibility of taking on the paper work that is necessitated by a death, especially one of this kind. The main task was to see if any of the life insurances would be effective; there were five small ones. I went to the funeral home to pick up the papers that would indicate his manner of death. I desperately prayed they would report it as a natural death. Due to the manner in which it was listed, only one insurance policy came through.

I was taken back to the seminary by my adopted priest, sobbing as I waved from the car to my mother. The sadness and utter wretchedness of the past week began to seep through the cracks of a well-defined wall. An uncontrollable flood was soon to follow. I was leaving a place where repression was a mandate for survival. The death of my father was one act of a long and pathological play. Unlike my siblings, I was leaving this stage with the hope I was returning to my home of choice.

9

A true teacher will never tell you what to do. But
he will give you the knowledge with which you
could decide what will be best for you to do.

—Christopher Pike

By THE TIME I completed by senior year in college, the second year
in the seminary, I had become a prolific reader. It was Steinbeck's *The
Grapes of Wrath* that cracked wide open the deeply-rooted conviction
I was not a student. Once I started to experience the excitement of
the written word, the reading became obsessive. I was infatuated by
the whole new world that exploded before me and had never known
existed. I had been living an extremely provincial life wedged in a tri-
angle of school, church, and ball fields, with the church and ball fields
occupying the majority of my time and interest. The inferior conception I had of myself regarding intellectual pursuits had imprisoned
me in a myopic and insular world. As if ejected from a plane hope-
lessly flying in circles I was saved by authors who had the brilliance to
paint with words a world that was both stimulating and expansive. As
if suddenly awakening from a slumber of procrastination, I became
addicted to ideas and the intricacies of people. As a veritable junkie
for more information, I could not wait for my next fix.

The seminary environment was an idyllic milieu for my newly
founded obsession. Aside from morning classes and the required
attendance in chapel, the stretch of open hours lay vacant and free
for a good part of the day. There was also the fact that I was beginning to isolate myself from the majority of the seminarians still in
attendance. When I began my first year at the seminary, the place

was bulging at the seams with over three hundred seminarians, so much so that another building had to be used for housing. By the time I reached my third year, the number was down to around a hundred and steadily shrinking on a semester by semester basis. The ones I identified with, and distinguished as worthy future priests, had either been ordained or left to go in another direction. I could not identify with the majority of those remaining in terms of what I thought the behavior of seminary life should be. The groundwork for an increasingly solitary life was also based on the advent of depression that silently yet lethally slipped into my pores. Undiagnosed by me and those around me, a melancholy state became more and more the norm in my daily existence at the seminary. Isolation became almost fitting and comfortable, enabling me to bury myself in books and hide from the realities of seminary life. Still undiagnosed and ignored, the emotional decline grew in intensity throughout the year.

Returning for my third year in the seminary meant I would begin taking theology classes. This would involve studies that included Scripture, Moral Theology, and Christology. I was looking forward to these classes since it would finally entail subjects that had to do with spirituality and the work I would do as a priest, something I failed to discover in the philosophy classes. My former teacher was correct that I would never be another Aristotle, even though he stated it as if I should be disappointed in myself. He was one of the few authority figures I could shake off as pure nonsense.

An opposite reaction immediately took hold of me during the first few weeks of the theology lectures. A few of the priest professors were deeply intelligent and charismatic, creating within me a desire and fascination that increasingly grew over the next two years. It was both an invigorating yet controversial time in the church. Tangible issues were being discussed that had to do with the everyday lives of church members. I finally had topics and a focus that could be applied to my future years in the priesthood.

The encyclical *Humane Vitae* had been published the year before and had created a storm of controversy throughout the church, including some of the seminary faculty and some of the seminarians. I wish I could say it was the majority of people, but that would mean the majority of people actually cared about the inner workings of the church, which was far from the case, sad to say. In order for a priest to remain in good standing and have the opportunity to move up the ladder of hierarchy, one had to operate under the umbrella of a mindless obedience. This was also the case for the seminarian who wanted to reach ordination.

The primary theme of the *Humane Vitae* encyclical that drew the most attention was the condemnation of the use of birth control by women seeking to avoid pregnancy. The encyclical was not written as an infallible work, meaning it did not come under the pretext of being the absolute truth; it was, nonetheless, accepted and treated this way by the majority of priests. The lay Catholic in good standing was expected to take this new dictum most seriously and follow its directives wholeheartedly. The expectation primarily centered on the abstinence of any form of birth control with the exception of the rhythm method, which the authorities stamped as permissible. This approach to the act of procreation became a laughingstock to anyone with even the slightest level of intelligence and basic common sense. The rhythm method was immediately referred to as the Vatican Roulette. Catholics were expected to play the game established by the single and fatherless males of the church.

A small number of priests throughout the country signed a petition disagreeing with the conclusions and demands of the encyclical. One priest at the seminary, my mentor and spiritual advisor at the time, had the courage to join this group. It was daring on his part because he was putting his priesthood on the line, especially in terms of achieving advancement in the ranks. The remaining priests supported the encyclical by openly agreeing and defending it or by remaining silent. The majority of seminarians did not care one way or another, for it did not affect their personal agenda one way or another.

Disagreeing with the pope was not in vogue at the time, not that it would ever be. Over time, the one priest in the seminary and others like him had to back off or else experience the wrath of a vengeful pope who demanded total loyalty. I was even questioned by a moral theology professor regarding my position, and I wisely, and somewhat condescendingly, claimed ignorance based on the fact that I had not as yet taken any theology courses. Of course, he knew I was being deceitful and hiding behind the shallow shield of academic ignorance. From my mentor, I found out this priest on several occasions pushed to have me expelled from the seminary as an unacceptable candidate for the priesthood. I was not alone living under this constant threat of expulsion. One of my peers verbalized the notion that perhaps consideration should be given to a married priesthood. The thanks he received for even entertaining this innovation was discussion among some faculty members on whether he should be allowed to remain in the seminary. So much for thinking outside the box.

Even though it involved a small minority reacting to this injurious encyclical, it could be argued it was at the center of the beginning of the modern church's downfall in terms of credibility and participation. Certainly, throughout the history of the church, there were other major controversies that led to critical reactions and, in some cases, schisms. For the modern church, *Humane Vitae* became an immediate fireball leading to a major polarization within the church and a lessening of active participation. The encyclical acted as a lid of repression and basically nullified the works of Vatican II, a work that emphasized individual responsibility and freedom of conscience. It is beyond the realm of ludicrous that the church authorities, with its myopic and distorted vision regarding the challenges of being human, would dictate to adults' issues of sexuality and having children. It is even more preposterous, if one considers the conditions of Third World countries living in poverty, dealing with overpopulation and the ever-growing disease of AIDS. It is no wonder that, in the ensuing years, there was an enormous number of priests leaving the priesthood, a major decline in seminary enrollment, and a substantial decline in active participation by the lay members of the church.

Over the next two years of taking theology courses, I would discover that any disagreement with the pronouncements and dictums of the hierarchy brought about immediate chastisement, including for some the request to leave. To remain in the good graces of those in charge, a passive acceptance of all that was taught was required.

Following this unwritten requirement of silent acquiescence to all that was taught, it also became a prerequisite for anyone wanting to be ordained a priest. A combination of fear or apathy permeated the basic atmosphere of the seminary. I was too enthralled and literally excited about what I was learning in some of the courses to even consider this position of stagnation. As a result, my first year of theology was just the beginning of my continuous clashes with certain professors, most especially those dealing with the controversial moral issues of the day.

Other than the moral theology professors who were mouthing concepts that lacked any common sense or applicable logic, I had the extraordinary experience to have brilliant teachers of Scripture expanding on the lives of the apostles and the life of Christ. Famous for his short but always inspiring sermons, one particular priest presented a class on the writings of St. Paul. I could not wait to get to his classes, for each one of them was profound and inspirational. I was not only learning the underlying meaning and significance of Paul's passages on an intellectual level, but more notably I was experiencing a spiritual growth of my faith. Even though St. Paul was not a priest himself, his faith and dedication to the life of Christ became a model for the person I wanted to be. Under threats of exoneration and the risk of being killed, he remained committed to preaching the message with an eagerness that was filled with an intense passion for his love of Jesus Christ. For seminarians, he was a prototype of what a priest should be. I am positive the majority of my classmates did not concur with my enthusiasm, much less even think about it.

Another professor had a unique way of presenting the life of Christ and the manner in which one might analyze living the Christian life. He chose six highly renowned American authors and discussed not only the story line itself as it unfolded but also emphasized the depth and strength of the key characters in each book. He listed six of each author's most famous works and assigned us the task of reading at least one novel of each author. With a masterful approach to each book, he unveiled the underlying Christian message in the underlying themes interwoven within each chapter. As each story progressed, he explored the development of each character both psychologically and spiritually. I sat in each of his classes spellbound by the depth of this priest's brilliance and the wisdom he shared regarding the art of being a true Christian.

Toward the end of the semester, the professor called us to his office individually to give us feedback on our papers. This meeting was like taking another one of his classes as once again there was so much to learn from this teacher with each interaction. At some point during our meeting he asked me which books I read from the list of the six authors. I responded by telling him I had read them all. He hesitated, most likely presuming I must have misunderstood the question. He asked again and I repeated my previous statement. He lowered his head momentarily and looked at me with an approving if not astonished smile. He was one of the few seminary priests that I cared what they thought of me. Receiving an endorsement from this particular priest made me feel I was on the right path to being the best priest I could be. I doubt he was aware of my addiction to books and how my self-imposed position of isolation made reading all these books possible. In any case it was overkill. I was learning a great deal, but the price was unknowingly detrimental. Either I was trying to rectify my educational iniquities of the past or compensating with the cave-like atmosphere I had imposed upon myself. Either way, I was in the middle of a breakdown.

The fact that this one priest and I related well as student-teacher laid the groundwork to avert what could have been a major crisis in my seminary life. Each year a well-known speaker would come to the seminary and speak to us all on one topic or another. On this particular occasion, the speaker was a high-ranking priest who held a number of leadership positions throughout America. The place was packed with not only seminarians and seminary professors but priests from outside parishes as well. At the end of the talk, as was the usual custom, he took questions from the audience. It lit a fuse in me, and I prepared to throw a bomb.

During the year, I had experienced a growing discontent for the hierarchy in the church, most especially those who took extremely conservative and what I thought to be incongruous stands on moral issues. Albeit with more emotion than thought, I thought that this speaking engagement was a good time to point out the unreasonableness of the church leadership, especially when it came to ministering to the needs of the everyday Catholic. He recognized me and I stood up with an extended outline comparing the Catholic hierarchy to the CEOS of major companies. My question, which was more of a statement, emphasized the point that the hierarchy, as with CEOS, cared more about power and the things power could give them than the real needs of the people they are supposedly serving. After fifteen minutes of my diatribe denouncing the majority higher-ups in positions of authority, I looked to the speaker in anticipation of his response. There was a deadly silence in the room, the kind where one is waiting in suspense for something dreadful to happen. Without even the slightest hesitation, the speaker coughed while muttering, "That's nice. Next question?" One would think laughter would follow his blatant dismissal of my statement, at least to break the raucous silence. Sensing that all eyes were on me, I was somewhere between embarrassment and rage.

Without being fully aware of it until after the fact, I became the talk of the seminary the next day. Most presumed I would be called in and asked to leave. To make matters worse, it was announced the previous night's speaker had been made a cardinal and his job was to oversee all seminaries and seminarians throughout the world. I wondered, once again cynically, whether I should send him a card of congratulations. I was obviously still not getting that I was a tiny peg in the middle of the ocean when it came to having any effect on church matters.

I am sure I would have been asked to leave if it were not for the intervention of the priest who taught the class involving all those novels. He called me into his office and at first questioned me about whether I actually made up the question myself. He was presuming it was my priestly mentor who had previously taken many liberal positions himself. I was a little taken back that he might think I was incapable of formulating the question I asked. He then explained to me that I had every right to formulate my own thoughts about the church, but he felt also there was a proper time and place to express them. He explained that the speaker was his guest and deserved some respect. I felt encouraged that he did not totally ostracize me for my behavior, while at the same time I did agree with him that my timing was irrational and totally inappropriate. The lesson, however, was short-lived and certainly not applied in many of the classes I would continue to take in the seminary.

The third professor I grew to admire was my Scripture professor. I had the opportunity to take his class in a tutorial format. Along with five other seminarians, I would meet weekly with this professor for about an hour and a half to discuss the readings assigned the previous week along with receiving readings for the coming week. It was a great deal of work and much more than we would have had in a regular class. The work, although overwhelming at times, was profoundly worth it. The two years of Scripture classes raised my level of understanding of the life of Jesus to new heights. It had a great effect on my prayer life in the sense I was getting to know the person I was talking to on a much deeper basis, which consequently led a greater depth in our relationship.

Under the direction of my seminary professors and the numerous readings they assigned, the intellectual pursuit of understanding the Gospels led me to a completely new understanding of what it meant to be a Christian, a follower of Christ. I was learning so much more about who Jesus was, often referred to by the scholars as the historical Jesus. Moving steadily away from my childlike vision, as in picturing a God residing in heaven, I began to learn of a God who was among us. Each day, and each week of classes, I was becoming more and more ecstatic about this faith community I wanted to be so much a part of.

One disturbing factor about the class was the professor's emphasis that we were not to share what we were learning with the people we would eventually serve. It was his belief that all the new discoveries regarding the writers and writings of the Bible would somehow interfere with the faith of the average Catholic. He was correct in the notion that the church for decades and decades had interpreted the writings of the Bible in a concrete and rigid manner, as if everything they taught was the definitive and final interpretation of the Bible stories. The authorities presented so-called truths as if they were permanent and never could change. In many cases this form of teaching is still taking place either in a direct misleading manner or by the silence or omission of discussion regarding these supposed truths. In doing so, the church has boxed itself into a corner and therefore cannot handle when new discoveries are made, which often alter previous interpretations in an alternative manner.

My problem with the suggested silence of these new facts, and keeping the lay people in the dark, was that it contradicted what I was experiencing regarding these new visions regarding the Scripture writings. Simply put, it transported me to another place. It was a place that brought life and a sense of excitement to my spiritual life. Because of the wonder and awe these new interpretations created, there was a natural urge to want to share it with others. Up until this time, the Bible stories had become routine and were often heard in a mindless fashion, similar perhaps to how the people in the pews hear and react to them. Learning what was on the minds of the writers, and how various communities envisioned their faith, made so much more sense in terms of how the Bible became the book it is. It did not threaten the beliefs I had; it enriched them. I wondered why our Scripture professor would have this fear about this new knowledge and believed it would hurt the average parishioner's faith. When I did become a parish priest, my plan was to offer them the same experience that was offered to me.

Almost from the beginning, my moral theology classes took on a very different tone than the Scripture and Christology classes. Where I was digesting everything I could with the other courses, I found the approach and conclusions to moral topics hard to swallow. The rigid and absolute positions the church took on regarding a number of ethical principles often lacked any common sense or practicality. Most especially, it lacked empathy for the human condition. The greater majority of the issues centered on sex and sexual practices, an area those in charge were obsessed with. They believed they were the final authority in terms of what was right or wrong when it came to sex.

Even though I was in continuous conflict with how these moral issues were being discussed in the seminary, I was immediately drawn to this area of study. I began to admire authors who had doctorates in moral theology, were experts in this area, and wrote opinions that were based on logic and had a lucid understanding of the challenges facing the individual Catholic. A few of those I admired had a master's in psychology along with their doctorates. It made sense if one wanted to have a better understanding for people intrinsically and have more of an insight into human behavior and decision-making. I therefore enrolled at the university for my master's in counseling and psychology.

By the end of my first semester, I easily concluded that the seminary professors' approach to each moral topic came with the final answer in hand and was to be accepted without discussion. It reminded me of the deductive method in plane geometry where an answer was given and one worked backward to prove it to be true. In such a method, all the variables that did not fit the answer, even if they were worthy of consideration, had to be ignored. I began to have a major problem with this blind and authoritative approach to solving crucial issues that affected all church members. It naturally followed that I would also have a problem with the conclusions reached through this method and was expected to accept without debate. Following so many class lectures, I often wondered how the moral theology professors considered this an education.

Thus began my openly combative nature with the moral theology professors. A mutual dislike grew steadily as the year went on. The majority of my classmates did not seem to mind the outdated and often obsolete conclusions the professors were imparting to us. They presumed that we would accept their conclusions whether it made sense or not, a common stance in the seminary. Perhaps some would consider these classmates wiser than I since they knew better not to rock the boat that was taking us to ordination. There were others who took on a submissive position because they simply did not care how these conclusions would affect the everyday Catholic. I had no respect or patience for either group, which once again led to further isolation.

Only years later did I realize my combative nature was not only a waste of time but, even worse, it did not matter to anyone involved.

Still not fully plugged in to the realities of where I was and what was expected of me if I was to remain in the seminary, my vehement nature toward these professors grew as a volcano ready to erupt. Imprudent would be a nice way of putting it, but in truth I was foolishly naïve. It was as if I was at West Point and against guns. Why I did not see this at the time I can only explain as my being somewhere out there in another and separate world.

10

We awaken by asking the right questions. We awaken when
we see knowledge being spread that goes against our own
personal experiences. We awaken when we see popular opinion
being wrong but accepted as being right, and what is right
being pushed as being wrong. We awaken by seeking answers
in corners that are not popular. And we awaken by turning
on the light inside when everything else outside feels dark.

—Suzy Kassem

My fourth year in the seminary, the second year of taking theology courses, was similar to the year before, but this time there was more intensity; it involved diverse stages of true madness on my part. The intensity mostly involved academic clashes with a couple of professors. I also continued to have a problem while the lunacy took place among some of the seminarians, each event having their own distinctive oddity and personal neurosis. Overall, the year was one that was permeated by a deepening depression and extreme sense of loneliness. I was still naïve about the symptoms of depression and, therefore, did not label my various moods as being severely unhealthy and detrimental. For the most part, the priest faculty also seemed unaware of what some of us were going through, unless they were just choosing to simply ignore it. They were there to ordain priests. If they looked too closely at any of us, or looked at themselves for that matter, very few would pass a mental health test successfully. The question was never raised that given the inhuman requirements to be a priest, celibacy being on top of the list, is it even possible to be healthy psychologically and still be a priest? Any type of questioning would put one in jeopardy of dismissal.

There was little to no time given to genuine introspection, most likely in fear of what I might discover. As with so many other avenues to mental health, I was oblivious to how important this practice was for one's mental health. As I learned to do during my childhood, I was more reacting as if a human pinball to the people and events taking place in the seminary. I had left a world behind that was as small-minded and limited as one could possibly imagine. Calling me provincial was more than an understatement. My childhood was constrained in terms of experience and personal evaluation, leaving myself in an ever-deepening pit of ignorance. My home life was a milieu of emotional poverty, imprisoning me in a fixed stage of adolescence. I did, however, become an expert to the various ways and means of survival, mostly by means of isolation from people and events. Going through the motions became an art form, giving people the impression I knew what I was doing. It was a talent that was not deliberately developed and formulated; it grew as if it had its own will. With no premeditation I was building layers of defensive walls that were meant as protection from shame and potential hurt. I activated these characteristics more intensely as I began this fourth year of seminary life. In the end, I found it to be personally useful and necessary, albeit extremely damaging, for my life in the seminary.

It was also a year when my vision of the church and the priesthood, as idyllic as it was through the teenage years, came crashing down. I recalled the previous year when a priest I highly respected said that the mature Christian should need the church only ten percent of the time for a strong and growing spirituality. I was shocked and dismayed when I heard him speak these fateful words. I had just written a paper with the opening line, "The church will never die." I wholeheartedly believed this to be true since the church had been my home of salvation, intellectually and emotionally, with the emotional being the greater part. To say that at some point I would need it only sparingly for my spiritual life seemed unfathomable. If a priest that I admired had not said these words, I might have considered it heretical.

The church was more than just a building, but the building itself embodied a haven I came to call home. It compensated the breach created by the place I slept every night. The church edifice, now the seminary chapel, is where I went to escape the chaos and the conflicts, enriching me with a sense of peace and belonging. It was a protected harbor I could enter and was able to spend hours healing the rejections and humiliations, feeling unconditionally accepted and loved by the Creator of all things. It was a community of people where we bonded under the umbrella of faith and with participation in the rituals of worship. It was a sanctuary where daily Mass began my day and a shelter I could return at any time to pray, truly believing I was being heard. It was a stage where I fervently played the role of altar boy as a young boy, knowing full well it was a stepping stone to the priesthood. Now, struggling as a seminarian, I still returned to the chapel for reassurance. It was my safe zone. It was my arena where I felt loved and could love in return.

All of this began to erode as I lived out a tumultuous and depressive fourth year in the seminary. I was ravaged with thoughts never experienced before and experienced behaviors on the part of others that belied what were meant to be a priestly preparation. It did not happen suddenly as in the rapid destructiveness of an earthquake or the massive ferocity of a powerful storm. At first, I was not even aware it was taking place as I was completely immersed in the theological courses and the shadowy confines of depression. As I became more aware, I simply isolated myself even more from the everyday interaction with most of the seminarians and ignored the contradictory behavior taking place among my peers.

As much as I ignored the reality of a massive depression and existed on the fine edge of a breakdown, I was aware of the symptoms. I accepted them as individual numerators without considering the common denominator of a clinical depression. I read frantically in attempts to understand myself and all that I was going through. There would be a phase where I would devour books on loneliness, trying to figure out why I felt so isolated from the majority of the population, priests and seminarians alike. Yet it was not as if I had this burning desire to be close to any of them, for the majority seemed to be so different from what I wanted to be. One day, my spiritual advisor at the seminary saw me reading one of these books on the nature of loneliness and suggested that I stop reading such books. He was correct but regrettably never bothered to ask the obvious question: Why was I so preoccupied with this theme?

I would go through this phase and then turn to books on love. I was desperate to find out what this word meant and why people could so easily speak about its nature. I had written a paper on the topic for one of my previous philosophy classes. The priest reading it was kind and gentle in his reaction, but he knew it was a paper written like an adolescent who only knew love as some juvenile fantasy. Yet I was starving for the experience and had no idea where to turn. It was during this time where I suffered a number of experiences, any one of which could have taken me to the insane side of life, as if living in someone else's body. There were many days during this fourth year that I was convinced a breakdown was a mere moment away. As I was mentally and emotionally shrinking, I downsized the seminary acreage to the confines of my seven-by-twelve-foot room. It was where I felt the safest.

During this fourth year in the seminary, the population decreased tremendously as it had the previous year. The representing numbers for the six class levels were down to around one hundred, one-third of what we started with during my first year. The majority of people whom I admired and could significantly identify with had either been ordained or had left for another career. Those interested in sports were basically non-existent, which resulted in my losing the one respite from tension and depression. Academically, most did not seem concerned with the theological issues being taught, and they most certainly were not bothered by the moral conclusions that we were forced to digest. Belying my previous approach to academics, I was immersed in each of the courses, but most particularly the classes involving moral issues. My perspective was always on how these moral conclusions would affect the everyday Catholic and whether they were viable, feasible, and practical. In a number of critical cases, many did not.

Toward the end of the first semester of this fourth year, I experienced a crisis of self-identity that sent me into an emotional turmoil. When I was not in my self-imposed isolation, I began to realize, for reasons I could not explain at the time, that a sizable number of my peers seemed to be more effeminate than I was accustomed to being with. There was this one seminarian, a few years younger than I, who was transparently effeminate. Unconsciously, at first, he became a major attraction to me. As the days went on, these feelings grew in intensity and passion. Even though I was enjoying a sense of exhilaration and a rebirth of feelings long buried by despair, a sense of terror overcame me. I had no idea what was taking place within me, or how to explain it to myself let alone anyone else. After a few months of mental and emotional anguish, I eventually turned to an older friend. He was the ex-Navy vet I sat with years before at orientation. With full trust in our friendship, I was able to explain to him what I was going through and my extreme attraction to this particular seminarian. Like the kind priest who read my paper on love, he also responded with what I deemed a sympathetic understanding. With much more knowledge than I could wish for myself at the time, he simply explained that when sailors were at sea for months at a time, some of the more effeminate officers would become an attraction to some of the men on the ship. It did not mean that all of a sudden they were becoming homosexual, but simply placing their sexual need on what was available due to a great deal of deprivation. My relief was immense!

Once I calmed down, I later considered that I was not the only seminarian going through what I called a harrowing and potentially devastating experience. Once again though, it was a situation that was never openly discussed by those in charge. There were warnings about having "particular friendships" and a rule we should not hang around in each other's rooms, but the underlying reasons for these rules were never discussed. I am sure it must have caused a great deal of inner misery to many seminarians who were purposely left in the dark by those who knew of these experiences. The only rationale I could think of at the time was that it would open up the proverbial can of worms. They, the priests in authority, had to know that squelching all sexual desires and failing to address one's personal sexuality would more than likely lead to some sort of neurotic response, if not perversion. Namely, by placing the irrational and, for the most part, the unattainable demand of celibacy on young men seeking the priesthood, compensations in various forms would necessarily have to be turned to. I was blessed to catch mine in time while I am sure there were those less fortunate than me who were dragged into a living nightmare.

Even though I was relieved to understand this one aspect of myself and why it occurred, it did not alleviate the depth of depression I was experiencing. I did everything to ignore it for fear of learning that I did not belong in the seminary. My goal was to tough it out with the hope that if I reached ordination everything would change for the better. My method for getting through this darkness was to obsessively throw every waking moment into reading. In one sense, it was fulfilling as I became part of the story I was presently reading and the characters became my social life. Having a non-life, they became my life.

The means to this end put me on a schedule that could not have been more injurious to both my physical and mental health. I went through a six-month period where I never saw daylight. The chapel was connected to the building where I lived enabling me to attend chapel requirements, spend hours making Holy Hours on my own, and then hibernate in my room the rest of the time. I began a master's program in psychology shadowing two moral theology professors I admired who had done this to support their doctorate in moral theology. Combining my seminary courses with the school outside the seminary brought the number of credits for each of the two semesters to twenty-seven credits. I was reading, studying, and doing papers throughout the day and night. I was totally unaware how neurotic I had become.

In order to achieve this irrational and obsessive schedule, I began to drink thirty to forty cups of black coffee each day. This practice not only interfered with sleeping, but my hands began to shake out of control. I avoided eating meals with my peers because I could no longer identify with the vast majority of seminarians I was living with. I felt I was different and wanted to be different. Now the physical condition of my shaking hands became another reason to isolate myself. I could no longer hold a fork with one hand and raise it to my mouth. If I did try, the embarrassment would have been too much. I was not about to make a fool out of myself, especially in front of people I did not respect.

Thanksgiving break quickly approached and most of my class-mates looked forward to a four-day break. To me, it was just another burden to deal with. Going home was a far cry from a welcoming mat. I had no idea how the day itself would be spent. As with so many other family functions, such things were not discussed. My two sisters were now married, leaving just my younger sister and brother at home with my mother. How they were handling the craziness of the household I never thought to ask. As in childhood, we all remained strangers to each other, living through our own individual fog. The severity of my mother's psychological issues was worsening, which meant she was more than likely driving my younger siblings insane.

Two nights before we were to leave the seminary, one of the older seminarians placed an unsigned note under everyone's door. In it, he claimed to be a homosexual. He informed us he still planned to be a priest and would take the same vows of chastity and celibacy that the heterosexuals would take at ordination. The contents of the note did not get much of a reaction as the daily events in the seminary were rarely along the lines of normal. Most of the hubbub came from participation in the guessing game of who wrote it. Personally, I did not care one way or another except that it was another reminder of how isolated I was from the majority of seminarians in the building. Like many of the other episodes taking place throughout the years in the seminary, I repressed most of what I saw and heard.

What did come as a shock was my conversation with the rector late that afternoon. I was not sure why he called me over, but my hunch was that he was trying to get to the bottom of who wrote the note and the purpose for leaving it under everyone's door. After a few minutes of polite small talk, he asked if I knew who the person was behind the note. I had found out earlier in the day, but I told the Monsignor I was uncomfortable revealing his name. He understood and seemed to honor my position.

What came next was the shocking part. The rector proceeded to tell me that he was aware of the number of homosexuals living in the other building; it was no secret to him. Therefore, the note was no great surprise. His awareness level was amazing to me. For some reason, I presumed those in authority were not aware of the nature of the seminarian population, as if it was underground secret. As I was listening, with some degree of bewilderment, he went on to describe certain aspects of seminary life that he was fully cognizant of. The final kicker was when he said, "Bill, I know at least half of the seminarians in the building are sleeping with each other. I am also aware that many go to hotels on their day off." I was stunned. All I could push myself to say was, "You know this?" He nodded and then added, "Bill, this is the priesthood. If you intend to stay, this is what you must accept."

I returned to my room in a daze. It was not the homosexual issue per se that astonished me; it was that those in authority were well-aware of the sexual lifestyles of both the homosexual population as well as the heterosexual. Even at this young and provincial stage that I was mentally and emotional existing in, I had no problem with a homosexual becoming a priest, no more than a heterosexual seeking the priesthood. It was the active sexual lifestyle that presented such a contradiction to how we were, I presumed, meant to be living. It seemed so hypocritical that none of it was called into question. As I did with all other incongruities up to this point regarding seminary life and the nature of the priesthood, I buried this whole subject somewhere in the hidden parts of my brain. I returned to my room, a place that by now had become my cave-like shelter. I discussed my conversation with the rector with no one. I was going to be a priest no matter what the situation.

The result of not dealing with the nature and reality of seminary life left me in an even deeper depression. I was still invigorated by the Scripture classes, but was in constant conflict with the absurdities presented in my moral theology classes. There was no logic to their lectures and I was convinced was an anathema to the life of Christ and his teachings. Human decision-making and activity, emphasizing mostly sexual issues, was judged on the proponents of Natural Law. These laws basically stated that anything that went against nature was wrong and sinful. The most significant problem with this conclusion was that this perspective was established so long ago and prior to years of prolific scientific advancement. The church authorities basically locked themselves into a corner with a number of definitive conclusions that sooner or later, as science progressed, lacked any common sense. Reaching conclusions regarding numerous activities and choices people were making, again most of them centering on sex, they presented so-called truths as they were the gospel. To be an active and faithful to seminary teachings was to abide by these to the letter of the law.

Among many of the moral issues that were being dictated to us in the classroom that made little to no sense was the issue of birth control. It took center stage for me. My two primary moral theology professors obviously had to teach the party line or they would not be given their teaching position in the first place or hold onto it if they spoke otherwise. Acts of sexual intercourse had to have the intent of having a baby and if it did not it would be considered as sinful. I found I could not just sit back and accept this antiquated and more importantly damaging position that the average lay member was expected to follow.

Most likely due to my deepening depression and choice for self-isolation, these classes became my primary focus and eventual obsession. If I was not as depressed as I was, I most likely would have taken a different approach from the one I did. My tactic to counteract much of what they were teaching was filled with an unnecessary and useless anger. This anger was borne from the darkness that I was barely surviving in. In an odd sense, these moral issues gave me a sense of life and purpose, something I lacked otherwise.

I was fascinated with each of the moral topics since they directly applied to the individual members of the church and the decisions we as future priests would be helping them make throughout their daily lives. I was putting myself in their place and knew that what the church authorities were asking of them was not only impossible but also idiotic and illogical. The two priests teaching the moral theology classes were not bad people. In so many ways, they had a great deal to offer. To say the least, I was not a favorite student to either of these professors. By the end of the first semester, I was raising my hand for the entire class wishing to debate the most recent topic of the day. I should have received the message. The priestly professors ignored me each day, which was a source of amusement to my fellow classmates. Nevertheless, my hand continued to be raised from the beginning of the class to the end.

Frustrated by being ignored and disappointed by my fellow classmates' apathy, I turned to another outlet. In the second semester, we were given an assignment to pick any moral topic and discuss it within five to six pages. I found my stage. Admittedly, I was also falling into an even deeper depression that was saturated with a great deal of anger. I had become disgusted with the entire lifestyle of the seminary, my classmates included. As a result of my seclusion from the majority of people in the seminary, I was able to devote every free minute to the writing of this paper.

I had difficulty choosing one moral topic and therefore chose a topic where I could include them all. All the moral positions basically came down from the reigning pope, primarily through major encyclicals. *Humane Vitae* was the most recent work and was on the topic of birth control. I decided to make the paper all-encompassing and entitled my work "The Right to Decent against the Pope." It contained, I am almost embarrassed to admit, thirty-five pages of bibliography. It took on a life of its own.

I was not that surprised when the paper was returned to me. On the margins of numerous pages, there were various comments on what I wrote. The majority were meaningless and some blatantly incorrect. He graded the work with a B. If translated properly it was a grand fuck you. I accepted his challenged with a fuck you of my own. I asked for a meeting with him to discuss the paper, and he made me wait for two weeks before finally agreeing to meet with me. It was one week after everyone else had left for the summer. I was intent on waiting him out.

I brought with me several books written by major theologians who were experts in their field. My intent was to respond to the professor's written comments and correct him with the backing of these experts. I knew very well he was out of his league and could not hold a candle to these famous theologians. We went back and forth for thirty minutes when he glaringly looked at me and said, "Ward,

I don't give a shit what you think." I had seen this glare before as my own father would often stare at me with a similar hate. I looked back at him and said, "Father, you are a disgrace as a priest." I gathered my books and walked out. I was obviously crazed. It was now me against the entire system—the church! I never considered myself to be an army of one. I had stacks of books written by brilliant theologians and lay writers who expressed a vision of the church I longed for. The writers became my nourishment and encouragement. Yet considering the academic atmosphere of the seminary, I would be returning as an army of one. Still wanting to be a priest, I never considered the consequences. I thought the truth would win out.

11

The seminary of the future must relate itself to flush out
blood men, or it provides a framework that only talks about
the people of God but never really shares life with them.

—Eugene Kennedy

WITHOUT ANY SENSE OF what would be considered logical awareness, I was making myself into a Sisyphus-like character, condemning myself into a hell where I was continually left to push a huge
boulder up a steep hill. The hill was located at the seminary, and the
boulder was the pope and his men. I actually believed that if I studied
diligently and continued my life of prayer to the priesthood, I could,
with the help of others of like mind, set straight the hideous and hypocritical nature of the church. I knew it would be an uphill battle but
felt confident that I could become part of the team of theologians
and lay people who were trying to affect a change in church methodology and the stagnant approach to one's faith. I ignored the ruthless
power that church hierarchy wielded in their attempts to silence so
many good men and women while I continued to see them as true
Christian heroes. The boulder had to be heavy for them, I thought,
but they kept moving forward and onward, with courage and a sense
of what was both logical and spiritual. The primary mistake I was
making at the time, while I was a seminarian, was I was not them,
most especially in terms of credentials and knowledge. As a seminarian, I had no influence or authority, something I so foolishly never
considered at the time. I did not picture myself as a Sisyphus character, but I most certainly was pushing an unyielding boulder.

I left the seminary that summer with a raging intent to learn as much as I could about a more expansive theology to pit against the authoritative workings of the church, more specifically my two moral theology teachers. I never questioned my ambition to be a priest or thought that I was putting myself at risk in being allowed to become a priest. My convictions overshadowed any such thoughts as my focus was on joining the small minority that knew change in church policy was mandatory if the message of Jesus Christ was to be effectively delivered and believed. The manner in which the church authorities were acting—the pope, cardinals, and local priests—had so little to do with the true message of Jesus Christ, especially when it came to moral dogma. Their narcissistic intent was not about the message of love and forgiveness expressed in the Gospels, but more about rules and regulations. The majority of the documents revealed an obsession with sex. Single men, supposed celibates, acted as the last word on the subject. Their sexual biases produced farcical documents and demands that few could logically follow nor should follow.

There were others who were outspoken about this sexual obsession and definitively felt the way I did regarding the hypocrisy and arrogance of church policy. I was aware the majority of those who did believe in a more rational message had left the seminary or priesthood fully sensing they did not belong in such a rigid-thinking environment. Many of those who remained were silenced or reassigned to the outer banks of nowhere or punished in some other fashion. These brave men and women knew full well they would never be bishops or cardinals or attain any position of significance having not played the game. Even while observing their prejudicial plight, I had not reached that point of understanding that I was on a similar path that would more than likely end in expulsion from the seminary. My myopic fixation was that I was going to be a priest, repeating my childhood lack of vision of not having a clue as to how I was to get there.

My antagonists were my priest professors, primarily in the area of moral theology who demanded loyalty to one way of thinking while disallowing any form of creative thinking. Making it worse was the isolation I felt among my fellow seminarians. It was not that they supported what was being taught, but more for the fact that they did not care one way or another. Stooped in apathy, their indifference to how the teachings affected the average Catholic drove me further into an isolated life at the seminary. In the academia life of the seminary one either had to go along or accept the consequences, which usually meant dismissal.

I worked at the brewery for the second summer in a row, once again with the promise that my second Mass would be said for the intention of the foreman. This time around, I did not mind the shift of three-thirty to eleven-thirty, for it left invaluable time for the work I desperately wanted to accomplish. Imprisoned in my self-created sickness, I began to read and study the more open-minded theologians of the time. They were certainly not popular among the higher church authorities, and some of them were openly reprimanded. They were the heroes I wanted to admire and the champions I wanted to emulate for their courage to bring about the necessary changes in church policy and attitude. The majority of them were priests who gave me the sense I too could be a priest even though I was at odds with much of church doctrine.

By the end of the summer, I had read about fifty books, primarily in the area of moral theology. Ten of the more significant ones I outlined chapter by chapter. To say I was obsessed was an obvious understatement, although at the time I would not have admitted to it. Convinced I was on the right track, it gave my summer meaning and purpose, even though I was spending the majority of time in isolation, as I did in my previous semester in the seminary.

For the most part, I read for the entire shift, energized with the notion I was arming myself with the ammunition to fight my moral theology teachers. I cannot say I was arrogant or narcissistic, mostly due to the fact I did not see myself as smart enough for that attitude. It was like I was living in some kind of self-contained bubble wrap, learning the thoughts of brilliant theologians. Irrational as it was, my intention was to bombard the unyielding walls of the seminary academia. I was too ignorant to know the futility of such a goal, especially given the powerless nature of my fragile bubble.

At the end of the summer and before returning to the seminary, I rented a Jersey shore home with several other seminarians and our spiritual advisor from the seminary. I always loved the Jersey shore and was looking forward to two weeks of just taking in the sun. Another seminarian and his family also rented a home a few doors from us. He had two younger sisters and both groups often got together for cookouts in the evening. During the first week, I began to spend time with one of the sisters, both during the day and in the evening. The feelings that were awakened in me during this first week were similar to the ones I would have on assignments outside the seminary. Perhaps, for this reason, I did not give the feelings much consideration and presumed they would go away as the other "falling in love" experiences simply dissipated in due time. Not much was said by my group or her family about the time we were spending together, all presuming my vocation to the priesthood was on track. In hindsight, a memorable line from her mother would become the statement of the week. She expressed, "Isn't it nice that Bill can spend time with girls but not get close?" I was not only fooling her but myself as well.

The second week was a totally different story. The physical gods of my male nature were taking over. In some circles, they refer to it as dopamine, that wonderful drug of lust. It was reinforced by the singing of the Carpenters' "We have only Just Begun" and Johnny Mathis's "Chances Are." I was off and running with pure emotion. Here was a pretty blonde in a purple bathing suit and everything else was out the window. I told her brother, three years behind me in the seminary, that I was leaving the seminary. I think he was shocked given his reaction to my announcement, and I began to wonder why I was not as surprised. My decision was firm and unwavering. Well thought out was not part of the equation.

I returned for my fourth year in order to prepare for my sudden change of life. As word slowly spread throughout the seminary, most of my peers had a similar stunned reaction. It was not as wild as when I announced I was going to be a priest in high school, for that contradiction between my behavior and vocational goal could not have been more opposite. Years later the contradiction was turned around. All my behavior, academically and spiritually, indicated that I was heading toward ordination, therefore making the decision to leave was both contradictory and baffling to all who knew me. My spiritual director asked me to think about it for a few months, a suggestion that certainly made sense. Yet I was adamant that this is what I needed to do. I was once again on pilot control destined to go in one direction. It did not make sense at the time, but in the long run, as I grew emotionally and mentally, it was the right decision.

The Viet Nam war was still raging at the time, and I knew that once I left I would be eligible for the draft immediately. In high school I thought I was going to go to Viet Nam, but since that time I grew to believe it was a war that needed to be stopped since it was not serving a rational purpose any longer. So I received counseling and eventually flunked the physical due to a bad back. I also knew I desperately needed to get a job and staying for a few months longer in the seminary helped me to achieve that goal. The job was a total bore, and I just worked my way through it until I became a college counselor.

The first year was chaotic. I was lost vocationally and was changing my mind about a career on a monthly basis. Since I had only six credits left for the completion of my master's in counseling, I returned to graduate school. It was at this time I had the luck, and the grace, to have a teacher who enlightened me to the wonders of psychotherapy. By the end of the class, I knew that helping people in this manner was what I exactly wanted to do. I eventually became a licensed psychologist in private practice, and I am grateful that I ended up in a career I find so meaningful.

The first year out of the seminary, however, I was like a lost puppy. I never considered another vocation other than the priesthood and, in many ways, missed my life as a seminarian and a future priest. During that year, I briefly broke off the relationship I had with the woman I met at the Jersey shore and began to rethink whether I should return to the seminary. In so many ways, the priesthood was never going to be out of my system, especially in the way I left so suddenly. At one point, I called the rector, the same one I had the conversation with about the seminarian who left a note under the door. I told him that I would like to come back and continue my studies for the priesthood. To this day, I consider him not only a good priest but one who had a deep understanding for what the priesthood was all about. He gently told me in so many words, "Bill, you do not belong here." It was not said in a derogatory way but more stated as a knowledgeable father who knew what was best for me. We talked at length, and I still said that I wanted to come back. Before we hung up he said that he would take me back but reiterated one again that it was a mistake for me to return.

I spent the next few days in turmoil. I had wanted to be a priest since my grammar school days and presumed that this is what I would be. I began to picture myself back in the seminary and having only two years left prior to ordination. The reality of the picture began to set in. It did not take much of an effort to recall the hours of loneliness and depression, and most especially the hours and days of self-imposed isolation. I also reached the conclusion, finally, that there was so much I disagreed with regarding moral doctrine that if I returned I would be left in the unhealthy states of frustration and anger. Spiritually, I loved the way of life, but in practical terms, I knew I could not sell the church package as it was so tightly wrapped to the lay people I would serve.

The desire to serve God as a priest was always a burning desire. As a child and as a teenager priests became my surrogate fathers and the church became my substitute family. Four and a half years ago, I was driven down the narrow roadway to what I believed would be a new beginning. I would proudly take on the identity of a seminarian preparing for the priesthood. All my hope and dreams rested on this choice. It was not meant to be. Most thankfully, I took away with me a new sense of spirituality, and through acts of grace, it has been growing ever since. The hardest part was coming to terms with my long-term desire to be a priest. The awareness I needed to reach, which I finally did, was the priesthood I sought, for the most part, did not exist.

Part 2

My New Testament
The Road to
Spirituality

Michangelo's Sistine Chapel

12

When I walked out of the seminary, I was like a
scared, frightened kid. I had no place to live, no
license, no clothes. I was just a lost soul.
—John Bradshaw

MANY YEARS HAVE PASSED since I left the seminary, forty-seven to
be exact. During this time, I raised four children, two boys and two
girls. It is said that the proudest accomplishment of any teacher is
to have their students surpass them in terms of growth and development. It is for this primary reason I am so proud to have been
a father and to have experienced four wonderful human beings go
from childhood and into adult life as intelligent, caring, and spiritual
people. The memories they have created for me, and are still creating
as they share with me their new lives as young families, has brought
tremendous fulfillment. In interacting with them today, I often have
to stand back in awe as they express their sensitivity regarding the
well-being of others and how they so willingly put their faith into
action knowing full well they are doing the work of God. I am confident, in the sphere of their own careers and lifestyles, that they will
make numerous and beneficial contributions to their generation.

I did marry the woman I met when leaving the seminary, but it
ended after thirty-six years of being together. Given the nature and
purpose of this book, I do not think it would be appropriate to go
through the details that led to this failure. I can say that its ending
was a correct decision on both our parts, for there is nothing worse
for any person to live in a destructive and draining atmosphere. I
did return to therapy in order to examine my role in the marriage's

demise. This in itself was a growth experience. I remain very close to my children, their spouses, and my grandchildren. Joy and pride fill my cup.

I do not regret leaving the seminary. The manner in which I did leave, however, certainly could have been done in a healthier and more mature way. Even though it was a swift and impulsive decision, surprising myself and many others, it definitively turned out to be the correct one. For I realize now my last two years before leaving that I was massively depressed and filled with anger. I was unaware that I was mentally and emotionally dying inside. Since I was a young child, the goal of becoming a priest was so engrained in my mind that it left room for no other option. What I was reading, studying, and most of all observing in terms of the realities of the church and the priesthood should have been enough of a message that I did not belong in the seminary nor did I in any way fit in to the church as an organization. Due to deeply rooted layers upon layers of developmental experiences, formed by both spiritual and psychological events, I was incapable of reversing the car drive to the seminary I had taken six years before. I was in desperate need of outside help.

I read somewhere that when we are not making the right decisions, or happen to be unknowingly going down the wrong path, God sometimes intervenes with a so-called holy hammer to set us straight. If there is any truth to this statement, which I believe there is, there is no question it was something I desperately needed. Steeped in anger and a massive depression, I was returning that year to the seminary with a tortured mind that intended to enter in an academic war with my moral theology professors. As I look back on these terribly naïve years, how and why I thought I could win such a battle, let alone affect the teachings of the Catholic Church, is beyond my comprehension. I therefore can accept with gratitude the workings of this holy hammer. It also saved me from the embarrassment of being asked to leave. Based on the papers I was writing, the questions I was asking, and the conflicts I was having with a few teachers, it is very doubtful I would have made it through the academic year. One day in each semester we all had to wait in our rooms with the anticipation there would be a knock on our door and told the rector would like to see us. Those who received the knock in the morning were given some kind of warning regarding their fitness for priestly life. Those who took the walk over to the administration building in the afternoon were asked to leave. If my exiting the seminary happened in this way, that is being asked to leave, I might have followed others in my situation and gone to another diocese. This type of decision would have prolonged the misery. What I needed was a complete change. I feel strongly, in hindsight, that grace was leading me to another vocational path.

The direction, after fumbling around for a year or so, brought me to a career that I truly consider a vocation. It is what I was meant to do. After getting my doctorate and studying under a number of brilliant mentors, I became a licensed psychologist and started my own private practice. Over the last forty years, I have met so many wonderful people who had the courage to share their lives with me at the deepest of levels. Within the confines of psychotherapy, not only were they able to personally grow mentally and emotionally, but they definitely added to my own growth as well. I am sure I could not have accomplished this duel achievement as a priest, given the rigid structure and restrictions of the Catholic Church.

I am not one of those who regret spending the years I did in the seminary. In so many ways it laid the groundwork for what I was to do in the future, not limited to academics but for my spiritual life as well. It was a wonderful gift to have had a number of theologians share their knowledge, expertise, and spirituality on a daily basis in the classroom. The Scripture professors were so incredibly knowledgeable, and I remember so many days waiting with anticipation for their next lecture. In the area of Christology, one professor was brilliant as he brought to everyday life the reality of Jesus in our midst. My spiritual advisor, patient and loving, was there for me whenever I needed to talk. He might have been disappointed at the time when I left, but I am sure he would recognize today it was the right decision.

Finally, the spiritual experiences of my childhood, as adolescent as they might have been, along with my years in the seminary, most surely lit a flame that burns intensely today; namely, the ever-growing relationship I have with Jesus Christ. I remained active in the church and raised my children as Catholics. As all parents can attest, the task of being a father and keeping a career profitable took a great deal of time on a daily basis. There was some time put aside for prayer and reading, but my formal tasks of being a father and psychologist demanded the majority of my time. As my children grew older and were more on their own, I returned with the same intensity I had in the seminary to understand what living a spiritual life really meant. Over the years, as difficult as this is to say, I found the formal workings of the Catholic Church a growing hindrance to this study and way of life. Referencing something I said earlier in the book, I was once again reminded of a statement one of my seminary professors made years before. Almost as an aside to his main theme for the day, he said the person attempting to live a full Christian life should need the church for about ten percent of their spirituality. In my youthful innocence and naiveté, I was shocked by what he had to say. Now, I fully understand what he meant and his statement, perhaps his advice, rings so true.

In my early years, I ignored the real facts about the functioning of the Catholic Church. In many ways, I was repeating my first years in the seminary by wanting to hold onto my established beliefs that I was attached to more emotionally than mentally. I was dependent on believing certain things to be the absolute truth as if my life relied on it for survival. More significantly, to retain the goal of being a priest there were certain things I had to ignore or deny. After leaving the seminary, I continued to read esteemed scholars in various theological and psychological fields. I began to contrast what they were saying and the amazing insights they had to offer versus what the church authorities were saying and what they had to offer. As in the seminary, I had, at first, a wall of defense to my unwillingness to let go of engrained beliefs. Over time, however, and a great deal of thought, the words of my seminary professor took on its own life. Eventually, I became convinced that if I was to grow spiritually I needed to look outside the walls of the Catholic Church to discover the true nature of Jesus Christ, both human and divine.

While in the seminary I was lucky enough to discover a wonderful book written by Victor Frankl. He was a legendary psychiatrist and Holocaust survivor who wrote the classic work entitled *Man's Search for Meaning*.[1] The book was written in two distinct parts. The first was about his experiences in the horrendous camps established by the Germans. He took the reader through his daily life, sharing deeply felt beliefs along with his painful heartaches. The second part of the book entailed the philosophy he developed as a direct result of his experiences in the camp. The philosophy, profoundly enriching and purposeful, became known as logotherapy. I found this book format not only informative but useful in application. It is for this reason I would like to borrow from Dr. Frankl's methodology for the second part of this book. In the first part of this book I wrote about my experiences with the Catholic Church, from my grammar school years all the way through my years in the seminary. In this second part of the book I would like to share with you the lessons I have learned from these experiences, emphasizing the journey I have taken since leaving the seminary. It is a journey that I could not have taken if I remained at the seminary, and most certainly, if I became a priest. Once again, I have realized how correct my theology professor was at the seminary. It was that one day when he advised that one can only find perhaps ten percent of their personal spiritual life with the confines of the bureaucratic Catholic Church. I cannot imagine where I would be today if that holy hammer—that moment of grace—did not occur. By leaving the seminary I was able to start on an entirely different journey. It has been a voyage where I have been introduced to many wonderful and profound people. They shared their spiritual message with me and have encouraged me to continue with this wonderful mission to know the human and divine Jesus Christ. As so many have done for me, I hope I can be a partner in your search for the holy.

13

Bureaucracies are inherently antidemocratic. Bureaucracies derive their power from their position in the structure, not from their relationship with the people they are supposed to serve. The people are not masters of the bureaucracy, but its clients.

—Alan Keyes

IT IS MY BELIEF, supported by numerous studies, that a vast number of people have ceased participating within an established church due primarily to their experiences with formal religion. I viewed a new Pew poll which compared religious participation over the last decade in America. The poll revealed a precipitous drop in the number of people calling themselves Christian, as well as three million fewer people calling themselves Catholic than in the 2007 poll. The Catholic Church, along with Protestant denominations, shed adherents faster than any other faith. Four in ten of those who received First Communion no longer identify with Catholicism. Additionally, as the millennials entered adulthood, they display much lower levels of religious affiliation. Fewer than six in ten millennials identify with any branch of Christianity, compared to seven in ten among older generations.

During the past decade I have observed people leaving formal churches in droves, but doing so they entered a spiritual desert. For many, once formal participation in church activities ceased, a thoughtful interest in spirituality never replaced it. My concern is not only for this group of people, but I am also concerned to what will happen to the children of these adults growing up in such a spiritual vacuum.

Back when I was in the seminary, I began to formulate ideas about the basic nature of the Catholic Church, the history of its development, and how it actually operates. I began to seriously study the reasoning and purpose underlying theological positions they take and then often turn such positions into must-believe doctrine. Shortly after I left the seminary, I realized this type of examination was something I would not have been allowed to continue to do openly if I remained in the seminary, or was ordained a priest. I was aware there were a number of priests that wanted me out of the seminary based on what I was saying and writing at the time. If I did not leave under my own volition, being asked to leave would have happened sooner than later.

My two moral theology professors, as I was informed by my spiritual advisor, did not want me to return in the year that I left. I was in constant conflict with them and strongly felt their lectures were something from a Cliff Notes outline, superficial and baseless.

They could not hold a candle to the moral theologians I was reading and studying on a daily basis. These authors, brilliant and extremely well-grounded, came under a great deal of wrath from the bureaucratic hierarchy. I witnessed too many of these men and women dismissed or explicitly ostracized if they wavered from any form of official church thinking. This arrogant attitude by church authorities toward men and women of good faith left me with a sickening feeling, and I readily admit, with various degrees of immature anger.

Following my years at the seminary, I continued with my search for a deeper understanding regarding the life of Jesus and comprehending, also at a deeper level, the meaning of his message. A psychologist may call it an obsession, which, I admit, my interest and drive does seem to fill this definition. But I considered it a most worthy obsession, and still do today. This passion to know more not only included the life of Jesus, but it involved evaluating interpretations and conclusions of many great writers along with what the church officials were proclaiming from their perspective.

With the assistance of many intelligent and spiritual gurus (those awesome people who lead us out of darkness), I finally concluded that the Catholic Church, more than anything else, is primarily a rigid bureaucracy that is concerned more about its own existence than it is in discovering a deeper truth. In so many of its actions and proclamations, it is an organization in which the true message of Jesus Christ takes second place to numerous manmade rules and regulations created by a self-serving business. As I was slow to learn in my seminary days, by all standards and perspectives, the Catholic Church stands out as an unyielding and close-ended structure, absorbed with its own need for supremacy and desire for dominance. In so many situations throughout its history, its actions and non-actions appeared to be predominantly intent on serving and protecting itself. At the same time, it repeatedly proclaims itself as the one true church.

The church leaders certainly had me buying the entire package the first twenty years of my life. My passive acceptance slowly began to change as I read numerous books on the history of the church. I found endless indications where the structure itself was put before the concerns and plight of others. This was most notable concerning the everyday faith and the challenges members face as they actively try to live out their faith. The recent pedophile crisis, horrendous in every aspect, is the latest example of the mind-set and attitude of those in charge. Authorities in the church, the popes, cardinals, bishops, and priests, deceitfully concealed the actions of hundreds of priests who had sexually abused children. This concealment is not a random hypothesis and by no means an exaggeration; it is a proven fact. It included the retired Pope Benedict, although he denies it to this day.

It also was not just a few bad apples, as the church authorities would want us to believe. It involved a conscious conspiracy on the part of hundreds of priests, bishops, cardinals, and popes to put the church structure above the safety and concern for its members. At the time I cannot say it was the last straw for me, for I was already well on my way in terms of having another spiritual direction. Matthew Fox, a former Dominican priest and author of numerous books, a man I tremendously admire for his courage and willingness to speak out, commented on this reality when he emphasized that, "I think this is why the pedophile-priest crisis developed as it did: because the church didn't appoint critical thinkers as bishops or cardinals; it appointed people who would toe the line. Yes, men."[1] Fox went on to accentuate that there is no question the needs of the institutional church were blatantly put ahead of the safety of young children. The bureaucratic church, from the pope on down, committed these criminal acts of deceit for one primary reason: to save their self-styled and self-created image. It was most certainly not the first time.

I did not reach these conclusions regarding viewing the church as a bureaucracy without a great deal of intellectual and emotional struggle. For so many years I considered the church, above everything else, as my foundation and the very substance to my everyday life. Like many my fellow Catholics, I considered it unfair to label the Catholic Church as first and foremost a rigid bureaucracy. Initially, I certainly resisted and was tempted to reject those who were critical of the church. With the help of many brilliant theologians, I was beginning to gain new information on the actual life of Jesus and the lives of his followers. I was reaching a new level of understanding than what I had previously been taught. This profound new material I was studying so often emphatically conflicted to what I previously accepted as hardcore facts presented by the formal church. Throughout my readings I continually encountered the psychological experience of *cognitive dissonance,* the intellectual and emotional clash between what I had assuredly believed to be gospel truth juxtaposed with the new ideas and perspectives regarding what Jesus actually taught.

By the time I reached my mid- to late twenties, I was more and more coming to terms with the fact that I had been passively dependent on the church for what I was to learn and to what I was to believe. Throughout my youthful years there was no place for doubt, no place for questioning. My spirituality was sterile, unbeknown to me, until I allowed myself to listen, really listen to people like Dr. Scott Peck, a psychiatrist who often spoke on the topic of spiritual growth. Along with others willing to speak out and challenge one's use of religion, Dr. Peck made so much sense to me when he emphasized that, "In weighing our thoughts and feelings, what matters most is whether we are willing to wrestle with the realization that we don't know it all. This means not only being introspective, but also experiencing doubt. Doubt, I believe, is the beginning of wisdom."[2] As I was entering my early thirties, doubting and questioning became a key component to my life, especially in the area of religion and spirituality. It was the personal beginning of concrete growth in making Jesus more alive to me, more real, more present. As referenced in the subtitle of this book, I was going through a spiritual growth one piece at a time.

This new and much more open perspective was a major spiritual turning point for me. From childhood and through my teenage years, I had accumulated numerous beliefs and principles that I accepted without questioning. I considered the formal church's teachings to be dogmas formulated from the time of Jesus Christ and passed down over the centuries to those in authority. These dogmatic truths were then passed down to us, the passive recipients of so-called truths. Gaining new insights and with an expanded awareness regarding the origins of these dogmas, I discovered most were manmade by the authorities of the Catholic Church. The new perspective I was having began to slowly contradict what I once held to be definitive truths. In many situations I often found that many of these facts, promulgated by the church hierarchy, demonstrated to be entire fabrications and were based on the needs of the bureaucracy and the politics that permeated the system. The acts of deceit, in other words, did not start with the pedophile crisis.

Gary Wills, an acclaimed bestseller of many religious books, did not have to worry about being ostracized by the church or have the burden of being called to Rome and questioned endlessly about his theological positions. He was not a priest and therefore was free from the concern of losing his position in the church or being silenced. He was unrestricted to call into question many of the theological principles and dogmas created by the church authorities over its long history. I remember one interesting example as he, along with others, questioned the concept of original sin, which held the underlying belief that we all were born into this world in sin as the result of the fall from grace of Adam and Eve. With the new openness I was expe-

140

riencing, I too began to also question this and other such concepts. I have, as many have, had the opportunity to hold little babies in my arms, sensing their innocence, vulnerability, and fullness of love. By following Scott Peck's suggestion, doubt was leading me toward a greater wisdom. To say they are in sin, I firmly concluded, is beyond illogical. However, in seeing the church from the perspective of being a bureaucracy, it is fathomable from the church's mind-set since it required for membership in the church to be forgiven for this proposed sin. The bureaucracy created a need for itself. If it was accepted as truth that one is born in sin, then it was too threatening not to ask for forgiveness.

Wills also questioned such concepts as the existence of purgatory, a place of suffering inhabited by souls of sinners who are expiating their sins before they can go to heaven. I can easily recall the hours I spent in grammar school repeating small prayers referred to as aspirations. While reciting each prayer, such as "My Jesus Mercy," I believed I was earning indulgences or actual days where I was freeing those in purgatory with less time spent there. My friends and I would carry around little pads checking off in groups of five the number of indulgences we recited. On any given day the number would reach into the thousands. I was proud of my daily accomplishments and felt it was a noble act by me as a Catholic. I never considered that the notion of whether there was actually a purgatory. From a new perspective I can now see that by having a purgatory it might have served the purpose of keeping us all in fear and therefore requiring the services of the church even more. Worse still was the forced belief that there was this fiery hell and the terror that was instilled that there was a possibility of any of us ending up in such a place. At one time I never saw the contradiction of believing in a God of mercy and love to a God that sent certain people to an eternal life in hell. All of this was followed by the rigid notion that there is only one true path to salvation, the Catholic Church.

The church, seen from the perspective of being a formal bureaucracy, created an endless number of rituals, laws, and requirements that held the prerequisite only church officials could perform them. If one is trying to build a bureaucracy with only a few are in a power position, this is certainly one way to do it. The most outstanding ritual is that of Mass and the experience of having bread and wine turned into the body and blood of Jesus Christ. As with so many other rituals created by the bureaucracy, it was one where only a priest could perform such duties. Perhaps more than any other required ritual, this particular one gave the bureaucracy exclusive power and therefore the demand for allegiance from its members. As many Scripture scholars stress, this was never the objective of Jesus nor was it the intention of the holy men who followed immediately after Jesus. Wills summarizes this point when he explains that, "Though there many charisms of service in the early Jesus movement—many functions, some inchoate offices—there were no priests and no priestly services; no male presider at the agape meal, no reenactment of Jesus's Last Supper, no 'sacrifice of the mass,' no concentrations of bread and wine, nothing that resembled what priests now claim to do."[3] Nonetheless, attending Mass is one of the major requirements of the bureaucracy for members to participate in if one wishes to belong as a member in good standing. Otherwise, the member is considered to be in a state of sin. A powerful obligation created by the bureaucracy, to say the very least.

I recall a conversation I had with a couple who were both Catholic. They just came from a funeral in a Methodist Church. A number of things impressed them, but what stood out the most was when it was time for the breaking of bread and the drinking of wine. The minister, welcoming throughout the ceremony, asked all to come forward to share in this ritual. As the couple and I reflected on their experience, we could not help but to compare this inclusive experience to that of the Catholic Mass. At the time of communion in the Catholic Church, especially at funerals and weddings when there is a diverse population, there is always the same directive from the priest. "If you are not Catholic or are not in the state of grace, please do not come forward to receive communion." Is it any wonder the pews of the Catholic Church are emptying out year by year?

As can be imagined by anyone who was raised in the Catholic tradition, when I first began to expand my faith to a deeper level, I went through phases where I was almost afraid to learn more. My childhood family, the Catholic Church, the one I had put my entire trust in as a child and young man, was being decimated before my eyes by insights that not only made more sense but also brought me to deeper levels of spirituality, a glorious experience in itself. The emotional struggle lasted for some time and, to some degree, still does. For me personally, it was like discovering the person you thought was your mother or father is actually someone else. It was both shocking and discouraging at the same time. However, once I got passed the initial emotional spiral, I reached levels of belief and closeness with Jesus I never thought possible.

When my thinking was simplified as a child, empowered by my emotional need to so desperately belong to something, I gave my full allegiance to the church and to the priests I interacted with on a daily basis. I never considered they, especially those with positions of authority, could be operating under another agenda and for another purpose. To put it more concisely, I was certainly unaware that they were forced to accept and operate under this agenda if they wanted to be part of the bureaucratic system. I considered the norm of the Catholic Church as normal, and never contemplated that individual thinking was a possibility or even healthy. Most certainly, I never considered it a necessity for spiritual growth. Presently, I can empathize with those Catholics who so rigidly hold onto the beliefs they were taught in childhood. For many, being a Catholic is so much a part of their identity, as it was mine. Sadly, though, so many remain stuck, as I once was, in a misdirected path as if still believing in Santa Claus and the tooth fairy. More sadly, and perhaps tragically, those stuck in the bureaucratic system are missing out in attaining greater depths to a more meaningful spirituality.

For the past number of years, I found criticizing the church as primarily a self-serving bureaucracy can be difficult if emphasis is also focused on the endless good works that have been carried out by numerous people who belong to the Catholic community. These works of Christian service can never be dismissed and most certainly act as models for me. More to the point, these actions of loving service are what Jesus wanted for us in the first place, and therefore should not be so unique. Yet given the vast number of practicing Catholics, they are rather unique. Most assuredly, Mother Teresa of Calcutta was a perfect example of saintly work done on this earth. Joseph Langford, author of an autobiography on Mother Teresa, reminds us of the intent that permeated all her good works. Referencing her daily acts of service, he emphasized that Mother Teresa's focus was based on the reality that, "We need our own personal epiphany, our ongoing encounter with the light of God and the God of light—renewed daily, always beckoning, ever fulfilling us."[4] This personal epiphany rarely takes place in a rigid environment that demands belief in definitive areas, and followed by rules and regulations for certain types of behavior. The tendency is to create followers not leaders. It is group conversion rather than individual conversion. I believe defining it as impersonal an understatement. It fosters thinking outside of oneself and it discourages individual and personal thinking.

I certainly honor Mother Teresa and others like her, and they will always have my highest respect. The fact remains, nonetheless, that those in authority principally operate, especially when there is controversy, within the realm of protecting the bureaucracy and do not allow the experience of individual thinking, much less a personal light, as Mother Teresa suggested. They operate under their own light, their own mind-set. The dire consequences for doing so can no longer be ignored, especially given the hundreds who have walked away. To follow the path outlined by the church bureaucracy and ignore the individual spiritual growth of people like Mother Teresa, we fail to understand the true nature and purpose of being a Christian. Langford once again reminds us, "Mother Teresa's example shows that by cultivating this encounter [with the light of God], we can successfully navigate the challenges of our own Calcutta and, as she, leave a legacy of light and goodness along our path."[5] Mother Teresa and others like her knew full well that goodness cannot be imposed from the outside, from the top down. It must grow internally from the bottom up.

During my time in the seminary and continuously after I left, I increasingly began to have difficulty in automatically accepting papal pronouncements, especially on moral issues. There was a time when I firmly believed in the structure of the Catholic Church, including having a pope as its chief spokesman. I readily accepted, without questioning, points of faith and morality as simply true, especially if it was instructions from those in higher authority. I never questioned the validity of the positions held by the formal church and just presumed it was a representation of what Jesus preached and wanted us to believe. As a child and through my teenage years, I passively accepted all that I was taught. As the orphan I was, the church was my family and therefore had every ounce of my loyalty. Like many other Catholics brought up in this tradition, I viewed the teachings of the formal church as not only true but required my belief, and as a good Catholic, my compliance. Looking back on my submissive development and committed willingness to conform in order to belong, I find it understandable that I went along with such a powerful bureaucracy. As the obedient child, who was I to question the pope? Who was I to question the entire church? How could I doubt any of it if I truly believed it was all coming from Jesus?

This hard-rock position of total adherence to the formal church began to crumble for me when I began to look more closely on how the rules and regulations were directly applied to the faith and activities of individual members. In my later years in the seminary, the encyclical *Humane Vitae* took center stage as the most controversial topic as it reaffirmed the orthodox teaching of the bureaucracy by rejecting all forms of artificial birth control. This is when I was sincerely driven, albeit somewhat insane, to write a paper entitled "The Right to Descent against the Pope." I was locked in a state of obsessiveness, both literally in my room and figuratively in my mind. Admittedly, only years later, I now see this as being illogical and certainly overly obsessive.

For months, I worked on the paper day and night. As noted previously the task was far from appreciated by my moral theology professor. In my ignorance, as I reflected in the first part of the book, it was like I was at West Point and was against the use of guns. Years later I came to realize that this professor, like all the others at the seminary, had no other choice but to preach and teach the bureaucratic mind. When this professor left the priesthood a year or so later, I wondered was he also in conflict. At the time I wrote the paper and he dismissed it with all sorts of degrading responses, I never considered that he was forced to present the party line if he wanted to remain a teacher. Speak about degrading yourself. Today, I might have been more empathetic toward his plight.

The mental and emotional rock that was cracking in my fourth year in the seminary was due to much more than the presentation of this particular encyclical. The encyclical itself did create a major controversy throughout the church, even though the majority of lay people simply ignored it in practice, as they still do today. The mood for some members in the church at the time led to other topical conflicts, mostly taking place between the bureaucracy and a small minority of theologians. However, the majority of theologians, along with the majority of bishops and priests, still remained silent in fear of losing their status in the bureaucracy. This fear was justified. For all they had to do was observe the treatment by the bureaucrats in power toward a number of brilliant theologians who had the courage to express their views. Once again, no personal epiphanies were allowed.

A few really good and brilliant people stood out to me as I was going through my personal spiritual crisis. I especially admired the writings of Fr. Charles Curran, who was a moral theology professor at the Catholic University of America. Because of his views on sexuality and medical ethics, the pope took away his license to teach theology and he was forced to leave the university. The church has traditionally been obsessed with sexual topics, which is remarkable considering they are single men supposedly living celibate and chaste lives.

Fr. Hans Kung, a Swiss-born theologian and author of the classic book entitled *The Church*,[6] also lost his license to teach Catholic theology after the Vatican condemned him for his views on papal infallibility. Fr. Edward Schillebeeckx, a Belgian Dominican, was initially investigated for questioning the virginity of Mary, even though he was supported by a number of theologians, including the renowned theologian Karl Rahner. All of these men I tremendously admired, not just because what they said made so much sense, but more for how they expressed what being a follower of Jesus Christ really meant. As my faith was growing, mostly due to the insights of such men and women, my faith in the formality and closed-mindedness of the Catholic Church was in a deep decline.

The treatment of these men and others like them by the church authorities leaves no doubt that the church is exceedingly powerful within its own confines. Through some sense of magical power, such as they own the "keys to heaven," those in authority are able to get so many to conform simply through the threat of dismissal. Andrew Greeley, a noted American sociologist, explained, "The Roman Catholic Church has traditionally been an organization with both a firm institutional structure and a strong concentration of power in the hands of both the pope and bishops."[7] An American sociologist, Robert Merton, who studied and wrote on the interactions between social and cultural structures, is particularly insightful in explaining the nature of a bureaucracy like the Catholic Church. His definition and description of a bureaucratic structure conveys in detail the formal structure of the Catholic Church and the format it has been operating under for decades. Merton defines an organized social structure, such as the Catholic Church, as "defined patterns of activity in which, ideally, every series of actions is functionally related to the purposes of the organization."[8] The part of Merton's explanation that bothered me the most was the emphasis placed on the "the purposes of the organization."

I was becoming more and more convinced that the core message of Jesus was being directly eclipsed by the needs and purposes of the organization, the bureaucratic Catholic Church. How and why the church reached this state of being a hardcore bureaucracy with so much power is one question. However, even beyond this question, I began to take a close look at the consequences for operating in this manner. As I was doing so, the gap between formal religion and a true sense of spirituality began to increasingly widen in me both emotionally and intellectually. The words of Philip Yancey, once editor-at-large for *Christianity Today* magazine, clearly makes the point how this gap was taking place within me. He explained, "I believe God insists on such restraint because no pyrotechnic displays of omnipotence will receive the response he desires. Although power can force obedience, only love can summon a response of love, which is the one thing God wants from us and the reason he created us."[9] In the end, I was seeing that the church was more about power and their obsession with keeping it. It was and is primarily about forced belief. Independent thinking is envisioned as threat, instead of being a possible contribution. Thus, the church comes up with the pope's infallibility; namely, he cannot be wrong on issues of faith and morals. This perspective regarding the so-called power of the pope drove me crazy even back in my seminary days.

By virtue of the church acting as a bureaucracy, the Catholic Church places the cardinals and bishops as direct successors to the apostles. Within this structure, the bishops are viewed as "presiding in place of God over the flock whose shepherds they are, as teachers of doctrine, priests of sacred worship, the officers of good order."[10] It is emphasized that he who rejects them, rejects the entire church.[11] The values of the group are considered before the values of any individual may hold. The organization's values, beliefs, and how they are adhered to, become the measuring rod for evaluating and accepting the individual as a member. If the individual considers the organization's needs and goals above his own, then he is viewing himself in the same manner as the organization views him. The Catholic Church strongly believes they meet the needs of most people by assisting them in their formation by way of obedience. In return they expect loyalty and a just return for what has been given to them. Such expectation by the Catholic Church is formed within the atmosphere that an ordered and disciplined response is mandatory for the organization to exist.

As I read and studied more about rigid bureaucracies, I discovered any formal bureaucracy like the church must always be assured that members will follow the rules presented. Since it is essential they do so, a great deal of emphasis is placed on the rules and directives themselves. Such an emphasis often causes the structure, in this case the Catholic Church, and its members to lose sight of the real message presented in the Scriptures. Adherence to rules, originally conceived as a means, becomes transformed into an end in itself. Based on the psychological state of the average Catholic, or any individual for that matter, it was not that difficult of a demand made by the church that its members follow long list of rules and belief systems. Most people, including myself at one time, are more comfortable with compliance to tradition. Standing away or against a primary group can be a lonely and threatening experience. Thomas Moore, a former monk who now is a psychotherapist, explains that, "For all its expressed championing of the individual, our culture in many ways favors conformity. We are pleasantly sedated by the flatness and predictability of modern life."[12] When I read these words of Thomas Moore, I cringed at the thought that my faith was based on a form of sedation and the comfortableness of conformity.

I discovered that when an individual member of the bureaucracy conforms to the rules and regulations it does not necessarily have to serve a purpose, but it becomes a value in and of itself. In time, the loyal members become so rigid they are unable to adjust to change or accept the possibility for new ideas. Yet most notably, it is not just the members who are affected by this rigid system. The original purpose of a Christian community begins to take second place to the actual conformity of its members to the rules. When such a situation occurs, which is often the case in the Catholic Church, the bureaucratic leaders are unable to assist those the organization is to serve, since all his actions and decisions are bound by specific rules, which are often unrelated to the specific needs of the individual. I found it interesting how Philip Yancey confirms the thoughts of Thomas Moore when he shares his experiences as an average Catholic responding to the bureaucratic teachings of the church. From his personal experience with his faith, he explained, "I often felt the victim of emotional pressures. Doctrine was dished out in a 'believe and don't ask questions' style. Wielding the power of miracle, mystery and authority, the church left no place for doubt."[13] Yancey continues that he was at one time taken in by this pressure to conform, as I certainly was at one time. Reflecting on his own past behavior, he confessed, "I also learned manipulative techniques for 'soul-winning,' some of which involved misrepresenting myself to the person I was talking to. Yet now I am unable to find any of these qualities in the life of Jesus."[14] Due to Yancey's honesty and conversion, he became one of my spiritual gurus.

Within the system of a bureaucracy, there is always an establishment of a hierarchy. Robert Presthus, author of *The Organizational Society*, explains that a hierarchy "is a system for ranking positions along a descending scale from the top to the bottom of the organization."[15] Authority, within a bureaucratic structure, takes precedence over all considerations, including those items that might be based on knowledge and common sense. Therefore, those in higher positions tend to become isolated from the rest of the members. Robert Merton explains, "Since they normally interact with near-equals in the hierarchy, the more complex the organization the greater the possibility that they will be shut off from changes in attitudes and norms in the lower (and not only the lower most) strata of the organization."[16]

I came to believe that as the size of the bureaucracy increases, the morale of the individual members will decrease. I have personally noticed this once I started to evaluate the average Catholic's approach to their faith. It is not just morale, but there is also a lack of excitement and a sense of fervor that one might find in other religious communities. The bureaucracy of the Catholic Church has created robots that are turned on, slightly I must add, for forty-five minutes on Sunday and turned off as they leave the parking lot. Some may complain how boring the sermon was, but never question the reasoning for their weekly attendance in robotic passivity. Since their First Communion days, Sunday Mass is considered an outward sign they are active Catholics in good standing. Unfortunately, for many it never goes beyond this weekly activity. The average Catholic, I believe, is trapped in their First Communion stage mentally, emotionally, and spiritually. Those that are not often just leave. The proof is in the numbers and the vast non-participation of the majority of Catholics.

For some bureaucracies, certainly true of the Catholic Church, the size and distance factor give to those in charge a particular level of prestige. The further away the authority (i.e., Rome) is from its members, there is a natural tendency to have them placed in a position of reverence, whether they have earned it or not. In organizations that are especially large, charismatic authority seems to become a presumed aspect of those in a leadership position. Since the hierarchy has the position of dominance and control, individual members often hold such figures of authority in awe.

I often wondered how such a system could last so long, until I realized how all bureaucracies are self-serving and are continuously reinforcing themselves. Attributing awe does not stop with the pope. Status within the bureaucracy takes on a life of its own. Since status is a value established by the structure, official members (priests) are placed in a position where they too must see it as a value. Unfortunately, many of these priests lose their autonomy in favor of keeping their status. In the organizational church, status becomes a regulator to the type of behavior the priest can perform or speak out on in public. The higher the status one has, the more authority he acquires. Individual priests are encouraged to play out their roles properly, especially if they wish to be rewarded with a higher status, perhaps bishop or cardinal.

Even under the slightest screening, it can be seen what does actually happen more often than not to the individual priest's autonomy, similar to the individual members he is supposedly serving. Passive obedience becomes the law for the priest also. The worship of authority is not only common, but expected. The person who chooses to belong to such a bureaucracy is expected to formulate their thinking and considerations that are in line with those in charge. At the same time, the bureaucracy itself rarely considers the ideas or opinions of those they manipulate.

I found it an interesting point when I realized the negative effect that such a system has on those in the lower echelons, as they begin to feel a tremendous sense of powerlessness the more they are removed from the decision-making. Robert Merton explains the process whereby the bureaucratic structure leads to over conformity and to the eventual trained incapacities of its members.

1. An effective bureaucracy demands reliability of response and strict devotion to regulations.
2. Such devotion to the rules leads to their transformation into absolutes; they are no longer conceived as relative to a set of purposes.
3. This interferes with ready adaptation under special conditions not clearly envisaged by those who drew up the general rules.
4. Thus, the very elements which conduce toward efficiency in general produce inefficiency in specific instances.

In most cases, members of a particular bureaucracy like the Catholic Church do not realize or wish to admit such inadequacies since they are tied so closely to the rules themselves and to the "rewards" which the bureaucracy holds for them. However, as Merton reminds us, "These very devices which increase the probability of conformance also lead to an over-concern with strict adherence to regulations which induces timidity and conservatism."[17] By focusing on this punishment/reward mentality, the average Catholic never actually learns how to grow spiritually.

One obvious result of the Catholic Church's bureaucratic structure is the depersonalized relationship between the bureaucrat, the leaders of the structure, and the members it serves (the lay member). The bureaucrat often looks to categorize the problem under some rule, while personal and individual cases are given low priority. The bureaucrat, even when his position is at the lower end of the hierarchy, takes on a dominating and authoritative attitude when making decisions. It is here where the average lay person has been lulled into a spiritual coma! Unless, of course, they have the courage and desire to grow in another place.

Pope Francis, the present pope as of this writing, seems to be making every effort to get away from the bureaucracy's form of depersonalization, which many Catholics are finding refreshing. However, the conservatives who want to hold onto the old ways are worried and angry. The present pope, I believe, is between a rock and a hard place. The pope's foundation and approach is pastoral, expressing full respect for the individual and for the challenges they face in their daily lives. In a letter to all Catholics, the pope addressed the issue of a second marriage following a divorce. It is here where he directs his priests to be more understanding, caring, and flexible toward those who have entered a second marriage. This pastoral focus, which is, for a change, both logical and realistic, but nonetheless creates a clash with formal church doctrine. Without a church annulment, the formal church considers this second marriage as adultery, and adultery is a mortal sin where one is condemned to hell. This is just one example of how detached the church has become from the everyday lives of the people they are supposedly serving.

How this pope will go forward in discussing other matters regarding the individual lives of average Catholics is bound to create major divisions in the church. In the past, previous popes emphasized again and again the mainline doctrine of the church, while many Catholics, in silence, went about making their personal decisions, contradictory or not. This is most obvious with the issue of birth control. The bureaucracy condemns it and the members ignore it. This pope, by voicing his pastoral approach, has brought some of these conflicting issues out in the open. I am sure this is bound to lead to a major collision between the authorities within the bureaucracy and the average practicing Catholic who is living their life knowingly in contradiction with church doctrine. In a sense, this pope has broken the silence that most knew about, accepted as a simple reality, but did not discuss. This pope has brought the ambiguity between the bureaucracy and the actual lives of members out in the open. Ross Douthat, a columnist for the *New York Times*, commenting on this major change, describes this present and future dilemma when he explains, "This means that the new truce may be even shakier than the old one. In effectively licensing innovation rather than merely tolerating it, and in transforming the papacy's keenest defenders into wary critics, it promises to heighten the church's contradictions rather than contain them."[18] From my perspective, it is about time to address these contradictions and the hypocrisies as well. If not, more and more members will continue to look elsewhere.

Based on the structure the bureaucrats of the Catholic Church developed, the members are expected to be mindless in regard to their personal spirituality; namely, in listening to and interpreting their personal sense of Christ's message. Elizabeth Johnson, professor of theology at Fordham University, reminds us of the core reason for being a Christian. She explains, "To be Christian now requires a personal decision, the kind of decision that brings about a change of heart and sustains long-term commitment."[19] The church's format put a halt to this type of spiritual growth and created a tremendous passivity for having a personal relationship with Jesus Christ. For the Catholic Church this was and is at the core of its downfall.

14

Every religion is true one way or another. It is true
when understood metaphorically. But when
it gets stuck in its own metaphors, interpreting
them as facts, then you are in trouble.
—Joseph Campbell

What I continually find so frustrating is how the bureaucratic church keeps emphasizing that their papal lineage, along with the priesthood itself, goes back to the time of the apostles. They incessantly refer to the statement made by Jesus when he said, "Upon this rock I will build my church." This Scriptural quote is unmistakably a metaphor. I intellectually agree with Thomas Moore when he reminds us that when reading the Scriptures, we must be careful not to make fixed interpretations of Scriptural stories and how we must get past the fundamentalist attitude about the spiritual life of the early Christians. He explains, "For the fundamentalist, the Bible is something to believe in; for the soul, it is a great stimulus for the religious imagination, for searching the heart for its deepest and most exalted possibilities."[1] I have learned through various readings on the interpretation of Scripture that by turning Scriptural metaphors into actual fact we lose the intent of what Jesus meant. Jesus used metaphors often, and they require our reflection so as to discover the incredible richness of his message. To do this, I know I must be careful not to take the stories literally.

I believe, as clearly revealed in the Scriptural stories following the death of Jesus, the early disciples and followers of Jesus never intended to have a formal bureaucracy, especially one that had tiers of authoritative power. If one follows the words and messages of Jesus Christ and the words and messages of his disciples following his death, the formal church as it exists today is a structure that was never meant to be. The author and teacher, Jay Parini, reminds us, "Jesus considered himself a devout Jew with ideas about reforming Judaism, not someone with designs on starting his own religion."[2]

Following the death of Jesus, as is well known, the early Christians followed the radical core of Jesus's message. They took literally the message to feed the hungry, clothe the naked, and visit those who were imprisoned. For doing so, also well-known, they were often persecuted by the Romans for their beliefs and their behavior. The first two hundred years of delivering the messages of Jesus Christ and experiencing persecution for doing so, this original movement, directed by the Spirit, experienced a major shift during the reign of the Roman Emperor Constantine the Great (AD 306–337). Not that I can pretend to be a historian, but just a casual review of that time period reveals that under his leadership and direction, Christianity was transformed into the dominant religion of the Roman Empire. It became part of the government and therefore part of the bureaucracy.

I kept searching for clues to how it was possible to dismantle the original message and intent of Jesus himself. It began to make more sense to me when I connected the dots and realized it was also during this period and the years that were to follow, where the formal church, while increasingly growing into a rigid organization, became more and more patriarchal—a men's only group. In due time, God himself was even depicted and believed to be a man with all the manly characteristics. It is one thing to refer to God metaphorically as Father, but it is another thing to take it literally, as the formal church began to preach during the Constantine era and continually preaches today. It became obvious to me that it was a grave turn of events that the church moved away from being primarily a discipleship to a doctrinal system of rules and regulations. There is no question that this new system is very much maintained and reinforced by the church today. Elizabeth Johnson warns us of the consequences that grew out of this bureaucratic shift, especially as it became exclusively male-orientated. She emphasized, "Exclusively male language leads us to forget the incomprehensibility of the holy mystery and instead reduces the living God to the fantasy of an infinitely ruling man."[3] As with other facts were brought into the picture, it became obvious to me that this male image was used to substantiate the movement toward a patriarchy and to the lessening of the role of women in the community. As I read the stories in the Bible, it is also quite obvious that Jesus interacted with women on many levels, and most certainly included them in his daily spiritual life. For sure, beyond my own perspective, the male leadership in the church unashamedly ignores this reality in favor of keeping its self-created status and male dominance.

As time progressed, and after the reign of Constantine, it seems to me that the church hierarchy continued to imply by their ongoing exclusion of women that maleness had more to do with God than femaleness. These hierarchal images of God as male causes to not only limit God, as I see it, but also to expand the unequal relation between man and woman, something the church bureaucracy fosters in the very way it functions. There is no doubt in my mind that if the Catholic Church is ever able to return to the roots of the apostle's message, this is one of the more important areas where the church needs to be transformed into a more equal community, especially in our response to the mysteries of God. Johnson once again explained this mandate perfectly when she said, "By naming God with female metaphors releases divine mystery from its age-old patriarchal cage so that God can truly be God—a comprehensible source and…the holy mystery that surrounds and supports the world."[4] To ignore this need for a major transformation, the church is discounting the very words of Scripture that I have so often read in one form or another. It directly explains we are bonded in mutual love. "There is no longer Jew or Greek, there is no longer slave or free, there is no longer male and female; for all of you are one in Jesus Christ" (Galatians 3:28).

In my thirties and forties, I kept returning to books that focused on the historical development of the church. Constantine's decision to cease the persecution of the early Christians and to accept the church as the major religion of the land was not only a major turning point for early Christianity but a force that had numerous consequences for the future church, especially in terms of building a bureaucracy. It is during this era that the church began to become part of the government and to begin its crossover into a formal bureaucracy. The spirit of Jesus's message was being overtaken by the hunger for power and the greed for wealth among the church leaders. I turn once again to the insights of Philip Yancey who expounded on this major shift from a community of equals to that of a layered bureaucratic system. He explained, "The good work continued until the triumph of Constantine, who legalized the faith and established an official imperial church. Over time the church itself became part of the wealthy establishment."[5] I will always remember the statement from one of the characters in Graham Greene's novel *The Power and the Glory.* In a dialog with a priest about religion a man by the name of Mr. Lehr said, "Of course my sister and I are Lutherans. We don't hold with your church, Father. Too much luxury, it seems to me, while the people starve."[6]

This switch in focus is reiterated by Thomas Moore. He explains, "I see no evidence that Jesus ever intended to create a formal religion and that he wasn't talking about the afterlife or another life. He was teaching how to live at a higher level in this life."[7] This statement hit a spiritual nerve in me. From the era of Constantine and the decades that were to follow, the church, as it became more formal and bureaucratic, began to issue decrees, doctrines, and encyclicals and proclaimed them to be nearly infallible, if not actually infallible. In his book, *Jesus, The Human Face of* God, Parini emphasizes the destructive nature of strict proclamations and quotes the brilliant theological work of Bonhoeffer in his work called *The Cost of Discipleship.* Bonhoeffer stated, in brace terms, "Discipleship means adherence to Christ, and, because Christ is the object of that adherence, it must take the form of discipleship. An abstract Christology, a doctrinal system, a general religious knowledge on the subject of grace or on the forgiveness of sins, render discipleship superfluous."[8] Another spiritual nerve was awakened. Parini follows these insightful words on the caustic nature of a doctrinal church by stressing, "It won't do simply to follow a doctrinal system, marking off things one has to believe in order to be saved."[9] Yet this is what this new Constantine bureaucratic church was attempting to do and continues to do today. No wonder I was so depressed as a young seminarian, and no wonder so many people are turning away.

These acts of forced belief placed on its members are evident in many statements by the church throughout its history. One outstanding example is on the nature of Mary's virginity. As the church became more bureaucratic, it placed a great deal of emphasis on this so-called miraculous event. In my own experience with what to believe or not to believe, I always had trouble with the exalted position Mary held in the church community and it seemed to me that she was often positioned at a higher place than Christ himself. This does not mean I demeaned Mary as the mother of God, but I felt the bureaucratic church went beyond what was necessary to honor her by demanding we believe her to be a virgin. I more agree with Jay Parini's viewpoint in terms of my own spiritual beliefs when he explains, "What matters in the Christmas story is that Jesus should have come into the world in a way that conveyed a sense of his unique connection to God as well as his deep-seated humanity. The Virgin Birth, as a mythical concept, delivers this message quite beautifully."[10] In other words, I wonder to myself, why ruin such beautiful messages by turning certain aspects into facts.

In my readings I discovered that the term virgin during the times of Jesus and shortly after his death could have meant a number of things and most certainly were not confined necessarily to women who had not experienced sexual intercourse. In both the Greek and Hebrew language, the word virgin could be translated in a number of ways, including simply using it as a label for a young girl or boy. I also learned that some important people throughout early history were often thought to be part divine and part human. The famous Roman emperor, Augustus, was believed to have no human father. The founders of Rome, Romulus and Remus, were supposedly children of Rhea Silvia and the god Mars. Even with this information, which certainly the church bureaucrats know about, the Virgin Birth remains a major doctrine in the Catholic Church, even though at the time many of the cardinals pleaded with the pope not to proclaim this a necessity to be believed. I most certainly believe and greatly appreciate the beauty of the Christmas story, especially the unique and divine relationship Jesus had with God. In my daily prayers, I am thankful to turn to the Holy Family for nurturing and grace. Yet in the deepest part of my faith, I personally do not need to be forced to believe it truths that belie logic. If anything, it decays once again the wonder and awesomeness of the gospel message.

It is expected that this proclamation of Mary's virginity and numerous other proclamations put forth by the church would not be questioned by its members. To be a Catholic, simply put, this is what you must believe. Those in authority, the popes and his colleagues, reached a point of belief that it was their responsibility to define God and to be the only specialist on interpreting Jesus's message. Adding further injury, it was demanded by all participants of the Catholic Church to accept their conclusions about God if membership was desired. Driving and thriving in this bureaucratic direction, Elizabeth Johnson explains how "Catholic theology tied the Spirit very tightly to church office and the teaching of the magisterium."[11] My own sense of sense of spirituality felt more and more confined. It seemed if I was to be a so-called worthy Catholic I had to turn off my brain and passively take on what I was told to believe by church authorities. Feeling suffocated, I thankfully looked outside the church for a breath of holiness. Doing otherwise would have left me in the horrible position of having a lifeless and monotonous spiritual existence. This is one reason why I refer to some members of the church as being in a spiritual coma.

I knew and believed strongly that if I was to seek the real truth regarding the core message of Jesus, I always needed to be in the process of growth and development. As the church remained rigidly bureaucratic, I discovered the theme Jesus and his disciples intended was eventually minimized and often buried beneath bureaucratic papers of laws and regulations. I had trouble with this even as a young Catholic in the seminary and often wonder why more practicing Catholics today do not have the same difficulty. In a very real sense authorities are saying, whatever the topic is at the time, this is what you must believe if you call yourself Catholic. This is what you must believe if you want to go to heaven! For me, this, at the very least, is a self-interested and self-created patriarchal formula constructed in arrogance and narcissism in its highest form.

There is no question that Jesus would be rather surprised, even humanly disappointed I believe, to witness the development of the Catholic Church since the time of Constantine. There is no place in Scripture, whether it be the active life of Jesus or the preaching of his followers after his death, where the creation of a formal Catholic Church is called for or planned for in the future. Prior to this major historical event under Constantine there were no priests, bishops, or popes. Gary Wills, author and Pulitzer Prize winner, makes the following valid point: "Isn't it odd that—with so many of Jesus's followers inspired by the Spirit to serve their brothers and sisters—none of these ministries was that of a priest."[12] I am reminded once again by Jay Parini, "It is worth noting that Jesus never meant to found a formal church with rituals and organized practices, to ordain priests, or to issue doctrinaire statements that formed a rigid program for salvation."[13] The Catholic Church is a manmade structure that lured in millions and millions of vulnerable people into believing that their way is the only way to be saved.

Throughout my Scriptural studies, it became more and more obvious to me how Jesus inspired his early followers to serve each other. I realized at some point that none of these services involved the presence of priests. Gary Wills explained, "All the followers of Jesus are, therefore, followers or leaners, and none is to be put above the other."[14] Willis supported this historical truth by referring to Scripture. Scripture states, "Do not address any man on earth as father, since you have only one Father, and he is in heaven. And you must not be addressed as leaders, since you have only one Leader, the Messiah. For whoever boosts himself up will be lowered, and whoever lowers himself down will be boosted up" (Matthew 23:5–12). Given this Scriptural insight, I began to wonder when and for what reason did priests take on the title Father, or even further the pope as Holy Father. I concluded the desire for power and to gain a sense of superiority is the only logical response.

As I got older, I began to question how one group of people, namely the higher authorities of the Catholic Church, could proclaim and then expect others to believe that the Catholic Church is the one true church. I have come to believe that this borders on a precarious and simplistic perspective. More importantly, I once again came to believe, it is enormously harmful to the spiritual life of any individual and to the community as a whole. When evaluated for what the formal church presently is and how it presently operates, this self-righteous position falls into the category of self-absorption and the need to feel superior. A system like this, hierarchal in nature, creates an environment of entitlement by proclaiming to know the real truth, above and beyond everyone else. Once again, Elizabeth Johnson reminds us that if you pretend to fully understand it, it is most likely is not God. For me, thankfully I have realized, the message of Jesus is ongoing, it is never static. Johnson reminded me of this truth when she states, "The concept of 'God' is not a grasp of God by which a person masters the mystery; but it is the means by which one lets oneself be grasped by the mystery which is present yet ever distant."[15] Sadly, the bureaucrats took the mystery out of faith, while portraying to the lay people they had all the answers, omitting their respect for mystery.

Elizabeth Johnson refers to the poignant observation made by the theologian Wolfhart Pannenberg who explained, "Religions die when the lights fail, that is, when their teachings no longer illuminate life as it is actually lived by their adherents. In such cases, the way the Holy is encountered stalls out and does not keep pace with changing human experience."[16] It is here where I am reminded of Mother Teresa's "seeking of the light."

The Catholic Church, as I have witnessed time and time again, expects loyalty and obedience to its laws and regulations. Even when these laws have no relevance and often have damaging effects (i.e., the banning of birth control, which in areas of poverty simply create more poverty). The authorities, ignoring such dire consequences, still proceed with their demands for obedience. The institution of the Catholic Church cannot afford to have individual members think and reflect on their own. As I and others have experienced, they interpret individual thinking as too threatening to the bureaucracy, even though this is what Jesus wanted: individual conversion.

The most damaging effect of a rigid and self-serving bureaucracy is the effect it has on the spiritual life of the individual. There are reasons people have left the church in droves. I was attending Mass one Saturday evening with my four children and wife. The presiding priest was young and newly ordained. The sermon was based on the Scriptural story of the shepherd and the sheep. At the beginning of his sermon the priest asked us all to reflect on the nature and functioning of sheep. He exclaimed, "My friends, have you ever considered that sheep are one of the dumbest animals on earth?" I sat in my pew amazed yet very pleased as the priest called us all to be shepherds, not dumb animals that just followed along. There was no doubt in my mind that this young priest was not going to be part of the bureaucracy for long. Six months later, I discovered he did resign from the priesthood.

While in the seminary and certainly in the ensuing years, I began to see how the Catholic hierarchy prefers we all be non-thinking sheep, obedient to our very core and always under the threat of losing membership. The average Catholic, if he or she wants to be a member in good standing, then becomes docile and submissive to their faith, allowing others to dictate the quality and tone of their spirituality. This type of religion discourages in-depth thinking and contemplation, as it would for me if I gave into it. Those that follow along become resistant to thinking for themselves. Scott Peck highlights the massive damage done when institutionalized thinking overtakes personal and individual thinking. He explains the damage that occurs as a direct result of rigid authoritarians demanding obedience that must be adhered to without any thought or self-reflection. Scott Peck states, "Rich versus poor, black versus white, pro-life versus pro-choice, straight versus gay—all are social, political, and economic conflicts fought under the banner of some ideology or deeply held belief."[17] Scott Peck challenged me to consider the destructive nature of these ideologies and to see how they are so often simply rationalizations for the continuation of the bureaucratic system. Scott Peck asks, "How often do we stop to think about what we believe? One of the major dilemmas we face both as individuals and as a society is simplistic thinking—or the failure to think at all. It isn't just *a* problem, it is *the* problem."[18]

Enforcing this notion of the non-thinking member of the church, power and the demand for obedience became the main thrust and purpose of the Catholic Church. A long list of rules, regulations, and items one had to believe in grew over the decades of operation. The church authorities moved slowly, but most decisively, away from Jesus's approach to never compel or demand belief. As a bureaucratic religious system, it became an arena for strict theological and ideological thinking and the church authorities, as I witnessed so often, would react with condemnation toward anyone you would question their position. This is why some of the things I express in this book I am rather sure will evoke anger on the part of those who have bought and continue to buy into the system. My response would be to those who are so enraged is how can you accept freewill and then demand a certain way of thinking? Did Jesus demand that his disciples and followers believe or did he prefer we make a personal choice? In reading the works of Thomas Moore, I was more than pleased that he encourages the latter and suggests envisioning spirituality as an act of personal creativity. He explains, "This new kind of religion asks that you move away from being a follower to being a creator. I foresee a new kind of spiritual creativity, in which we no longer decide whether to believe in a given creed and follow a certain tradition blindly. Most important, we no longer feel pressure to choose one tradition over another but rather are able to appreciate many routes to spiritual richness."[19]

I believe by prohibiting individual choice and the freedom of individual thinking, the formal church became a system of requirements and rewards. Of course, the dangling carrot is the ultimate reward of getting into heaven, preceded by the ongoing fear during one's life of not getting there. The Catholic Church, canonizing itself as all-knowing, proposes and blatantly maintains that it knows the way to this glorious reward. I recall years ago hearing on television an interview an arrogant newsman was having with Dr. Scott Peck. Following this notion of punishment versus a heavenly reward, the newsman, in a mocking fashion, asked Scott Peck, "So God is up there in heaven and when someone dies he chooses whether they deserve, have earned, this heavenly reward?" Scott Peck paused for a moment and said, "No, my friend, you choose, here on earth, whether you want to go or not." I sat there thrilled and so proud of his answer.

I was just as delighted and inspired when I read Marcus Borg's comments on the nature of having an individualized faith as opposed to emphasizing rules and regulations. Borg, a distinguished professor of religious studies, emphasized, "Faith as *fidelitas* does not mean faithfulness to statements about God, whether biblical, creedal, or doctrinal. *Fidelitas* refers to a radical centering in God."[20] Borg resented all the emphasis displayed by the formal church on rules and regulations. He was fully aware of how it depersonalized faith and left an individual's belief system in shallow waters and, as Peck affirmed, overly simplistic. For Borg, faith in Jesus necessitated a most personal involvement and a personal response. In describing the true person of faith, he explained, "Faith as faithfulness means loyalty, allegiance, the commitment of self at its deepest level, the commitment of the 'heart.'"[21] I came to believe, years after leaving the seminary, that faith is our personal relationship with God and we need to be consistently focused on that relationship. It is a far cry, as the bureaucratic church would like us to believe, trusting so much in so-called truths or following a list of regulations. The wonderful guru and holy mystic, Paramahansa Yogananda, hit home to me when he proclaimed, "New hope for new men! Divine union is possible through self-effort, and is not dependent on theological beliefs or the arbitrary will of a Cosmic Dictator."[22]

I feel strongly, more strongly than I do about anything else, that I need to continually reevaluate my religious and spiritual experience. I feel Thomas Moore was speaking about what has been taking place within me for a number of years. In his book, *A Religion of One's Own*, he describes what is going through the minds, hearts, and souls of many people. He states, "Fewer are willing to do whatever the priest, rabbi, or minister tells them. Fewer want to pack into a crowded church and go through the motions of a meaningless rite. Fewer want to curtail their sexual interests because a celibate or sexually repressed or obsessed cleric tells them to. Fewer women want to remain second-class observers to a male hierarchy. And so many of the churches are emptying and graying."[23] The Catholic Church officials are painfully trying to explain why church attendance is down. They come up with explanations that, of course, have nothing to do with them. It is time, and I sincerely hope there is still time, that they take a serious look in the mirror.

When the author Thomas Moore speaks to this issue he is not suggesting or encouraging a mass exit from all formal churches that have become more bureaucracies than houses of worship. He is strongly proposing that each individual must rethink their religious experience. They must ask themselves in the privacy of their own meditation whether and when does the church allow for growth and, more importantly, when does it encourage growth? I am left with the question, does the bureaucratic church breathe new life into a spiritual experience or does it get in the way of spiritual growth? Up to this point, I personally think it does get in the way in so many areas of having a faith-full life. This does not mean that I intend to exit my church of childhood and never return again. What it means is that I can no longer depend on the church, as it operates as a bureaucracy, for my spiritual fulfillment and spiritual growth. I need, actually crave, to expand. This is why I believe in the perspective of Elizabeth Johnson when she explains, "This is the grace of our age: encountering multiple religious traditions widens the horizon wherein we catch sight of God's loving plenitude. Thus, we are able to approach the mystery ever more deeply."[24]

By expanding beyond the sterile and often destructive bureaucratic system, I have finally recognized that so much of the church's belief system and doctrinal proclamations were based on self-serving needs and had very little to do with a spiritual life. As with many bureaucracies, the church has become overplayed with useless procedures and regulations. Obsessed with all areas of sexual life, the church has enacted rules that are at the very least immature and in some cases pathological. Pompous authorities have created a major disconnect with the people, which is why so many are bored to death by meaningless weekly sermons. So often they have nothing to do with what the average person is going through—emotionally, mentally, psychologically, and spiritually. I personally do not plan to completely abandon all aspects of the church, but I know I have to follow the advice of Thomas Moore when he advises, "Don't take the traditions as they are offered. Struggle with them, work hard at extracting only what is valuable in them, and be ready to discard the dross."[25]

I personally have taken Thomas Moore's advice and so many other great writers' since my seminary days. My main concern, however, is it too late for a vast number of Catholics. Because of my background, I am able to throw out the dirty bath water but keep the baby. I am able to discard many of the bureaucratic beliefs and demands as pure nonsense and even harmful, but still hold onto the messages of Jesus Christ. Many Catholics, were not as lucky as I was in being able to study Scripture and other areas of my faith. The average Catholic's faith comes from what the bureaucracy has passed onto them. From my viewpoint, we are all left with a much-divided church community. The first group, who could be referred to as traditionalist, simply accept everything the church proposes. They may in the privacy of their own lives make personal choices that defy these teachings, but up front they act as if they agree with the bureaucratic message. The second group, I refer to them as sociological Catholics, participate in church activities up to a point, but eventually leave once these activities or rituals are completed. For psychological reasons, certainly not spiritual, they feel the need to have their children baptized, receive Holy Communion, and be confirmed. They may attend weekly Mass, especially if it is required by their local parish in order to participate in these rituals. Once they have attained the necessities of membership, they go in another direction. The third group, by far the largest representation of Catholics, has stopped attending church all together and do not see the need to have their children go through the rituals to attain membership. Some may decide to join other church denominations, but my guess is that most do not. The shame here and something I firmly worry about is as they throw out the dirty bath water, have they attained enough of a spiritual foundation to live their lives by? If not, where will they and their children hear Jesus's message?

As a result of the divisions within the church and as a result of the mass exodus from church participation, it may very well be too late for the bureaucratic church to be become believable and effective as a Christian church of leadership. As I discovered over time, as many Catholics have also experienced, the formal church, when it operates as a bureaucracy, has very little to do with spirituality. As a young boy who was immersed in the daily rituals of the church and most assuredly considered it my home, the new awareness that I and others have reached has created a major disappointment. In some ways it can be compared to the death of a loved one or in having to face one's own death. I actually experienced the various psychological stages that one goes through in facing the end of life. Kubla Ross defined these stages extremely well in her book entitled *On Death and Dying*,[26] and I believe these stages can be applied to other significant forms of death.

Reflecting on my own stages of spiritual growth, at first there was denial. Steeped in ignorance and naiveté, I refused to accept what I was seeing and hearing. Even if something going on within the church did not feel right or seem logical, I would ignore it. I would never let new information impinge on the purity in which I envisioned the church and the priesthood.

Then there was anger, where I was lashing out at those who were such a disappointment in terms of their ideas and actions, their hypocrisy and lack of caring for an individual's plight. Looking back on it, there were times when this anger could be labeled as irrational and most certainly a waste of energy. Most of the anger was based on frustration and disappointment. I was a round peg trying to fit into a square hole. I was refusing to accept the "square hole" and wanted it changed. The failures in these efforts often led to more frustration and anger.

Then the stage of depression and sadness came into the picture. This took place in the last two years in the seminary, where I spent days, weeks, and months in isolation. I was aware that my eyes were blood shot and had various tones of purple under them. I knew that my hands were constantly shaking and that I was sleep-deprived. Unaware of the benefits of psychology, I did not know I was on the verge of a major breakdown. I could only identify with a few of my professors and hardly any of my fellow seminarians. Finally, it had to be grace, I was able to accept this death. The priesthood I sought did not exist, and I left the seminary. It took me years to put all the pieces together. Looking back, even though it was painful, I am grateful for the experience. I am finally enjoying and thriving on the process.

Many of the members of the Catholic Church are now going through a similar type of experience regarding their personal faith while being a member of a formal church. The stages from denial to anger and depression and then finally to acceptance have created a major crisis of faith for those who have the courage to face the realities of the bureaucratic church. In order to avoid the mistake of throwing out the baby (our core faith) with the dirty bath water (the major missteps of the church), it is necessary to make a distinction between religion and the vibrant life of spirituality.

There is no doubt that a formal religion can be a part of one's personal spirituality, but it must be recognized that too often the structure of the organization falls short of its primary purpose and goals. Many scholars have noted how the Catholic Church, as has many organized religions, has the tendency to become like a business, concerned with its own well-being and its own survival. Thomas Moore explained it perfectly for me when he clearly explains, "Formal religions are often overdone, with useless formalities, immature psychological notions, and pompous authorities."[27] This is easily exposed in how so many of us are forced to sit through meaningless sermons that have nothing to do with what people are going through emotionally, mentally, and above all spiritually.

A new approach is needed if we are to return to the core messages of Scripture. This new approach can include a formal religion but must never be confined by it. Once again Thomas Moore reminds us, "We are assailed by people ordained by the society to convince us of its beliefs and values, leaving us with a pseudo religion."[28] When this does happen, religion becomes destructive to the very nature and core of spirituality. A formal religion, as long as it remains rigid and self-serving, needs to be placed to the side and most certainly no longer be considered as the primary source of being spiritual.

There are a number of things that can be done to turn this in another direction. If the Catholic Church chooses to be more a part of the spiritual life of individuals, a number of changes in the structure are required. Among the first of these is priestly celibacy.

The law forbidding marriage for priests is manmade and served the purpose of church leaders and had nothing to do with spirituality. The church authorities know all the apostles were married.

The negative consequences of mandating celibacy in the priesthood create numerous problems both for the priests and the people they serve. These problems must finally be taken seriously since they are far worse than any argument for keeping it. When celibacy is discontinued as a requirement, I am positive the priesthood would attract a much different person than the church has been ordaining and continues to do so today. It might very well stop the major decline in the priesthood and a more well-rounded and spiritual group might consider it.

Another major change must involve the inclusion of women in the priesthood. It only takes common sense to recognize the pitfalls of an all-male organization. Women obviously have a great deal to offer. Spirituality needs their perspective, ideas, and leadership. The bureaucracy must cease their token acceptance of women and give them an equal place in every level of the church community. This is going to be a tremendous challenge for the present pope. Even though he expressed numerous times the need to be open to all people, he nonetheless is still representing a patriarchal structure. Matthew Fox clearly and pungently addresses this issue when he states, "There is no reason, other than patriarchy, that women can't be priests. I find the argument that Jesus did not ordain women is ridiculous. Jesus didn't ordain anyone. I believe the church's refusal to give women positions of power is about the patriarchy's desire for control, pure and simple."[29]

In my reading of the Scripture stories, I can easily see that Jesus enjoyed being around women. Parini reminds us, "Women followed him eagerly, and many became leaders in the early Christian church. It was much later—many decades after his death—that misogyny took root in the church."[30] There is no question the church authorities have ignored the reality that Jesus himself never shied away participating with women and assumed they would take on a spiritual authority in his name. Mary Magdalene, for one, was certainly a key figure in Jesus's life and played a defining role in the ministry of Jesus.

She was not only at the foot of the cross, but she was the first to see him after his resurrection. So the question I feel must be asked: how did the church authorities marginalize women in the church even though they were very much part of Jesus's ministry and the spreading of his message? Elizabeth Johnson reminds us, as those in authority most certainly need to be reminded, that the early Christians were "a community of brothers and sisters bonded in mutual love."[31]

These are just a few of the changes that must be considered if the bureaucracy is to return to a more spiritual structure. It certainly will attract a healthier person for leadership, allow for more realistic perspectives regarding the issues we all face, and will be a means to cease some of the built-in pathologies that occur as a result of the present system. But I feel the need to be realistic, it can be assumed that these changes will not come from within. Those enjoying the luxuries and pleasures of rectory life are not going to want it changed. The changes must come from the demands of the lay community who must stop enabling the present pathological system. The ways of going about this require the input from people from all walks of life.

Those who have left the church need to be encouraged to return. The community needs them. For those still active, they need to stop yessing Father to death, especially when they feel so differently in their silence. When I do attend church, the complaints of the lay person leaving church that day so often far outweigh any positive thoughts about the priests or the church itself.

It has been my experience, even though I feel strongly that these bureaucratic changes need to be made, that I cannot wait for the formal church to do so. As a matter of defined purpose, I have also looked outside the church for a stronger spiritual life and a better understanding of Jesus's message. I do realize that the bureaucracy is set up to be stable and predictable, but a true spiritual life needs to be constantly evolving. Thomas Moore explains it by ceasing from being a follower and becoming a creator. Rather than keeping your spiritual life in a structured cathedral, the building and all that it entails, he suggests that we build our own cathedral. I was so encouraged when I read Moore explain, "The religion I am putting forth is not the domesticated, tame, rehearsed, and constantly repeated variety. It is ever revealing and renewing itself. When I say that it is your own, that's what I mean. It is not someone else's summary of what you should do or be. It is the constant new revelation of the deep truths that can shape your life."[32]

This is my challenge. I hope it is clear in this book that I feel the need to encourage each person. We need to encourage each other to open our eyes, be educated, and to be open to a deeper spiritual growth. As problems in the formal church become more and more obvious, we all must have the courage to confront them openly and honestly. For today's spiritual man and woman, who often sit alone with his or her thoughts of holiness and grace, this is the modern challenge of spirituality. Marcus Borg reminded me of this challenge when he expresses, "The Christian life is not about believing or doing what we need to do so that we can be saved. Rather, it is about seeing what is already true—that God loves us already—and then beginning to live in this relationship."[33]

For me, the very dynamic of this relationship is depicted in one of the paintings in the Sistine Chapel where God is reaching down to man and man is reaching back. It is a painting that is full of action. It reveals the collaboration throughout history between God and man that is constant and enduring. It reveals that we are on a journey moving toward God but also with God. It is the duality of God's divine grace and our individual effort in response. Borg reminds us once again that our individual journey involves our entire lives and "its destination is life in the presence of God. Yet God is simply not the destination, but one who is known on the journey."[34]

In her introduction, Elizabeth Johnson speaks to this open-ended partnership when she explains, "The phrase 'the living God' elicits a sense of ineffable divine mystery on the move in history, calling forth our own efforts in partnership while nourishing a loving relationship at the center of our being."[35] For sure God has been doing his part and sent us Jesus Christ to make sure we know the way. My daily question to myself and my question to others is, how serious are we about reaching back?

15

God has fallen out of containment in religion and into human hearts—God is incarnating. Our whole unconscious is in an uproar from the God who wants to know and to be known.

—Carl Jung

As a psychologist in private practice for over forty years, I have reached the conclusion that the science of psychology is not the comprehensive remedy or ultimate answer to all the challenges we face as human beings. Psychology, most assuredly a benefit in so many ways, still fell short in my attempts to discover the true meaning and purpose of my life. Due to my experience with psychotherapy, I acknowledge it is a valuable path to problem-solving and creative growth. However, I found it can only take us so far. Even when the experience of therapy came to a successful conclusion, I, and many of my clients, was left with the question, "What else?"

There is no doubt, however, it was my involvement with the field of psychology, especially as a client in therapy, that enabled me to even reach the place where I could even ask, what else? In the years of weekly therapy sessions, I experienced how therapy released me from many of my demons and placed me in a life direction that is now both mentally and emotionally rewarding. It took time and a patient therapist, but was well worth it. As anyone who has gone through therapy will certainly attest to, the process itself is no easy task. I was often tempted to edit or downplay what I was feeling or thinking. There was often the embarrassment about discussing certain topics, along with wondering how my therapist would react to what I was telling him. After years of being a therapist myself, I have come to respect the amount of courage and hard work it takes to address ourselves openly. It is truly the brave souls who are willing to dig deeply into their thoughts and feelings, discover how they originated, and then examine them for what they are. Once reaching new levels of insight, it takes enormous resolution to make the necessary changes for living a healthier life. Thomas Moore emphasizes the importance of this experience when he states, "Therapy involves an exploration of these hidden presences that affect us so profoundly. The people and events of our past and the archetypal figures that shape us and make up our own periodic table, the basic stuff out of which we make a life and become a person."[1]

Yet even as I accepted and responded to the challenges of therapy, I slowly reached the conclusion that there is more that needs to complete the task of self-awareness. I say this not as a complaint. In a very authentic way, it is a good thing. I have determined that through the process of self-analysis, I was free to go to a higher and even more fulfilling level. Unconstrained from worrying about my own limitations and allowing my inferior feelings to dictate my mood and decision-making, I could finally focus on my gifts and creative side. The spiritual leader, Paramahansa Yogananda, said it profoundly when he explained, "To humble the ego or false self is to discover one's eternal identity."[2] This is the opportunity that therapy offered me and I have presented to my clients.

When I was in the seminary, the first two years of academics involved various classes in a wide range of philosophical topics. It was believed by those in charge of academics that philosophy created the groundwork for the theology classes we would take the following four years. Studying philosophers such as Plato, Aristotle, and Kierkegaard formed a foundation for the numerous levels and diverse ways of thinking and problem-solving. Once this was accomplished, this new knowledge would be applied to when our course work turned to theological issues and to the formation of theological principles.

In a very similar vein, I view the field of psychology and the experience of psychotherapy as an essential precursor to allowing me to focus and to begin living within a spiritual life. The study of the human mind and emotions were the primary tool that enabled me to redefine and completely alter my mental and emotional make-up; these included areas I was once unaware of having. In turn, the therapeutic experience acted as the primary instrument to changing my behaviors from ones that were unfulfilling and destructive to ones that were creative and purposeful. Referencing especially the use of cognitive therapy, Deepak Chopra, the preeminent teacher of Eastern philosophy, described how the most powerful instrument for change exists in the beliefs and assumptions we have of ourselves. Chopra explained, "We suffer because we have mistaken ideas about ourselves (I don't deserve happiness; Nothing ever works out)."[3] Therapy helped me replace these distorted concepts about myself with more realistic ones. For example, I do deserve happiness; things have a way of working out. Ridding myself of distorted thoughts that were corrosive to my well-being brought about the openness to move to higher levels of thinking, especially about the true meaning of life and my purpose in it.

Accepting psychology as a precursor to spiritual awareness, Elizabeth Johnson made the point, "People who courageously accept themselves, who accept their own life with all its quirks, beauty and agony, in point of fact accept holy mystery who abides within him— the more you know and accept self the more you accept God."[4] The years I spent in therapy brought me to a place where I was more comfortable with myself, something that was definitively missing in my teenage years and early twenties. While agreeing with Johnson, I do know for sure that it was not an automatic transition. Though the process of therapy, I was brought to a place mentally where I became aware of an invitation to become more. This invitation came in many forms and called for me to make a personal decision on whether to respond with a yes. I could not resist and I am grateful to the many voices calling me forth. I could finally open the doors that I once thought were protecting me from all forms of vulnerability and feelings of being inferior. Because of therapy, my eyes were able to see so much beauty in my soul.

Toward the end of my doctorate program, a turning point in my career occurred. I met two brilliant psychologists who invited me to join them in their private practice. Both of these psychologists were involved with the Alfred Adler Institute in New York City. Alfred Adler developed a unique theory regarding the growth and development of the human being from a psycho-social point of view. It is referred to as "The Individual Psychology of Alfred Adler." As I was completing my doctorate, I knew I was not learning enough about how to apply the principles of psychology to the actual work of being a therapist. Influenced by the psychologists I was now working with, I enrolled in the Adler Institute and attended classes for three years. One of the psychologists I was working with was a dean and professor at the institute and, when I completed my personal therapy, I began weekly supervision sessions with him for five years. One year was only required to get a license to practice, but I was learning so much I extended my supervisory sessions for a number of years. I would not be the psychologist I am today without this training.

*****

When seeing clients on a weekly basis, I always have a game plan on what I think needs to be accomplished in therapy. In the first few sessions of therapy, the client explains his or her issues that led him or her to seek therapy. Once they have expressed their personal predicaments and I feel the time is right, I explain to them that along with wanting to help them with their specific problems, I have a secondary goal. This secondary task, which I believe is imminently crucial to the success of therapy, involves the comprehension of a concrete philosophy about what makes us who we are, what issues underlie the adults we have become and, most notably, how and why we make our everyday decisions. These choices include whom we decide to marry and how we relate to our partner in marriage, our career choice and our attitudes toward the work experience, and the people we choose to socialize with and the manner we interact with them. Intertwined with these life-altering decisions, there is the task of how we would define the meaning and purpose of our behavior within each of these challenges. I have a plaque in my office containing a Mark Twain quote where he pointedly stated, "There are two crucial days in our lives: the day we were born and the day we figured out why we were born."

Based on my own personal experience in weekly therapy sessions and then as a therapist myself, I found learning a specific philosophy gave me the opportunity to put my life into a tangible framework. It also allowed me to reach a deeper understanding for the thoughts and feelings I was experiencing at the time. In performing my role as a psychologist, I feel it is vital that all my clients have a philosophical structure to not only understand and assess themselves, but also to understand the underlying nature of all the people they interact with on a regular basis. It serves the purpose of making them better people, a better spouse, better parents, a better friend, and a more productive contributor to society. I came to believe that therapy, based within a theoretical framework, has the potential to free all of us from our self-created prisons that once emotionally handcuffed us to what we once beheld as a life of limitations. With this newly found freedom which therapy offers, we all are in a better position to turn to our creative side and fulfill our personal dreams. It is a goal I wish for all of us.

Certainly, the Adlerian approach is not the only or decisive approach. In graduate school, I found there were many philosophies to choose from. The main advice I received was to choose a philosophy that I was most comfortable with and then allow the other viewpoints to contribute to these basic tenets. As I went through this training, I was encouraged never to stop the learning process, even after formal therapy is completed. Formal therapy was certainly a good start in the route to understanding myself, but the process has to be a lifetime experience. By attaining a vision of my basic nature within a philosophical structure, the ongoing therapeutic process of introspection is nurtured and fostered in a much more organized and progressive fashion. The end result opens the doors to our spiritual side.

In stressing the need for ongoing nourishment, I am thankful that I fell in love with reading. I encourage all my clients to read as much as they can and to use brilliant authors as gurus, people who literally show us the way out of darkness. Eknath Easwaran emphasizes this point when he explains, "To reignite enthusiasm when it is slowly fading, the best thing you can do is to spend time with a passionately enthusiastic teacher."[5] For my own self-knowledge as a therapist, along with studying the works of Alfred Adler, I lean heavily on such authors as Karen Horney, Carl Jung, Scott Peck, Thomas Moore, Eknath Easwran, Elizabeth Johnson, Paramahansa Yoganda, Jay Parini, Joseph Campbell, Henri Nouwen, Deepak Chopra, Marcus Borg, and Philip Yancey. I love the novelists Pat Conroy and Leon Uris, and many more. I find novels, when written well, are great examples of individual character traits and lifestyles; they reveal how human beings can live in fear, trepidation, and self-dislike or with courage and love.

The above authors revealed to me that there is always a pattern to our lives. In my therapy, it was stressed that each situation discussed in therapy must never be seen in isolation. Everything must be interpreted in light of me as a whole person. The way I interpreted therapy was somewhat like working on a thousand-piece puzzle, each piece being significant but must always be seen in terms of how it fits into the big picture. In my personal application of the Adlerian philosophy, it encouraged more in-depth understanding about my personal ways of thinking and added clarity to the types of choices I made. Scott Peck explains the path of therapy as one where "we begin by distrusting what we already believe, by actively seeking the threatening and unfamiliar, by deliberately challenging the validity of what we have previously been taught and hold dear."[6] Along with other authors I studied, Scott Peck made me aware of how I developed an erroneous belief system that dominated my emotions and ruled my mind. Unbeknown to me at the time, the major consequence was that it hindered me from constructive growth. By the time I reached my midtwenties, I was operating in an ongoing and endless rut.

As I took on this task of self-discovery in therapy, I was presented with an outline of the Adlerian model. Early on, I could see this philosophy was aligned to the Judeo-Christian approach to life, which was already very much part of my life. Adler believed that the highest form of mental health is having genuine interest in the welfare of others. In maintaining this point of view, he coined the term

"Social Interest." Highlighting the importance of caring for others, Adler believed that in living within the tradition of social interest, "The individual feels at home in life and feels his existence to be worthwhile just so far as he is useful to others."[7] I became convinced that if I strove to live my life under the banner of genuine interest in the well-being of others, I would have the opportunity to become a more whole and completed person myself. It struck me early in my studies how this Adlerian perspective corresponded so well with the basic Christian message that we are to love our neighbor as we love ourselves.

My experience in learning the Adlerian philosophy took time to digest. I better understood it when I could actually see it operating in my life. This took a great deal of introspection, discussion, and application. Therapy does not involve speed, although I do admit that at times I wished it could be faster. There were weeks where I lost motivation and times that I found it difficult to discuss certain issues. Even as a therapist, I sometimes wish I was more like a dentist. The individual comes in suffering from a specific pain. I find the origins of the problem. Then I drill and fill and the patient walks out relieved and pleased. Unlike dentistry, therapy is a long and complex process. It took me months of reflection to unravel the layers upon layers of defensive barriers I had formed, along with the many distorted self-perceptions I carried around with me on a daily basis. Karen Horney emphasizes the worthiness of the therapy when she explains, "The therapeutic value of the disillusioning process lies in the possibility that, with the weakening of obstructive voices, the constructive forces of the real self have a chance to grow."[8] It is not mandatory that every individual experience the process of individual therapy, but I found it extremely helpful in knocking down my defensive walls so I could get back to the very essence of who I am. Even though I was tempted to use a quick fix, the reality remained that discovering my true self took time, courage, and hard work.

After having experienced therapy for a number of years, I have always wanted to replicate what was done for me with all my clients. I especially want each of my clients to get some idea of the game plan and the direction that we will take together in order for us to attain our therapeutic goals. Before explaining the philosophy, I emphasize to each client two major points. First, this philosophy applies to every human being, not just those coming for therapy. It is universal in its essence and can be used to understand how we all think, feel, and behave the way we do. Secondly, most of what I am about to tell them about the philosophy exists in the subconscious; namely, there are numerous perceptions and attitudes we have about ourselves that we are not aware of having. This is the main point for participating in therapy. We want to bring our core thoughts about ourselves into our conscious state so we can judge each of them as either being true or categorically distorted. Yogananda references the existence of these misleading subconscious thoughts as our inner enemies, and with the strongest of words, he states, "Man can understand no eternal verity unless he has freed himself from pretensions. The human mind is teeming with the repulsive life of countless world-delusions. Struggles in the battlefield pale into insignificance here, when man first contends with inner enemies!"[9]

The therapeutic goal that was presented to me was to reach a heightened realization about how many of my unconscious and repressed thoughts were affecting my life. I was finally able to grasp that I had developed numerous misperceptions about myself and was often misled by these thoughts. In referencing these subconscious perceptions as our "shadow," a Carl Jung theme, Deepak Chopra warns that there is a heavy price to pay for not becoming aware of our personally developed shadow. He explains, "The shadow is a region of the psyche. Nothing exists in it that is beyond our power to dissolve. Instead of allowing the shadow to victimize us, we must seize the control switch and reclaim our true function as creators."[10] Yogananda once again underscores this premise, this time more poetically, while speaking to one of his students. He states, "Come with me; I will teach you to subdue the beasts of ignorance roaming in the jungles of the human mind."[11] This is what my therapist helped me to do and I want to accomplish for all my clients.

Therapy is very much like teaching. It involves the learning of a specific philosophy and the key components of what it means to be a human. Paraphrasing the Adlerian viewpoint, I explain to my clients the philosophy starts with this one simple yet all-important statement: No human being fully has what it takes to handle life. When most of my clients hear this statement, they usually agree with what seems to them an obvious human condition; namely, we are not Supermen or Wonder Women figures. I then explain to all my clients, somewhat to their surprise, that even though this first concept may be obvious and easily acceptable when initially voiced, this opening phrase may be the most important sentence I ever say to them. The reason behind its importance is the fact we all spend part of our lives trying to deny this reality. The basic reason we all fall into various intensities of denial is due to the fact we all experience, from the early stages of our lives, a sense of physical, mental, and emotional vulnerability, coupled with a deep sensation of being inferior. Some of these thoughts and feelings may be conscious and clearly evident to us, but many are not. In my therapy, I discovered how I often denied or repressed painful feelings and how the majority of them became my personal shadow. I was not in control; my demeaning thoughts ran the show.

My experience of having inferior feelings and a powerful sense I was vulnerable to being damaged came about in two primary ways. First, by how I interpreted early life events and the conclusions I reached about myself once each of these events had been experienced. Secondly, the type of environment I was born into and the manner in which I was socialized, played a tremendous role in the values and goals I formulated. When I did not achieve these societal goals, I became extremely critical of my self-worth. Marcus Borg warns us that we must all be aware how "systems affect how we think, including our perception of ourselves and others."[12] In this case, his using the term *systems* was a reference to society's values and norms. When younger, I was convinced I needed to meet and achieve these standards.

I fell into the trap of emphasizing how I looked, the degree to which I succeeded, and the level of affluence I had attained. Yoganda warns of the consequences for making these our primary goals. He states, "How quickly we are weary of earthly pleasures! Desire for material things is endless; man is never satisfied completely, and pursues one goal after another."[13] As true as Yoganda's words are, I, nevertheless, took the bait and began comparing myself to the values and goals of our society; this often led, again unbeknown to me, to the beginning stages of feeling inferior and inept.

It is almost as if I was born into this world with a blank slate. I say almost because genetic make-up and our neuron development certainly affected the outcome of my development. While these important factors need to be taken into consideration, I still was compelled to examine how the people I interacted with, and the cultural environment I existed in, wrote on my blank slate with statements about my basic characteristics, both my strengths and limitations. The perceived limitations, I often erroneously accepted as pure facts. I despised all feelings of being vulnerable or inferior.

By the time I reached my teenage years, my slate was rather full of convictions regarding myself as a person. Because I did not reach the personal standards I set for myself and presumed I was supposed to meet, powerful feelings of inferiority and vulnerability became part of my personal slate. Not matching up to the criteria of my particular culture only added to these thoughts. In due time, these self-perceptions began to take on a life of their own. Often detesting how I felt about myself and not wanting to face this self-imposed image, the process of denial and repression became a common practice, most of the time without my realization. Not wanting to see myself as inferior or vulnerable, I bottled up as much of these feelings as possible and avoided as many situations that might give rise to these feelings. Thus, the birth of my shadow!

Based on conversations in therapy, I can see how these inferior self-perceptions and the feelings of vulnerability began very early in my life. It is hard to say when I left the innocence of being a baby and began to have these feelings, but through the use of early recollections, I can now see it clearly. Now that I am attuned to the Adlerian philosophy, I can observe it taking place in young children. I was recently playing the game of *Candy Land* with a five-year-old one Friday afternoon. As the game went on we were laughing and having fun, moving our pegs along the board. Then the crushing blow occurred. My young friend lost the game. The disappointment was written all over his face. The next week when I arrived at his home and suggested we play the game again, his response carried a telling message. He said, "Why don't you and Mom play and I will watch?" He clearly was reacting to the loss the week before and most likely interpreted it as a personal failure. As a result of this reaction, he may have concluded he was lacking in some way. By his interpretation, the result of how the game ended made him feel inadequate and therefore inferior. Unless this conclusion was corrected, future games and contests, once again via his perception of himself, would ignite various degrees of vulnerability. Without his conscious awareness of doing so, he would come up with a way not to repeat this so-called negative experience again. Perhaps he would choose the psychological solution he initiated with me. "I'll just watch." His reaction made me think of how many adults carry such a solution into their adult lives and "just watch."

A similar scenario took place when I asked a ten-year-old if he played sports. He said, "No, I am not good at sports." I asked him when did he came to this conclusion. He responded, "When I was five." I can guess that at this young age he either experienced a failure in some sporting activity, or was laughed at by his peers, or possibly received a harsh statement from an adult about his abilities. I am reminded once again how early inferior feelings are born and then are reacted to with a self-created solution to avoid a re-experience of these feelings. Sadly, so many of my adult clients report back to me their own personal perceptions of themselves: "I can't read"; "I don't know how to write"; "I'm an introvert"; or "I'm not good socially." I have found the possibilities for self-recriminations are endless.

The first ten to fifteen years of life are crucial. Through my own interpretations of events and most certainly the influence of how I was treated by those around me, convictions of myself began to formulate. Areas of vulnerability and the times I felt inferior became my main focus. These perceptions became engrained and highly influenced the decisions I made or did not make. The limitations, or my exaggerated misinterpretations of them, are what led to nagging feelings of inferiority and vulnerability. Chopra explains, "If we are honest with ourselves, dark impulses are free to roam our minds at will, and the price for being a good person—something we all aspire to—is that the bad person who might ruin everything must be kept under wraps."[14] Debbie Ford, who conducted workshops around the world on this subject, explains we all have gifts along with inadequacies. It is the duality of our human nature. She explains, "If we know courage, it is because we have experienced fear; if we can recognize honesty, it is because we have encountered deceit. And yet most of us deny or ignore our dualistic nature."[15] During the first twenty or thirty years of my life I did not handle this duality well. It was a notion I found very difficult to accept; namely, I had limitations but I also had gifts. As a consequence, I continued to deny my duality's existence and tended to focus on keeping any form of imperfection from being revealed, both to me and most certainly to others.

Yes, I believe there was a time when I was an innocent little baby, free to love and be loved, free to touch and be touched, and free to laugh and experience pure joy. However, a new reality began to take form. I began to interact with others as an imperfect and wounded person in a world that I often perceived as harsh. Questions started to arise as to how well I fit in versus not fit in, how lovable was I versus how well am I loved. I rated myself, intensely, according to my successes and failures. I allowed the people and the values of my environment to rate and judge me, and then accepted their evaluation as an indication of my worth. How good I am coincided with am I good enough. This eventually led, as I grew older, to being haunted by internal emotional and mental conflicts on a regular basis. The innocent and pure child I once was became replaced by feelings of being inferior in one fashion or another. Mistakenly, due to the fact I did not want to see myself as being both inferior and vulnerable, I began to spend a great deal of time and energy doing everything in my power to ignore these feelings and the situations that might bring them about. The feelings of being inferior and vulnerable eventually brought about a variety of anxieties and fears, which often controlled all aspects of my life. Ford, referring once again to Jung's theory of our shadow, reiterates that "instead of being able to have control over it, the shadow winds up having control over us."[16]

It is the primary task of therapy to bring our self-perceptions into our conscious state. We need to reach a level of awareness that many of our self-perceptions have been developed in a distorted fashion. Yes, inferiority may be a reality, but it does not have to be our main focus. In therapy, through discovery of my repressed shadow, I was able to come to terms that many of my self-perceptions were distorted and, in some cases, totally wrong.

The primary task of my therapy experience was to discover the degree in which I experienced a sense of inferiority and shame. I discerned how these feelings were formulated through my interpretations of my childhood experiences, along with the influence of the values and beliefs of those around me. There is no doubt that if I was born in another time and place, surrounded by totally different group of people, I would not be who I am today. My surroundings, including parents, teachers, relatives, friends, and coaches and the characteristics of my entire environment, all had a tremendous effect on how I felt about myself. Marcus Borg highlights this effect when he explains, "By the time we are in early adolescence, perhaps earlier, our sense of who we are is increasingly the product of our culture."[17] My socialization involved questions as to whether I was attractive enough, to whether had I achieved enough, and to whether I was significant enough. Influenced by my cultural values and the fact I often did not achieve what was considered valuable goals, my sense of being inferior grew in strength. Success, popularity, and all forms of power presented a tremendous temptation in terms of goals to achieve, especially when the fear of not being good enough, at least by society's standards, took form. Henri Nouwen, a spiritual writer, explains, "These negative voices are so loud and so persistent that it is easy to believe in them. That's the great trap. It is the trap of self-rejection."[18]

Some fears and vulnerabilities we all share in common, such as the fear of getting cancer, experiencing a major accident, or even the fear of death. However, the ones that I needed to be most concerned about, as others need to do, are the ones that were personal to me. I often ask my clients to picture a list of forty possible inferior feelings written on my office wall. The list may include the fear of rejection, of not being included, the fear of being ignorant, of not being handsome or pretty, all levels of not achieving, etc., etc. The imagined list on the wall basically involves negative human thoughts and feelings that most can easily recognize, for they are all human possibilities. The main point I want to make to my clients, however, is two or three from that list might be my primary feelings of inferiority, two or three might be the ones they hold onto, and two or three might be someone else's. The types of interpretation we make or the conclusions we reach about ourselves is very personal to each individual. The key is to bring them out of our shadow and judge them in a more logical fashion. I found both required a great deal of study and examination on my part in order to understand the person I became.

Once I have recognized that an inferior or vulnerable feeling has been awakened, I then must then come to terms with the psychological reality that I have basically two primary yet very different choices in response to a challenge. The first response has only one purpose, and that is to eliminate, as much as possible, the inferior or vulnerable feelings I may be experiencing. I came to recognize this as my unhealthy path which, if it is used a great deal, can possibly turn into being a major neurosis. Even though there are numerous types of neurotic solutions, they all have one thing in common: the denial of our humanness. In this regard, Nouwen reminds us, "Neurosis is often the psychic manifestation of a much deeper human darkness: the darkness of not feeling truly welcome in human existence."[19]

The common denominator of not feeling welcome is what the feeling of inferiority is all about. The unhealthy solution is an attempt to repress all such feelings as they occur. It is a solution that is totally dictated by my fears and vulnerabilities; it overshadows any of the talents I may have at my disposal. Scott Peck references how so often people choose to avoid challenges or problems; he explains, "The tendency to avoid problems and the emotional suffering inherent in them is the primary basis of all psychological illness."[20]

Nouwen takes this one step further regarding this unhealthy choice and helps to explain the main point of this chapter regarding psychology and the experience of psychotherapy as being the precursor to having a spiritual life. He explains, "Self-rejection is the greatest enemy of the spiritual life because it contradicts the sacred voice that calls us the 'beloved.' Being beloved expresses the core truth of our existence."[21] One of the primary goals of my therapy was first of all to recognize I have this type of solution and to recognize it as a crucial mistake to use it. If I did not recognize it as a sickness, I cannot be cured. Secondly, I needed to come to terms with how destructive this solution is, most especially in terms of growing and reaching higher levels of my human potential. Thomas Moore reminded me that the feelings of vulnerability are part of my human nature from childhood and not something I should ignore or run from, and most certainly not allow to dictate my life. Moore encourages me when he states, "We approach the power of this child not by fleeing its vulnerability, but by claiming it."[22] Therapy taught me one definition of being healthy involves the admission of having feelings of inferiority and vulnerability, along with having a solution that desires to ignore all minus feelings, no matter what the cost. For me to have a chance of being healthy, I needed to realize its destructive nature and wisely choose not to use this as a solution.

The other choice I have experiences the vulnerability but is not dictated by it. This choice is freed from denying my real or imagined inferiorities. It is a choice that can fully respond to the task at hand without any prejudice or bias. It is a path that moves away from focusing on personal negativity, real or imagined, in order to be in a position to concentrate on my gifts. The author, Langford, reminds me of how a person like Mother Teresa was able to perform her wonderful and spiritual works. He explains, "Mother Teresa realized that our greatest suffering is not our need or weakness itself, but the feeling of uselessness, of being worthless, unappreciated, and unloved."[23] By turning to my healthy solution, I am choosing to turn my attention to my creative talents, and without the self-depreciation that inferiority creates.

As I progressed through therapy in my late twenties, I was encouraged to discover my personal shadow and the inferiority convictions I presently carried within me. Later, as a therapist, I would share some of the contents of my shadow with clients. I did this not just to give a prime example of how Adlerian philosophy works, but I also want my clients to know we all suffer in one way or another with some form of inferiority, including their therapist. For example, early in my life I grew to believe that I was inferior intellectually. This perception was formed not because of one or two events but came about and was consistently reinforced for numerous reasons. Some of the reasons included the fact that my two older sisters and younger sister achieved, by a long shot, better grades than I did. I was often repeatedly told by my teachers that I was nothing like my sisters; and eventually, I was discouraged enough to believe their perceptions of me were true. Because I was not responding to everyday classroom challenges, I consistently received poor grades, which only reinforced the perception of being inferior intellectually.

In my grammar school and high school years, I never formulated in a concrete way what the purpose of school was or was meant to be. As a result, I did not do much more than physically show up. Envisioning school as somewhat like a circus, I was hyperactive in the classroom; I drove my teachers crazy. I carried this perception of myself as a non-student into high school. Throughout my four years, I rarely opened a book. I easily recall getting my books in my senior year, putting them in my locker for nine months untouched, and then returning them at the end of the school year. The perceived inferiorities were dictating my life.

Years later in therapy, I came to recognize if there are any absolutes in life, one is surely true. I believe it almost always takes place when I allowed inferiority perceptions to rule my life. Simply stated, it is the absolute that predicts what I try to avoid at all costs I eventually become. Namely, I was trying to avoid my inferior feeling of being inept academically by not participating in school with the fear I would embarrass myself by exposing my level of ignorance. Eventually, I created the very thing I was afraid of being. I became ignorant. Through therapy I was able to challenge this engrained inferior perception and come to terms with how distorted it was. In doing so, I was able to approach academic challenges in a totally different way.

I compensated for this major inferiority by turning all my attention to sports. However, since I was living my life dictated by fears and feelings of being inferior, sports was something that I not only wanted to do well in, but had to do well in. As Nouwen explained,

I was still listening to the louder voice within me rather than to the voice of logic. Winning became my ideal goal to counter all other minus feelings, especially the inferiority I experienced in the classroom. Nouwen pinpointed the voice I was listening to and the solution I was immersed in when he said, "Prove that you are worth something; do something relevant, spectacular, or powerful, and then you will earn the love you so desire."[24] It took me years to begin listening to another voice.

There were at least three inherent problems with this self-imposed solution concerning sports. First, when I did lose at something, I experienced severe depression, believing I was a total loser. Second, I experienced major anxiety before any game due to the pressure of having to achieve my idealistic goal of having to win. I sometimes turned to some obsessive-compulsive behavior to counter the anxiety. On the day of a game I would close my eyes and then look at the classroom clock. If the hand was on the right side of the clock, I interpreted it to mean I was going to win. As foolish as this activity was, it, nonetheless, brought about a degree of relief. Third, even when I won, the reward was short-lived. I immediately started to worry about the next game. It was only years later that I understood the wise words of Easwaran when he explained, "As long as we believe that we are happy when some external condition is fulfilled, another one comes along that needs to be fulfilled."[25]

I am certainly not proud of this part of my life and wish in many ways it could have been experienced much differently. Entering therapy in my twenties, I discovered how I had this engrained, yet unconscious perception that I was literally inadequate when it came to learning. Through conversations with my therapist, I discovered how I formed this perception at a very young age and then how I came up with ways to repress this particular inferior feeling. School became a place of vulnerability for me in the sense that it had the power to expose my personal sense of being inferior. Not wanting to expose this shameful part of me to others, or even to myself, I protected it by repressing this perception and avoided all participation in academic assignments. Before my experience in therapy, I never considered to look for the underlying reasons for the way I approached school. Receiving very little to no help from the outside, including my parents and teachers, I was simply labeled as being lazy and it was left at that. At the end of my senior year, I was told by one of my teachers, who had recently found out my IQ, that I should have had all A's with even the slightest of an effort. At the time, it meant nothing to me. I accepted the label of being lazy and concluded that was my basic problem.

While in therapy, and through the use of the Adlerian philosophy, I learned that laziness was not my problem. It was my solution! My unconscious inferior feeling created a biased and totally distorted picture of the academic challenge. It was something to be avoided at all cost if I was to keep from being more ashamed than I already was at the time. I presumed, once again in an unconscious manner, that school was not for me. The lack of introspection allowed me to achieve this goal of avoidance through continuous acts of repression. I would find, or I so hoped, my self-worth through sports. Bottom line: I fooled myself into thinking I could beat inferiority.

The second choice in response to a challenge, the healthy one, experiences the vulnerability but is not dictated by it. This choice requires a degree of courage since it is carried out with no guarantees for success. It is a choice that focuses more on my talents and capabilities rather than my limitations or faults. At this point in therapy, I know no human being can grow and develop unless they are willing to accept the reality we all have inherent talents along with limitations. Scott Peck emphasizes the need to recognize it is a choice, if we are to be healthy, and one that we must all make. He explains, "I have repeatedly said that we have a choice of whether to grow or not."[26] Peck then added, "One of the greatest psychologists of this century, Abraham Maslow, coined the term 'self-actualization,' by which he meant human beings' capacity to grow and evolve into higher levels of psychosocial and spiritual functioning, autonomy, and personal power."[27] All philosophies of psychology emphasize the need to recognize the importance of making this choice.

My challenge in therapy was to discover what my personal vulnerabilities and fears were and then take ownership of them. I was born into this world and slowly developed numerous fears. They emerged as a result of my interactions with key figures (parents, siblings, authority figures, etc.) and the perspective I developed of myself as a result of these interactions. This is one of the reasons I cannot stand the concept, developed by the bureaucratic church, of original sin. The fact that the church subscribes to the notion a five-day-old baby is a sinner is ludicrous. I much rather believe the perspective presented by Henri Nouwen when he explains, "We were innocent before we started feeling guilty; we were in the light before we entered into the darkness; we were at home before we started to search for a home."[28]

*****

Considered by some to be the father of cognitive-behavioral therapy, Albert Ellis created a paradigm that is uniquely applicable both inside and outside of formal therapy.[29] It is a theoretical model that I teach my clients so they can better understand how to apply the Adlerian philosophy. Ellis's theory is formulated with the use of three columns, each labeled A, B, and C. The "A" column represents the specific challenge or experience we are facing at any particular time. The "C" column represents the feelings we have about the challenge. The natural reaction is to be highly influenced by this column as we more often than not allow feelings to dictate the manner in which we respond to the challenge at hand. My goal is to show each client why adhering to this habit is a crucial mistake. Feelings are important and make us aware that a challenge is before us, but we must never allow feelings to be the determining factor in how we respond to challenges.

I do not want a client to ignore their feelings but to realize the content of the "B" column, which always precedes the feelings contained in the "C" column. The "B" column is where we would find the thoughts and perceptions we have about "A." These thoughts and perceptions are what create the feelings we have at the moment. In other words, you cannot have a feeling without a thought. However, our thoughts and perceptions can either be logical or illogical; and both are capable of producing a particular feeling. This is why it is a mistake to react just to our feelings. They could be based on illogical thinking and therefore lead us to mistaken choices. Easwaran warns us, "This is where the trouble starts, for the senses are wonderful servants, but poor masters."[30] The advice Easwaran puts forth, therefore, counsels us to pay attention to our feelings, but do not presume they based on factual thinking.

Years ago, I had a thirty-three-year-old client come to therapy complaining he often felt depressed and overwhelmed. The depression, he explained, was not ongoing, but seemed to start up for no reason at all. He also expressed he tended to have an explosive anger that, when it occurred, he had no control over the rage he felt. With various Adlerian diagnostics questions, we were able to discover that client suffered with two prominent feelings of inferiority: he had a strong sense of being insignificant and not being able to fit in with his peers. He explained, "I never feel as if I belong to any particular group of people, and believe people are better and more talented." He also had a fear, almost an expectation, of being abandoned, even with those he considered friends. As with all inferiority feelings clients have, myself included, these two fears of vulnerability did come about because of one or two events. They had their origins based on our subjective interpretations of childhood experiences. As an adult, many of our interactions with others, along with the many challenges we face, have the potential to tap into any of our inferior feelings and fears of vulnerability.

My client reported one experience when he was sitting at his desk at work and it was approaching lunchtime. Two or three of his colleagues, people he was friendly with for years, went by his office on their way to lunch, and they did not include him. My client expressed his immediate reaction. He said, "I, at first, felt angry that they did not ask me to lunch. Within a minute or two, the anger turned into what I would call a mild depression. I felt awful for the rest of the day."

During the session that this conversation took place, I reminded my client that he suffered with two major feelings of inferiority that made him very sensitive to many of his interactions. Using the A-B-C paradigm articulated by Albert Ellis, the "A" column would be the two or three friends going by my client's office and not including him for lunch. The feelings first of anger and then depression would be placed in the "C" column. As with many people, my client was in the habit of reacting to his feelings without any consideration as to why they were occurring. When I asked him what were his thoughts about this particular interplay, he thought about it for a few moments and then said, "I immediately felt a strong rejection and thought they did not think of me as important enough to be included."

My client's conclusions of this brief scenario may or may not have been true, but in his biased thinking, he automatically presumed they were factual just by listening to his feelings and believing in his distorted thoughts. After discussing the situation from another perspective, my client was able to see that his feelings of vulnerability—an inferior self-image of being insignificant—might have distorted the experience completely. Adler refers to this human experience as reflecting the possibility for all humans to have a biased perception when it comes to experiences in life. He explains, "I am convinced that a person's behavior springs from his opinion. We should not be surprised at this, because our senses do not receive actual facts, merely a subjective image of them."[31] It is the continual task of this client, and all my clients, to make use of the lessons taught by both Adler and Ellis. Easwaran also addresses this issue when he cautions us to not automatically believe that our feelings are based on logical thinking, and the real work must be done cognitively. Easwaran gracefully explains, "I like to think of the mind as the Big Boss and the senses as the five secretaries."[32]

By keeping in touch with my mental images and the engrained perceptions I had about myself, I was in a much better position to think more clearly about my place in life and the experiences I had interacting within life events. Through this process of being mentally aware, I was freed from the prison of emotional captivity caused by my obsession with vulnerability and inferiority. The key was to be in touch with when I was feeling vulnerable or when I did experience a feeling of being inferior. A good tool, I found, was having a "pause button," which kept me from automatically reacting to the feelings occurring during a challenging experience. Too often, anxiety and depression, emotions that arise from vulnerability, were viewed as my enemies. I have learned my personal depression is often nothing more than my cup needs to be filled. I am feeling empty and need to be nourished. It is a voice that reminds me something is off-kilter. Rather than simply swimming in the pool of depression, it might very well be a call to a more in-depth way of viewing the meaning and purpose of my life.

I have also learned that anxiety is also not my adversary, but more of a feeling that is awakening me to the fact I have a challenge before me. My challenge is to go deeper and not make the mistake of staying on the surface. People make the mistake of existing in the shallow end of the pool and yet believe they are in the middle of the ocean. When I was younger and immediately reacted to any anxiety feelings, I felt that I was nothing more than a stick in a stream and allowed my first impulse to direct my way. By training my mind to pause, I did not have to go with the first feeling. I can wisely realize my anxious feelings are calling me to new horizons, perhaps once again to the life of being less worldly and more spiritual.

I opened this chapter with the proposition that psychology can act as a precursor to the spiritual life. The field of psychology, especially the experience of psychotherapy, brings us to the point of realization that as humans we have limitations along with having gifts and capabilities. Psychology teaches us how to be not afraid when we are uncomfortable. It teaches us that many times we are distorting our experiences through the prism of vulnerability. Psychology, in other words, frees us to move to another and higher form of living.

In part 1, I talked about how I allowed my environment to place me into a position of passivity and silence. I could put some of the blame on my youthful ignorance, but I still needed to take responsibility for it lasting so long. For me, repression became the norm. No one knew about my home life, and might not have believed it if they heard even hints of it. Within and outside my family life, I was living on an island that was destroying my spirit. My environment did not teach me how to love, but it did instill in me the fear of the human touch. I was captive soul in the very circumstances of my birth. By the time I reached my teenage years, my identity seemed shaped as if fixed in concrete. There was no thought of ever changing. In my youth, I never considered there was another choice. In so many ways, the people around me and the interpretations of my childhood experiences made me feel alienated from the parts of myself that were crying to be heard.

I searched for a surrogate family and found it in the church. I developed a clinging connection to the priests around me. My early role as an altar boy and then as a seminarian defined my path. Living away from my parents and the agonies of my environment, I thought I would find a new freedom, one of acceptance and love. Yet the seminary itself had its own imposed rules of silence and, while massively disappointed, I discovered the priesthood I desired did not exist. While in the seminary, I witnessed a huge paradox between what was being preached and the behavior of the priest faculty and of my peers. I was told what to believe in, and in the process of this forced learning, a new kind of silence was required: acceptance of all that was taught or you were asked to leave. I soon discovered that the seminary and the church, when acting as a bureaucracy, was into its own self-worship and made the needs and ideas of the members secondary. Intrinsic sexual conflicts created more shame about who I was and what I was becoming. I was left to question my own masculinity, seemingly neutered by seminary life. I was wearing the collar during the day, but never truly felt part of the organization. For me, the seminary created more isolation and loneliness. Depression and anger were the consequences.

I had turned to the church for comfort and peace of mind, and perhaps mostly for acceptance. The term codependency, for me at least, could have been conceived here. Yet I do not want to sound like an ungrateful brat, for I will always be thankful and indebted to those members of the church who got me through years of turmoil and a deep and chronic depression. As I grew older and with years of encountering the works of spiritual gurus, I determined a change was necessary. I would later agree with the personal experiences of Thomas Moore when he explained in his writings, "Let me say clearly that the gist of this book, the discovery or creation of a religion of your own, is not an option. It is a necessary step in your spiritual unfolding. Resist it and hide either in a religious institution or in a fully secular world, and your soul would be stuck."[33] Freed in a new way by rejecting the punitive rules and regulations and the distorted theological principles of the formal church, made me not less religious but more so.

During all the weeks and months of therapy and supervision, I absorbed the painful reality that I had not a clue as to who I was or was meant to be. Deeply seeded feelings of inferiority and a fear of all things that made me feel vulnerable was running and ruining my life. My formal therapy was the primary facilitator in seeing the wrongness of my life and how I was looking in all the wrong places for some sense of satisfaction and worth. Even though I am most certainly a work in progress, I do very much now see the light, both psychologically and spiritually. I recall the works of Eknath Easwaran as he reflected on the words of Saint Augustine. Augustine said, "Our whole business in life is to restore to health the eye of the heart, where God may be seen."[34] I also truly believe what Easwaran then stated when he uttered, "We are all born with this eye, only sheer disuse keeps it closed."[35] My plan and purpose became never to close my eyes ever again, nor to allow my vision to be overshadowed by thoughts and feelings of inferiority. As I moved away from focusing on my limitations and fears of failure, I was finally in the glorious place of restoring the eyes of my heart in order to see the wonders of God.

16

You have to learn to intake, to imbibe, to nourish yourself
and not be afraid of fullness. The fullness is like a tidal wave
which then carries you, sweeps you into experience.

—Anais Nin

As I slowly accepted the nature of my humanness in its entirety, the duality of having both strengths and limitations, I was in a much better position to formulate the true meaning and purpose of my life. In so doing, I had to unlearn the habit of focusing on my sense of being inferior, along with the fears I had of being physically, mentally, and emotionally vulnerable. I had to also let go of mistakes I made in the past, even though some of them were painfully embarrassing. As I went through this process, I developed a clearer and more open mind. This led to a unique freedom to discover my gifts and the courage to put them into action. Through the assistance individual therapy offered me and the insights offered by self-help writers, I found all the psychological self-reflections acted as a precursor to living a more complete life. Most importantly, it led me to a new perspective on spirituality. Scripture references this process: "Be transformed by the renewal of your mind" (Romans 12:2).

I also realized how my thinking had been trained to seek worldly things and accomplishments and to focus on them as goals. When I was younger, winning at everything became my obsession. It could involve a state championship game all the way down to a friendly game of ping-pong in someone's basement. However, with each contest, even when I won, the satisfaction was always short-lived. I came to understand the development of these goals was simply but quite

196

destructively a reaction to personal feelings of being inferior and vulnerable. I presumed I had to be superior in something in order to like who I was. Not comprehending it at the time, I was attempting to fill my ego cup, unaware there was that proverbial hole in the bottom. It needed constant refilling as I nervously waited, sometimes desperately, for the next competition. Nouwen reminded me of this frustrating cyclic truth when he stated, "When we come to believe in the voices that call us worthless and unlovable, then success, popularity, and power are easily perceived as attractive solutions."[1] Coming to terms with how my sense of being inferior was driving my life, I was able to find another way to deal with this part of my humanness. I came to see the infected cavity I dug for myself was one of self-rejection, reinforced by placing all my chips on the absolute mandate to roll for the dice of success.

By the time I ended formal therapy, I knew that the process of self-examination needed to continue and required my constant attention. I learned, sometimes the hard way, that therapy is not a process that brings about a total cure. There are always new things to discover and new connections to make regarding past experiences and their influence on the present. Yet the introspective process did allow for a deeper awareness of when I was experiencing a sense of vulnerability. Most especially, when I did feel vulnerable I had the option of not being dictated by it. I also reached the point that since vulnerability and fear, along with anxiety and depression, are always a possibility, then the use of my unhealthy response is also always a possibility. My primary task, therefore, if I was to stay healthy and creative, was not to allow any form of inferiority or fear to become my obsession. I needed to constantly remind myself that if and when I fell into this rut of self-depreciation that I was accomplishing nothing more than overshadowing any of my possible gifts and abilities. As a therapist, I would remind my clients that without constant vigilance there is always the possibility for us to allow vulnerable feelings to be our primary focus. This new perspective of mine is found in the words of Joseph Langford when he expressed, "Our sins and flaws are not the truest thing about us. Our failings hamper, but do not define us."[2]

As I continue to make every effort to stay away from my unhealthy reaction to being vulnerable, I encountered another primary task that required my attention: the task of nourishment. With a totally different mind-set of what it means to be human, I began to see how my spiritual life was also being affected by this change. No longer operating from a fear of being worthless, it was replaced by a sense of gratitude for the person I was and was becoming. I realized that loving and accepting myself as I am and recognizing I have the ability and responsibility to love others must be the foundation of my Christian experience. Scott Peck explains this process; he states, "If you work long enough and hard enough to understand yourself, you will come to discover the vast part of your mind, of which you have little awareness, contains riches beyond imagination."[3]

The process of becoming a more complete person became a stable part of my everyday life. It was not complete when formal therapy was over, but now I was more in the position to keep growing, most especially in a spiritual way. The ability to keep discovering and expanding myself in terms of my meaning and purpose in life was dependent on me, and this is where the notion of a continual need for nourishment entered my life. I began referring to my spiritual side as my inner soul; it needed to be fed not only continually but in the proper way. Thomas Moore defined the soul in a noteworthy manner; he explained, "Soul is the invisible, mysterious and softly radiant element that infuses your being and makes you human. Like plasma in your veins, it gives you a sense of meaning, feeling, connection, and depth."[4] In such an inspiring manner, Moore continued, "If you have a soul, you have a visible glow and are alive and present. When people encounter you, they see a real person."[5] Thus the importance for all of us to nourish this precious part of ourselves.

I often tell my clients that if, after leaving my office, they indulge in eating ten Milky Ways, I can guarantee them they will feel a definitive physical sickness. Just as we must be careful of the foods we eat as we choose how to nourish our bodies, the same is true of what we allow to enter our mind and soul. The modern world, especially with all its technology and calls to be successful, has useful purposes, but in the end, it does little for the soul. In order not to be swayed by worldly temptations that promised glorious triumphs, I found that I needed to become a student of spirituality. In other words, I needed to learn what kind of spiritual diet was necessary if I wanted to walk down a more meaningful and lasting path. Marcus Borg emphasized the importance of this pursuit; he explained, "Education also matters for adults, particularly in our time of change and transition…it will involve reeducation from a way of seeing Christianity learned as children to a way of seeing Christianity that makes persuasive sense to us as adults."[6] As I was making the choice to feed my soul and learn the art of being a true Christian, I soon discovered that motivation was not enough. I needed to be taught on how to be spiritual and to find the methods that would enhance this process. Whatever these spiritual substances were, I needed to take them on my spiritual journey and make them my constant travel companions.

With advice and direction from others, I discovered the map to make my spiritual life less fragmented to one of holistic and enduring nourishment. I discovered that worship nourishes, prayer nourishes, reading the Bible nourishes, reading spiritual writers nourishes, a retreat nourishes, and meditation nourishes. None of these items are a one-time experience or just acted out some of the time; they need ongoing practice and personal involvement. In one of her beautifully written books, Oriah Mountain Dreamer makes this point; she explains, "A practice, a regularly repeated and at least minimally structured way of connecting with our sense of the Mystery of which we are a part, gives us a way to open to that which sustains us when everything falls away."[7] Practice, and an ongoing effort, have to be a part of my spiritual nourishment. I found this to be especially true when it comes to prayer and meditation.

Praying has become the center point of my life. Thankfully, I am so past the way I use to pray when younger. During the younger period of my life, I would mostly pray to get or accomplish something, as in winning a game, passing a test, or making more money. As I went through my spiritual phases of growth, the way I prayed also changed. I now see it primarily as having a conversation with God, or for the most part a conversation with Jesus. He, in his holiness, made God more recognizable to me. It is a time where I put myself in a position to pay attention to Jesus and ask for grace, which was defined for me as asking for his presence. I remain determined to become more and more aware of his presence in my life. I now see prayer as time to be filled with Jesus's love and to let him know how grateful I am that he is in my life. In reading the Bible, the message is straightforward on how Jesus put prayer at the center of his life and how often he went off by himself to pray to the Father.

Sometimes, I will use formal prayers as a means of communication, but most of the time I use my own words in conversation with the Father, or Jesus, or the Holy Spirit. I feel that when I start in the morning with the Our Father, when I say it slowly and with intent, the prayer contains phrases that put me in the right place to begin my conversation with God.

Our Father—not just my Father, for we all are his children. This opening of the prayer is recognition that I am addressing our Father and that we all are a part of his family. I am part of a community who looks to God, our Father.

Who art in heaven—the Father is everywhere. Our true place here on earth is a part of heaven, where our Father also exists. The Father is never far from us.

Hallowed be thy name—I recognize our Father as holy and sacred; I treat our Father as the Holy One; I want to admire him for who he is and for what he has done; I want to let myself be drawn into this holiness; to grow in holiness myself.

Your kingdom come and Your will be done on earth as it is in heaven—I am asking the Father to be my king. I choose to accept his ruling authority and to think and act the way the Father wants me to. The world, to be sure, is not as the Father intended. In recognition of his power and intent, I want to allow my Father to be the ruler of my domain. His will be done here on earth, which involves goodness, truth, and love for one another.

Give us this day our daily bread—bread symbolizes everything I may need for my life. I know I need our Father's support. If I am to walk a spiritual path, I need to depend on our Father for an ongoing supply of nourishment.

And forgive us our trespasses—with our Father's forgiveness and his acts of mercy, I am made free from my wrongs. The manner in which our Father created us, he knew we would most likely sin; all we have to do is ask for his forgiveness and get back on the right path.

As we forgive those who trespass against us—with our Father as our example, we must forgive if we expect to be forgiven. We must, by example, show the Father's will to others.

And lead us not into temptation—never forgetting my human possibilities and how I can be pulled in the wrong direction, I ask for help in dealing with wrongful enticements that might momentarily attract me on this day.

But deliver us from evil—recognition that evil is real, and that all forms of evilness are an attempt to destroy life. It is for this very reason that the existence of evilness must be taken seriously.

Amen—so be it. I want to really mean it.

Saying the Our Father sets the stage for a more personal conversation. Someone long ago suggested that I should pray before I pray. Somewhat like the preparation I do on the way over to a friend's house. I think about what I want to say to him, what I want to share, what I want to ask him about. When I pray, I want to share with Jesus as if he were a best friend. If I am wondering about something and do not understand a particular aspect of my life, I want to be able to ask Jesus questions and to listen to his response. I want to tell him about my family, my friends, and the work that I do. If I am fearful about the future, I want to share this with him. I want to feel good about being with this very special friend. I wholeheartedly agree with Joseph Langford when he explains, "Praying with the heart is principally about depth in prayer. Praying at the level of the heart requires the effort to go beneath the surface of awareness, where we spend the majority of our conscious lives, to find God who abides within, at the center of our being."[8]

Another instrument I have found to be crucial for living a nourishing spiritual life is meditation. For me, it acts as a primary means to contemplate the existence of the Father, Son, and Holy Spirit. In the Bible, Jesus often said, "I am the light" (John 9:5). Deepak

Chopra, reflecting on this statement, explains, "Physically, light is what you see when you wake up in the morning. Mystically, it is what you see when you wake up to your soul. Light gives life, and it shows the way through the darkness."[9] This is what Jesus meant when he said he was the light. Furthermore, he wanted me, and all of us, to join him in this light. Jesus said to all of us in a very personal way: "You are the Light of the world" (Matthew 5:12). I often feel this statement difficult to believe, unless, through acts of nourishment, I find the Spirit within me.

The primary purpose of meditation is to be in contact with the presence of God. Through the exercise of meditation, I am able to slow down, to stop speeding through life. I often share with my clients we are so often like a pinball stuck in a machine. When we rise for the day, the lever pushes us up to the top and we bounce off one object after another, each dictating the next direction we take. Work pushes us to rush off in urgency in one direction or another. We rush around in our cars and get annoyed if we are delayed. We sprint mindlessly around with a long list of errands and flash through quick conversations with friends. Nowadays, it involves the impersonal use of a text message, which sadly keeps us from looking into each other's eyes. We are like gerbils on a raging wheel. In a definitive manner, meditation offers to stop the nonsense and the often meaningless actions of our day. Joseph Campbell takes it one step further as he emphasizes the importance of meditation.

> An absolute necessity for anybody today. You must have a room, or a certain hour or so a day, where you don't know what is in the newspapers that morning, you don't know who your friends are, you don't know what you owe anybody, you don't know what anybody owes you. This is a place where you can simply experience and bring forth what you are and what you might be. This is a place of creative incubation.[10]

I found the primary purpose of meditation is to calm my mind. To quiet all the voices screaming in my ear, including the predisposed voices that are often coming from me. It allows me to get out of my cyclic rut, come to a halt, and expand my inner mind. It is a time when I can listen to what my inner heart is telling me. Most importantly, I can listen for the voice of God within me. To accomplish this, I need to experience the consequences of solitude and silence, all of which meditation offers. Neale Walsch, who lives on a retreat site and formed the organization ReCreation, made a pointed suggestion regarding the practice of meditation. He explains, "Begin by being still. Quiet the outer world, so that the inner world might bring you sight. This insight is what you seek, yet you cannot have it while you are so deeply concerned with your outer reality. Seek, therefore, to go within as much as possible. If you do not go within, you go without."[11]

Along with prayer and meditation, I have found a number of other ways to call Jesus into my life. I believe he is always there, but it is up to me to recognize that reality. The main point is that I must invite him first, since I do not believe that Jesus forces me to love him. He gives me a choice. I have found that daily meditation and daily prayer works for me in terms of responding to his invitation. At other times, reading the Bible and contemplating the words and the true meaning behind all the spiritual messages adds a great deal to my spiritual perspective and faith. Reading spiritual books are a tremendous aid in getting to know who Jesus was and is, which always enhances my relationship with him.

I have found that when I am open to the notion of spiritual nourishment, the essential component is my perspective and attitude. What am I looking for in life and what is my mind-set while I am searching? While sincerely believing he is here, I must be looking for him in everything I do. There are many ways God reveals himself, all involving love and nourishment for the life I am living, the life we all are living. In one his books, Neale Walsh offers us a hint of what God might be saying to all of us.

Watch. Listen. The words to the next song you hear. The information in the next article you read. The story line of the next movie you watch. The chance utterance of the next person you meet. Or the whisper of the next river, the next ocean, the next breeze that caresses your ear—all these devices are Mine; all these avenues are open to Me. I will I will show you then that I have always been there. All ways.[12]

This is my intention in terms of being spiritually nourished. I know Our Lord will come before me in an endless amount of ways each and every day. My response must be to watch and listen.

17

There is nothing like returning to a place that remains unchanged and to find the ways in which you yourself have altered.
—Nelson Mandela

ALONG WITH THE NECESSITY of being nourished, I believe my next responsibility is to make sure I am an active participant in my own spiritual development. I must not be content with just going through the motions or, God forbid, ever think I have arrived. Some people say they do not believe, but what they do not realize is that faith takes a genuine effort. It does not somehow magically come to us in our sleep, or in the forty-five minutes we spend at church on Sunday. This I learned, gratefully, in my seminary studies and the spiritual readings that followed. I am constantly reminded of this need for development when I think of one section of Michelangelo's work painted on the ceiling in the Sistine Chapel. It is the scene where God is reaching down to man and man is reaching back. Their fingers do not touch, for it is an activity still in progress. It helps me a great deal to picture myself in this scene and reminds me that I must be an ongoing part of my spiritual progression; I must evolve toward knowing him more.

In order to advance forward spiritually—to evolve—I must recognize that the grace to do so is always present to help me fulfill my part in working at my own spiritual growth. Eknath Easwaran explains, "It can be baffling, this mysterious interplay of divine grace and individual effort. The truth is, both are absolutely necessary."[1] The good news is that as long as I am doing everything possible to seek spiritual truths, the work is always one of partnership. Easwaran quotes Robert Browning in his use of a geometrical simile when he states, "All the Lord expects us to do is to draw the arc; the Lord Himself will complete the circle."[2]

My spiritual past helps to confirm the reality and authenticity of evolving. Each stage of my spiritual life had its own inherent worthiness, leading me next to another level of intellectual and spiritual growth. Starting with my spiritual experiences as an altar boy, through my years of Catholic education, my experiences in seminary life, my studies in psychology for my doctorate, my years of personal therapy and meditation on spiritual writings: all encompassed the process of evolving. My first step to evolving was the belief that I could. The Pulitzer Prize winner, Ernest Becker, makes this valid point when he states, "If there is tragic limitation in life there is also possibility. What we call maturity is the ability to see the two in some kind of balance into which we can fit creativity."[3]

Evolving sometimes entails an emotional and mental tug of war, often leading to a certain kind of lethargy or desire to give up. There were also times that an uncertainty or even a fear overcame me as some of my engrained beliefs were challenged. I soon realized that in growing, whether psychologically or spiritually, that there would be gaps between the stages. It was somewhat of a scary place when I was leaving the security of what I thought were facts and had not yet replaced them with new insights. But I am often reminded, whether through acts of prayer, meditation, or reading, that I must continuously allow hope and faith to find me, even on those days that I am lost, confused, doubtful, or not paying attention.

I have found that faith is a matter of grace, recognizing, as in the painting in the Sistine Chapel, that God is reaching out to me. Faith is there for the asking, if and when I choose to make the effort. Knowing the importance of spiritually evolving and desiring to do so is my responsibility. Oriah Mountain Dreamer defines this obligation; she states, "It is an attempt to find our inner authority, to resist giving over our authority in our lives to something external—church or state, family or business—all those voices who profess to know what is best for us."[4] I truly believe, through such encouraging thoughts from Oriah and others, my spiritual development is nothing less than a personal mandate.

I believe that Jesus himself had to evolve. Logically, as I accept the human part of his nature, how could he have possibly known he was the Son of God as a five-year-old? At the same time, I do not believe that Jesus was simply just a carpenter. When he reached adulthood, he did not all of a sudden become a Scripture scholar or an esteemed teacher. Even though there is not much known about the life of Jesus's boyhood, I have to presume, based on his last three years of life, that he had, as a young man, to throw himself into Scriptural studies. He was, at the same time, an active participant in the wealth of ideas permeating the area at the time. Jay Parani describes the intellectual and spiritual arena that Jesus had the opportunity to immerse himself in on a daily basis. Parini explains, "Living on the Silk Road, a trading thoroughfare between East and West, He would have encountered Hellenistic notions of the soul's immortality that poured in from the West, from Greece and Rome, and felt the heady winds of mysticism blowing from Persia and the East."[5] By age twelve, Jesus must have had an inkling to his future purpose when he responded in a concrete manner to his mother, Mary, who was searching for him at the time and eventually found him in the temple. Jesus told her, "I must now be about my Father's business." I believe Jesus was present in the temple as part of his evolving. The distinguished author, Marcus Borg, with intellectual authority states, "He no doubt observed the Sabbath, which included attending the synagogue for Torah study and prayer."[6]

Jesus's evolvement became evident at his baptism. People did not yet know who he was at the time, but it clearly revealed that Jesus, at this crucial time of his life, knew who he was and what he was becoming. His closeness with John the Baptist underscored the level of spiritual awareness Jesus had achieved. Marcus Borg described this singular event when he explains the most likely mind-set Jesus had at this moment in his life. Borg states, "But something led him to leave conventional wisdom behind and go out into the wilderness to become a follower of John the Baptizer."[7] It is here where Jesus began his public life as he revealed himself as being more than simply a human spirit. As Scripture discloses, a voice was heard to exclaim, "This is my beloved son, in whom I am well-pleased" (Matthew 3:16–17). Parini explains this baptism moment, whether it was an actual voice or not, that "Jesus was filled with God's spirit, experiencing a sense of rebirth, renewal, and mission."[8] At this moment, Jesus might have realized his divinity, reaching the climax of his spiritual evolution. In explaining the personal experience Jesus endured, Marcus Borg explains, "We may further surmise that Jesus underwent what William James calls a 'conversion experience.'"[9] Further, as Borg states, "It is reasonable to suppose that Jesus experienced such an internal transformation, which led him to undertake the ministry he did."[10]

What Jesus did for himself, he wanted us to do also for ourselves. Deepak Chopra makes this point well; he explains, "Perception creates reality, and all of Jesus's sayings have one thing in common: They try to make our perceptions shift."[11] Just as the theme of perception is so important to understanding the psychology of who I am as a human being, it is also equally essential to understanding who I am spiritually. Psychologically, my personal goal is to be evolving toward what Abraham Maslow describes as "self-actualization."[12] It involves moving from basic psychological needs (food, water, warmth), to a sense of belongingness and lovingness, to the highest form of humanness where I reach my full potential. Sadly, most people stop growing at an early age and flat-line when it comes to understanding who they truly are. As a result, they not only do not understand the underlying reasons for choices they make, but they also lose out on the opportunity to discover their gifts. For a number of reasons, I do not believe I am capable of reaching the highest level of development, yet I want to always be moving toward it as much as I am capable.

Spiritually, my goal is to evolve through the various stages of growth moving toward what Paramahansa Yogananda refers to as self-realization or God-consciousness. Yogananda explains, "One must drink deep from the fountain of Truth—God. Self-realization means just that: direct experience of God."[13] Once again, and just as regrettable, most people flat-line on this most important area of their life as well. For the majority, once they have received confirmation, or even earlier, all growth ceases. I listened carefully to Joseph Campbell's warning that we all must get beyond our elementary image of Jesus since it acts as a dangerous barrier to further growth.

Campbell explains, "You hold onto your own ideology, your own little manner of thinking, and when a larger experience of God approaches, an experience greater than you are prepared to receive, you take flight from it by clinging to the image in your mind. This is known as preserving the faith."[14]

There came a point in my life when I knew that my spiritual life was more than being a good Catholic who passively followed along with rules, regulations, and a pre-scripted image of Jesus. In order to evolve, I needed to break out of my rigid form of thinking and see that Jesus was much more than rules and laws. My job was not so much to preserve the faith, but to evolve within it. Just as I realistically know I am not capable of reaching the psychological goal of full self-actualization, I can presume I will not attain full God-consciousness. That is okay with me, but I want to be doing the work of moving toward it! Seeing my life as one of wanting to evolve, I am encouraged by the words of Yogananda: "No such barrier exists, I came to understand, save in man's spiritual unadventurousness."[15]

By reaching full God-consciousness and realizing that he was sent by God as his Son, Jesus increasingly became my model to follow. As Parini notes, Jesus urged his followers "to open their hearts and minds to the spiritual realities he had himself experienced."[16] For me, this was the main purpose for Jesus's appearance on earth. I do not believe that Jesus came to die for our sins. His death, his execution, was a direct result of what he was teaching and preaching. As a client in therapy, I came to know that I must get beyond the engrained image I had of myself due to childhood experiences. So too, I came to see, that I needed to get beyond the embedded image I had of Jesus from my early days in catechism class or even at the seminary. I know now that my reason for being here on earth is to evolve, psychologically and spiritually, not just to memorize an established set of answers or beliefs. By emphasizing my own spiritual growth, I am led to believe in the words of Marcus Borg when he explains, "The Christian life moves beyond believing in God to being in a relationship with God."[17] I do believe that if I continue to work on this relationship, especially through the life Jesus led, that it will transform my entire life in the present.

The purpose of evolving is to give a mundane or business-as-usual life more depth. Jesus, throughout the Gospels, called, even insisted, for a change of heart. Through my studies of Scripture, I began to see these writings not so much as historical documents as they were stories of developing beliefs of the early followers of Jesus. They were accounts of individuals and communities evolving in their own faith. Marcus Borg puts Scripture in a much more practical and logical fashion when he explains that the Gospels "are not divine products inspired directly by God, whose contents therefore are to be believed (as I had thought prior to this). Nor are they eyewitness accounts written by people who had accompanied Jesus and simply sought to report what they had seen or heard. Rather, I learned, the gospels represent the developing traditions of the early Christian movement."[18]

Having this perspective of the Gospels does not downplay the importance of the messages it contains. Jesus, perhaps the greatest teacher of all time, used parables and metaphors to reveal to us the radical message God wanted us to have to live our lives in the most meaningful manner. Matthew Kelly, an international speaker and best-selling author, reflected on the genius of the Gospel message; he explains, "In many ways reading the Gospels is a tour through the mind of God. Each parable or teaching, each encounter Jesus has with a person highlights what God cares about and what he doesn't."[19] In other words, the communities that put these stories together in Gospel form were also evolving. They set the example for the communities I am presently involved with today. The life of Jesus was also a journey of evolving. As Marcus Borg states as he reflects on the life of Jesus, "Its destination is life in the presence of God. Yet God is simply not the destination, but one who is known on the journey. It is journeying *toward* God that is also *with* God."[20] I believe that in seeing Jesus's life in this way, and the communities that followed him, directs me to ask continually, what is my spiritual purpose?

In my seminary days, there was a movement among some of my classmates that referred to the need to be "born again." I had trouble with this concept and more often than not rejected it as foolish talk.

In my young twenties at the time, I was simply sticking to what I was taught in grammar school and high school. I thought there was not much more to know about Jesus or spirituality in general. I was naïve regarding my personal vision of spirituality and was hesitant to even consider new information. It was only years later, after reading numerous theological books and authors' writing about having a livelier and cultivating spiritual life, that I began to see the light.

One day, I was thinking about the plane geometry class I took in high school. Out of deep respect, and definitively some fear of the priest teaching the class, plane geometry became one of the few classes I took seriously. Thinking about some of the things I learned in the class, I recalled two of the methodologies to solving geometric problems, one referred to as the deductive method and the other was called the inductive method. The deductive method involved having the answer first and then one had to work backward to discover the steps that led to this answer. In the inductive method, one did not know the answer exactly and had to go through certain steps to reach a solution. As I was thinking about this, something else came to mind. I began to examine how I approached resolving serious questions or problems in my life, especially when it came to spiritual issues. Up to my early twenties, I could easily see that, for the most part, I approached my spiritual life using the deductive method. I was told a specific theological belief, usually by some authority figure, and then I only looked for the steps, or in this case, the rationale that would confirm this belief. Any other thought or possibility, no matter how interesting or confirming it might be, was discarded if it did not match the answer I already had in mind.

In my younger years, using a so-called inductive method was too frightening and perhaps threatened the belief system I had already established. Even though I was reading and hearing many profound ideas on the topic of spirituality, I gave them little credence; they did not match the answer I already had in hand. However, the more I read and the more I contemplated new perspectives, I reached a point that I could no longer ignore them. A statement made by Joseph Campbell, along with many other gifted writers, encouraged me to change my approach, which up to this time was rather sterile and stagnant. Campbell identified my crucial mistake when he explains, "You have to break past your image of God to get through to the connoted illumination. The mystery has been reduced to a set of concepts and ideas, and emphasizing these concepts and ideas can short-circuit the transcendent, connoted experience. An intense experience of mystery is what one has to regard as the ultimate religious experience."[21]

Once I was free from approaching my spiritual life and belief system from a deductive method, which presumed I had the correct answer before me, I was able to see many more ideas in a new light. One definitive notion was the necessity for me to be "born again" if I was ever able to progress and evolve spiritually. I also came to believe that this process of being reborn is not just a one-time event, but is more of a gradual and ongoing process. Marcus Borg explains, "Dying to an old identity and being born into a new identity, dying to an old way of being and living into a new way of being, is a process that continues through a lifetime."[22]

I also came to believe that this is an experience that I cannot force to happen; I must, nonetheless, always put myself in a place where it can happen. Whether it is through times of prayer, meditation, conversation, or reading, I must continually be open to seeing and hearing a new message so I myself can be renewed. Deepak Chopra explains this point well when he states, "The most reliable thing we can say is that Jesus pointed the way to a seeker's heaven. Finding God was a mystery, but in more mundane terms it was a process, not a leap or a promise that would automatically be filled at the sound of the last trumpet."[23] The notion of evolving and being reborn returned me to the notion that spirituality is a collaboration involving my effort and hearing God's response. It brought me to the awareness of the need to move away from my catechism-like thinking and to realize that revelation is a robust and ongoing process. Jesus himself, as clearly seen in the Scriptures, did not want us to blindly worship or to follow dozens of rules and regulations. By showing us the way, he simply wanted us to be enlightened. Reflecting on those Jesus interacted with, Philip Yancey explains, "Jesus directs most of his comments not to the masses but to these serious thinkers. He constantly pushes them toward a deeper level of commitment, with strong words that would bring anyone up short. 'Forsake the love of money and the pleasures the world has to offer. Deny yourself. Serve others.'"[24]

To be able to listen to the challenges Jesus presented, I once again had to remind myself that an ongoing personal evolution and rebirth was necessary. If I was to evolve psychologically, I had to bring a death to my childhood desires and wants. An open-ended rebirthing was a requirement if I was to live a healthy and creative life. This is most surely true for spiritual growth as well. Joseph Campbell speaks of this necessity when he explains, "To evolve out of this position of psychological immaturity to the courage of self-responsibility and assurance requires a death and resurrection. That is the basic motif of the universal hero's journey—leaving one condition and finding the source of life to bring you forth into a richer and mature condition.[25]

Elizabeth Johnson describes what is inherent in the process of evolving; she explains, "At root we experience that we are orientated to something more. Let us not, for the moment, say what this more is. It is something like a horizon that opens up the landscape and beckons us onward."[26] This opening to a new landscape is what has encouraged me to seek more. It is like experiencing a sunrise or sunset once again. I know that I have witnessed both before, but each new experience of another newly presented sunrise or sunset on the horizon brings another moment of grace and the presence of the Almighty. I do not want to be shy, hesitant, or be afraid to say that I am striving to be holy. When I read about the lives of saintly people, I am fortified spiritually by the courage they openly had about their own evolvement. This was most evident in the life of Mother Teresa, who undoubtedly saw the light while working through her personal darkness. Her life was one of encouragement for all those who are seeking a spiritual rebirth. As Joseph Langford expresses so well, "The fact that Mother Teresa was not born the same person she became, not already imbued with the qualities for which she became famous, means that the rest of us, too, have hope to change and improve."[27]

Like other saints before her, Mother Teresa's spiritual journey was anything but easy. It was filled with sacrifice and personal struggles. In the end, however, she became a model to not only admire but to follow as well. Langford emphasized this point about her life when he explains, "No matter our present foibles or lack of human qualities, we all can hope to arrive at a deeper intimacy with God and deeper care for our neighbor; to live more generously and whole-heartedly, even in the midst of our own trials, and to make a difference with our life; to leave a legacy."[28]

I have found the seeking of a higher and more in-depth holiness creates a vision of what all of us can become and continue to become. There is always a need for intellectualism and a bit of skepticism, but more importantly there is a need to take excursions from reality. We all must prepare ourselves to seek and recognize all the mysteries around us, sometimes forcing us to live outside the perimeters of reason. Profoundly, being spiritual leads us to an awareness of a relationship that already exists. The path that Jesus showed us is one of enlightenment. Deepak Chopra explains this overwhelming experience when he states, "Our second birth occurs on this subtle level, where perception shifts and a person suddenly notices that spirit has always been there, like the wind that has been taken for granted."[29]

18

We are all mosaics. Pieces of light, love, history, stars—
Glued together with magic and music and words.

—Anita Krizzan

WHILE TRYING TO NOURISH myself for the very purpose of evolving spiritually, I kept having trouble with the Scriptural statement, "Behold, the kingdom of God is within you" (Luke 17:20–21). From my younger years growing up and educated in the Catholic Church, I believed that my primary goal was to get to heaven, somehow earn it, and return to the Father by following the example given by Jesus Christ. This would be accomplished, I was convinced, by obeying the rules of the church. As I began to read more and more spiritual books, so many of the authors kept referring to the term individual God-consciousness. This specific reference referred not to some external heaven that I must be aiming for but stressed more the need for the inner transformation of each individual. As I was getting a better sense of what "the Kingdom of God is within you" meant, I began to realize that it required each individual believer to reach a higher level of God-consciousness within himself. Deepak Chopra explains, "Jesus will not return to raise the dead from their grave. Instead, the Second Coming will be a shift in consciousness that renews human nature by raising it to the level of the divine."[1] Coupled with my sense of having to be in a constant state of evolvement, this perspective of seeing my faith as a movement toward God-consciousness and all that it entailed seemed to be more logical. For me, it certainly held a clearer sense of what it meant to be spiritually growing as an individual. It encouraged me to live more in the present rather than waiting for the so-called reward waiting in a heavenly existence. This new perspective was a huge change on my outlook in terms of developing a more meaningful spiritual life.

As I noted in the previous chapter, my growth in what it means to be spiritual was not one of a giant leap; it was and remains a process requiring ongoing growth. Chopra explains, "When we join this injunction with the one about the Kingdom of God being within, the implication is that going within requires a person to wake up. In fact, that's the only way to live any spiritual path to the fullest."[2] The "waking up" is a reference to the fact that I must be continually growing to higher levels of who God is and not be complacent with what I think I already know. Joseph Campbell emphasizes this point; he explains, "We are all manifestations of Buddha consciousness, or Christ consciousness, only we don't know it. The word Buddha means 'the one who is waked up.' We are all to do that, to wake up to the Christ or Buddha consciousness within us."[3]

Observing the life of Jesus as presented in the Bible, it is Jesus himself who presents us with insight about what it means to reach God-consciousness, especially when he talked about himself. In his personal growth and evolvement, Jesus realized that the Father was within him and he wanted each individual to follow him in this regard as set forth by his example. In Scripture, Jesus expresses, "You call me Teacher and Lord—and you are right, for that is what I am. So, if I, your Lord and Teacher, have washed your feet, you also ought to wash one another's feet. For I have set you an example that you should also do as I have done to you" (John 13:13–15). Jesus reached a full level of God-consciousness within himself, and I have come to believe that he wanted us to wake up to the notion that we are to follow him and do the same.

I do not know if I will ever reach the full level of God-consciousness. I think that is relegated to a special few, those who are living their lives on a different level than I am living. For me, it almost does not matter, for I am so much enjoying the searching and reaching the new levels of belief evolving brings me to. I relate well to the words of Jay Parina when he explains, "I emphasize throughout what I call the *gradually realizing kingdom of God*—a process of transformation, like that of an underdeveloped photograph dipped in chemicals. The process itself adds detail and depth to the image, which grows more distinct and plausible by the moment."[4] Moving away from personal condemnation of who I think I should be to a place of wondering who I am and who I am becoming is so much more of a pleasant and richer way of living. Moving away from a punitive God to a God that wants me to discover him by being personally transformed is so much more of a positive and encouraging choice. Marcus Borg seemed to have a similar experience when he reflected on his own personal growth. He explains, "I realized that God does not refer to a supernatural being out there (which is where I had put God ever since my childhood musings about God up in heaven). I began to see the word God refers to the sacred at the center of existence, the holy mystery that is all around us and within us."[5]

To achieve what Marcus Borg has achieved, I know I must get beyond what authorities say are the truths necessary for faith to a faith that is more involved in having a relationship with Our Lord. Following Jesus's life, it is not that difficult to recognize how God was the center of his life, while his relationship with the Spirit of God was the source of everything in his life. As Parini explains, "What matters is the way God moved in the life of Jesus, who showed us how to find this spirit within ourselves."[6] This is why one of the most meaningful prayers at Mass in reference to Jesus is stated in the prayer, "Through him, with him, and in him, in the unity of the Holy Spirit, all honor and glory is given to you Holy Father." It is also why I love the quote referenced by Easwaran of a statement made by Saint Augustine, "You were inside, Lord, all the while I was looking in all the wrong places."[7]

As noted in other parts of this book, I often get captivated by simply the title of a book or a movie and then run with it. One such title was a movie I saw long ago entitled *Pieces of a Dream*. My ensuing thoughts had nothing to do with the content of the movie, but I associated it to other spiritual readings and changed the title to *Pieces of God*. When I apply this title to the concept of the Kingdom of God existing in us all, if I cannot fully achieve full God-conscious I can, at the very least, achieve awareness of pieces of this kingdom.

As a result of this thinking, I began to envision that an actual mosaic lives within me; each tile represents a God-like piece of who God is. Each piece represents values and morals I have, over time, made my own and are now a permanent part of who I am. All these pieces, I believe, represent the divine. Elizabeth Johnson explains, "It is not the case that divine nearness is checkered, close to some, far from others. Rather, with loving generosity holy mystery graciously offers the gift of divine life to everyone, everywhere, and at all times."[8]

The more and more I contemplated the spiritual path I must take, the more I realized that it must start from within. I must rethink the profound notion that we all are made according to the image and likeness of God, an idea in my earlier years I ignored or never took seriously due to some form of self-loathing. Early on in my spiritual education, I was instructed to believe that I was some kind of sinner and when left on my own was basically inept. Heavy emphasis was also placed on the potential for me to being corrupt and immoral, unless I was extremely careful and followed the rules put forth. I even had the thoughts and actions to confirm my sense of self, which were only relieved, and supposedly erased, by weekly confessions. This perspective was engrained as early as seven years old as I prepared, in trepidation, for my first confession. It continued throughout my teenage years as I was unrelenting in search for how bad I was during any given week. The underlying fear was not being in God's good graces. As I was to learn, the Buddhist approach to spirituality was closer to the truth. For the practicing Buddhist, their Nirvana was more a state of mind, not a place somewhere like heaven. As Joseph Campbell explains, their heaven "is right here, in the midst of the turmoil of life. It is the state you find when you are no longer driven by compelling desires, fears, and social commitments, when you have found your center of freedom and can act by choice out of that."[9]

Most thankfully, through the process of psychologically and spiritually evolving, and through regular acts of nourishment, I reached a totally different level of thought. It is not a place, most certainly, where I believe I am incapable of sinning, but more to a place where that is not what is emphasized or is my primary focus. It has been replaced by the profound viewpoint that the Kingdom of God is within us all. Joseph Langford emphasizes this new perspective when he explains, "Despite what our failures and inadequacies may suggest, our God-given dignity is *innate* and cannot be lost, neither at our own hand, nor taken away by society, nor by abuse of others, for it is immutable."[10] I need to constantly remind myself that when I do feel extreme tension or do experience a sense of falling apart it is only because I have moved away from the center within me.

I came to believe we are all born as children of God yet over time were misled by religions and the effects of socialization. Religions would like us to believe we are born in sin and then, more than just by coincidence, they created the need for their existence by having us believe they are the only means to salvation. Society sends us the message that we are only a good person if we have achieved fame or fortune. Both forms of these organizational pulls are a manipulation of the worst kind; it emphasizes achievement from the outside in. I came to wonder how these organizations, religious and societal, would respond to the notion that the Kingdom of God is found within not from without. How would they defend themselves if they read the words of Marcus Borg when he explains the Kingdom of God as "what life would be like on earth if God were king and the rulers of the world were not. The Kingdom of God is about God's justice in contrast to the systematic injustice of the kingdoms and dominations of this world."[11]

I like to envision the Kingdom of God within me as my personal mosaic. A mosaic, I believe, that exists in all of us. I am fully aware that I am more than likely never to achieve or discover this full mosaic. I do believe, however, that God has given me the grace to recognize one piece at a time, as long as I am looking for it. It is similar to what I often tell my clients. Psychologically, we all are like a thousand-piece puzzle. Formal therapy or even a lifetime of self-reflection will never achieve a full picture of our personal puzzle. What therapy did for me was to give me a good start, along with the tools to continue the discovery of my personal puzzle. Once formal therapy was done, it was my responsibility to continue the process of discovering who I truly am. I view spiritual introspection to be a similar process. Through both formal and informal spiritual education, I have been given the tools to discover the Kingdom of God within me: my mosaic. Joseph Langford emphasizes this point when he explains, "We are never more authentically human, never more living in our dignity as temples of the Almighty, then when communicating with the God within. This conviction, this awareness of God's indwelling is the starting point for prayer."[12]

In his biographical story of Mother Teresa's life, Langford painted a beautiful picture of how one person, albeit one incredibly special person, was able to live out her life in the discovery of her own inner mosaic. Langford, reflecting on the day-to-day life of Mother Teresa, explains, "She went about mirroring the light she carried within. In pondering this mosaic of light, reflected in the various qualities and aspects of her own life, we can come closer to beholding the light and love of her inner fire."[13]

This image of Mother Teresa's spiritual mind-set reminded me of the novel *All the Light We Cannot See*, written by Anthony Doerr.[14] The story centered on the lives of two children: one blind girl and a German boy who was part of the Hitler youth. The young girl, even though blind, was able to grow in wisdom and insight in spite of her incapacity to actually see the activities and events around her. The author pondered such an achievement by marveling how her brain, which was without a spark of light, could build for her a world of light—all the light she could not see. So it was so for Mother Teresa. As Langford so accurately pointed out, even though her outside world was so often darkened by sickness, despair, and tragedy, Teresa was able to carve out an intrinsic mind-set that was totally different. Langford explained, "Faith became a way of seeing in the dark, of seeing a divine reality ever present and unchangeable, though beyond the grasp of the senses."[15]

The author Yogananda continues with this manner of thinking when he states, "The land of healing lies within, radiant with the happiness that is blindly sought in a thousand outer directions."[16] This manner of thinking, along with numerous other wake-up calls, changed my spiritual world and the manner in which I was trying to create it. I too was seeking truths, for the most part, in all the wrong places. When I was younger, a great deal of my faith was based on the fear of possibly going to hell and the dire need of wanting to get to heaven. This reversal in thinking did not mean I had to give up being a Christian, or even my Catholic participation. I relate to the story told by Marcus Borg of the Christian who asked the Dalai Lama whether she needed to become a Buddhist. He simply yet definitively responded to just go deeper in the faith you are living. Borg advises, to which I agree, that he personally chose as a Christian to live more deeply in his own tradition. He uses the metaphor of digging a well: "If what you are looking for is water, better to dig one well sixty feet deep than to dig six wells ten feet deep."[17] Changing my way of thinking and the manner I was trying to be more faithful gave me a chance to go deeper in my own faith, especially in hearing the messages of Jesus from a totally different perspective.

As I learned over time, I needed to stop allowing the formal church and its teachers to determine whether I was worthy or not; I was already one of God's chosen ones, as we all are. By confining myself to the influences of my outer world, I was being suffocated by an order that accepted or rejected me according to its own agenda and whim. When I was young, I was too blind and indoctrinated to read with understanding the Scriptural passage, "Behold, what manner of love the Father has bestowed upon us, that we shall be called the sons of God" (1 John 3:1). Prior to this change of heart and spiritual perspective I was more living my life trying to earn or prove that I deserved to be loved. Discovering my own inner mosaic, those pieces of God within me, has brought me to a place where I can believe in the words of Henri Nouwen when he states, "Life is a God-given opportunity to become who we are, to affirm our own true spiritual nature, claim our truth, appropriate and integrate the reality of our being, but, most of all, to say Yes to the One who calls us Beloved."[18]

The two primary essentials for me has been first to recognize the existence of an intrinsic mosaic within me and the worthiness of each and every piece. Secondly, to know that I must always be active in the process of becoming more, adding more pieces of Godly awareness. This must be the spiritual handle I must continuously grip as I do my best in responding to the daily challenges of life. Stated simply in one

Scriptural passage, "And God saw everything he made, and behold, it was very good" (Genesis 1). I need to believe that I am truly part of this profound creation, along with all my brothers and sisters. The bottom line for me regarding my intrinsic mosaic is found in the words of Joseph Campbell as he explains, "When you know this, then you have identified with the creative principle, which is the God power in the world, which means in you. It is beautiful."[19]

There is no question. It is a beautiful way to envision the entire notion of spirituality. As Marcus Borg states, "We are in God, we live in God, we move and have our being in God. God is a non-material layer of reality all around us, right here and more than right here."[20] Once I owned this very notion, spirituality moved from a place of negative thinking and worry to a positive and reassuring way to live. It is a view that I am part of God's creation and that through this very fact God not only lives within me but also with every human I interact with on a daily basis. Joseph Campbell witnesses this when he observes the behavior of many groups in India. He saw that when they greeted each other they often held out their palms together as if they were in prayer. Campbell explains, "It is a greeting which says that the god that is in you recognizes the god in the other. These people are aware of the divine presence in all things."[21]

This form of greeting I often reference with the reception of communion at Mass, an activity I have often participated in with many members of my community. As a child, I was taught that this was the actual body and blood of Christ. Whether I accept this notion today is secondary to me, for even if it is a symbol or to be taken as a metaphor, it remains to be a real opportunity to turn inward and to realize that Jesus Christ lives actively within me. It also is an opportunity to be keenly aware that it is the same experience for each member of my community. As with the beautiful greeting the Buddhist gives to his visitor, it is an opportunity, through the actual reception of bread, that we must be bread for each other.

It is also a reminder for me of how I live in a country that blatantly and even boastfully contradicts this message. The inane fighting over immigration and the obsessive need for so many to reject entire groups of people based simply on how they seem from the outside, or the judgments made on the religion they practice. All forms of racism are still thriving is not only an inherent social flaw, but a spiritual one as well. These mindless movements are a sign of inner individual fear; it is so far from the notion that we all are instruments of the Divine. I only need to be reminded of the profound Scriptural story of the fishes and loaves. As a metaphor, the message is clear. Jesus, the bread of life, is there for us all, not just a self-appointed chosen few. Referring to the miracle of loaves, Henri Nouwen expresses the Christian concept of genuine interest in all mankind; he explains, "How different our life would be if we could but believe that every little act of faithfulness, every gesture of love, every little bit of joy and peace will multiply and multiply as long as there are people to receive it...and that—even then—there will be leftovers!"[22]

I came to believe that the expungement of the evils of racism can only be achieved with the recognition we all are children of God. To lift the veil of hatred I need to realize that salvation is not just personal, it is also social. Marcus Borg explains, "Salvation is about life together. Salvation is about peace and justice within community and beyond community."[23] This starts with the acknowledgment of our inner mosaic, our unique and priceless stones, which is part of all human existence. Once again, we only have to turn to Mother Teresa as a model who truly believed, as Langford reflects, "We are all called and equipped by God not only to survive our personal Calcutta, but to serve there—to contribute to those around us whose individual Calcuttas intersect our own."[24]

As I am getting older and can no longer deny that I am on the other side of the mountain, I think more of death than I ever have before. Not that I am some kind of hero, certainly far from it; the fears I had when younger have faded, or certainly have lessened. This is totally due to the reality, acquired with the help of many great people, that my faith perspective has completely changed. For years, I chased after objects of desire that I thought would soothe me, even save me. None of them attained the end I was searching for. For this failure, I am thankful; it forced me to search in another direction. From my deeply seeded needs and yearnings, always vibrantly alive but never satisfied, also allowed me to turn, faintly at times, to a new image I had of God. I truly believe that by understanding the messages of Jesus in a different light, I changed also the image I had of God. This new image of God then ultimately led to changing the image I had of myself. The Pulitzer Prize winner, Ernest Becker, states, "Once a person begins to look into his relationship to the Ultimate Power, to infinitude, and to refashion his links from those around him to that Ultimate Power, he opens up to himself the horizon of unlimited possibility, or real freedom."[25]

It all comes down to my personal mosaic, which ultimately and most definitively is the presence of God within me. Tempted throughout my life in so many other directions, I have realized that striving to a higher level of God-consciousness is the ultimate purpose of life, not just for me but for all of us. I certainly want to live a number of more years, but the terror of dying no longer exists as it once did. I believe that by knowing my inner life, the vibrant life of my mosaic, and knowing of its existence, I have few regrets. Aging is never easy, but I turn to the wisdom presented by Joseph Campbell when he expresses the challenge aging presents. He states, "When the body has reached its climax of power and begins to decline, is to identify yourself not with the body, but with the consciousness of which it is a vehicle. Am I the bulb that carries the light, or am I the light of which the bulb is a vehicle?"[26]

I believe, it is the light within—my mosaic—that will never go out. To all those who took the time to read my personal journey from religion to spirituality—thank you. I greet you with my hands folded, as if in prayer, recognizing your divinity. Know this: your personal mosaic is your eternal flame.

PEACE PRAYER OF SAINT FRANCIS

Lord, make me an instrument of your peace:
where there is hatred, let be sow love;
where there is injury, pardon;
where there is doubt, faith;
where there is despair, hope;
where there is darkness, light;
where there is sadness, joy.
O divine Master, grant that I may not so much seek
to be consoled as to console,
to be understood as to understand,
to be loved as to love.
For it is in giving that we receive,
it is in pardoning that we are pardoned,
and it is in dying that we are born to eternal life.
Amen.

NOTES

Front Page
[1] Mosaic Cross by Kate Sutcliff Katesutcliffmosaic).

Prologue
[1] Mary Karr, *The Art of the Memoir* (New York: HarperCollins Publishers, 2015), 127.
[2] Thomas Moore, *A Religion of One's Own* (New York: Penguin Books, 2014), 4.

Part 1
Chapter 4
[1] Maya Angelou, *I Know Why the Caged Bird Sings* (New York: Ballantine Books, 1997).

Chapter 8
[1] Graham Greene, *The Power and the Glory* (New York: Penguin Books, 2003), 92.

Part 2
Chapter 12
[1] Victor Frankl, *Man's Search for Meaning* (New York: Beacon Press, 2006).

Chapter 13
[1] Matthew Fox, "The Mystic," *The Sun*, July 20, 2015: Issue 475 (Chapel Hill, NC: The Sun Publishing Company), 6.
[2] Scott Peck, *The Road Less Traveled and Beyond* (New York: Simon and Shuster, 1997), 46.
[3] Gary Wills, *Why Priests* (New York: Penguin Books, 2013), 17.
[4] Joseph Langford, *Mother Teresa's Secret Fire* (Huntington, IN: Our Sunday Visitor Publishing, 2008) 110.
[5] Ibid., 110.
[6] Hans Kung, *The Church* (New York: Image Books, 1976).

[7] Andrew Greeley, "The Catholic Priest in the United States: Sociological Investigations," *The National Opinion Research Center Study* (Washington DC: United States Catholic Conference, 1963), 133.

[8] Robert Merton, *Social Theory and Social Structure* (New York: The Free Press, 1957), 196.

[9] Philip Yancey, *The Jesus I Never Knew* (Michigan: Zondervan, 1995), 78.

[10] Walter Abbott, ed., *The Documents of Vatican II* (New York: The American Press, 1966), 40.

[11] Ibid., 40.

[12] Thomas Moore, *A Religion of One's Own*, 125-126.

[13]

[14]

[15] Robert Presthus, *The Organizational Society* (New York: Random House, 1962), 31.

[16] Robert Merton, *Social Theory and Social Structure*, 345.

[17] Ibid., 201.

[18] Ross Douthat, "Week in Review," (New York Times: April 10, 2016), 9.

[19] Elizabeth Johnson, *Quest for a Living God* (New York: Continuum International Publishing Group, 2007), 23.

Chapter 14

[1] Thomas Moore, *Care of the Soul* (New York: HarperCollins Publisher, 1962), 239.

[2] Jay Parini, *Jesus, The Human Face of God* (New York: Houghton Mifflin Harcourt Publishing, 2013), 5.

[3] Elizabeth Johnson, *Quest for a Living God*, 98.

[4] Ibid., 99.

[5] Philip Yancey, *The Jesus I Never Knew*, 156.

[6] Graham Greene, *The Power and the Glory*, 219.

[7] Thomas Moore, *Care of the Soul*, 172.

[8] Jay Parini, *The Human Face of God*, xii.

[9] Ibid., xii.

[10] Ibid., 20.

[11] Elizabeth Johnson, *Quest for a Living God*, 182.

[12] Gary Wills, *Why Priests*, 7.

[13] Jay Parini, *The Human Face of God*, 152.

[14] Gary Wills, *Why Priests*, 9.

[15] Elizabeth Johnson, *Quest for a Living God*, 36.

[16] Ibid., 23.

[17] Scott Peck, *The Road Less Traveled and Beyond*, 23.

[18] Ibid., 23.

[19] Thomas Moore, *Care of the Soul*, 8.

[20] Marcus Borg, *The Heart of Christianity* (New York: HarperCollins Publishers, 2004), 32-33.

[21] Ibid., 32.

[22] Paramahansa Yogananda, *The Auto Biography of a Yogi* (California: Self-Realization Fellowship, 1974) 370.

[23] Thomas Moore, *A Religion of One's Own*, 21.

[24] Elizabeth Johnson, *Quest for a Living God*, 163.

[25] Thomas Moore, *A Religion of One's Own*, 31.

[26] Elizabeth Kubla-Ross, *On Death and Dying* (New York: Scribner, 1969).

[27] Thomas Moore, *A Religion of One's Own*, 31.

[28] Ibid., 12.

[29] Matthew Fox, *The Sun*, 12.

[30] Jay Parini, *The Human Face of God*, 49.

[31] Elizabeth Johnson, *Quest for the Living God*, 91.

[32] Thomas Moore, *A Religion of One's Own*, 31.

[33] Marcus Borg, *The Heart of Christianity*, 77.

[34] Marcus Borg, *Meeting Jesus Again for the First Time* (New York: HarperCollins Publishing, 1994), 125.

[35] Elizabeth Johnson, *Quest for the Living God*, 4.

Chapter 15

[1] Thomas Moore, *A Religion of One's Own*, 90.

[2] Paramagansa Yogananda, *Autobiography of a Yogi*, 355.

[3] Deepak Chopra, *The Third Jesus* (New York: Random House, 2008), 169.

[4] Elizabeth Johnson, *Quest for a Living God*, 45.

[5] Eknath Easwaran, *Seeing with the Eyes of Love* (California: Nilgri Press, 1966), 155.

[6] Scott Peck, *The Road Less Traveled* (New York: Touchstone, 1978), 194.

[7] Heinz and Rowena Ansbacher, *The Individual Psychology of Alfred Adler* (New York: Harper Torchbooks, 1956), 155.

[8] Karen Horney, *Neurosis and Human Growth* (New York: W.W. Norton and Company, 1950), 348.

[9] Paramahansa Yogananda, *The Autobiography of a Yogi*, 49.

[10] Deepak Chopra, *The Shadow Effect* (New York: HarperCollins Publishers, 2010), 34.

[11] Paramahansa Yogananda, *The Autobiography of a Yogi*, 66.

[12] Marcus Borg, *The Heart of Christianity*, 140.

[13] Paramahansa Yogananda, *The Autobiography of a Yogi*, 167.

[14] Deepak Chopra, *The Shadow Effect*, 9.

[15] Debbie Ford, *The Shadow Effect* (New York: HarperCollins Publishers, 2010), 1.

[16] Ibid., 2.

[17] Marcus Borg, *The Heart of Christianity*, 116.

[18] Henri Nouwen, *Life of the Beloved* (New York: The Crossroad Publishing Company, 1992), 31.

[19] Ibid., 33.

[20] Scott Peck, *The Road Less Traveled and Beyond*, 144.

[21] Henri Nouwen, *Life of the Beloved*, 33.

[22] Thomas Moore, *Care of the Soul*, 50.

[23] Joseph Langford, *Mother Teresa's Secret Fire*, 251.

[24] Henri Nouwen, *Life of the Beloved*, 34.

[25] Eknath Easawan, *Seeing with the Eyes of Love*, 30.

[26] Scott Peck, *The Road Less Traveled*, 98.

[27] Ibid., 98.

[28] Henri Nouwen, *Life of the Beloved*, 44.

[29] Albert Ellis, *Overcoming Destructive Beliefs, Feelings and Behavior* (New York: Prometheus Books, 2001).

[30] Eknath Easawan, *Seeing with the Eyes of Love*, 56.

[31] Heinz and Rowena Ansbacher, *The Individual Psychology of Alfred Adler*, 182.

[32] Eknath Easawan, *Seeing with the Eyes of Love*, 57.

[33] Thomas Moore, *A Religion of One's Own*, 207.

[34] Eknath Easawan, *Seeing with the Eyes of Love*, 108.

[35] Ibid., 108.

Chapter 16

[1] Henri Nouwen, *Life of the Beloved*, 32.

[2] Joseph Langford, *Mother Teresa's Secret Fire*, 228.

[3] Scott Peck, *The Road Less Traveled*, 243.

[4] Thomas Moore, *Care of the Soul*, 2.

[5] Ibid., 2.

[6] Marcus Borg, *The Heart of Christianity*, 195.

[7] Oriah Mountain Dreamer, *The Invitation* London: HarperCollins Publishers, 1999), 120.

[8] Joseph Langford, *Mother Teresa's Secret Fire*, 190.

[9] Deepak Chopra, *The Third Jesus*, 21.

[10] Matthew 5:12.

[11] Joseph Campbell, *The Power of Myth* (New York: Doubleday, 1988), 92.

[12] Neale Donald Walsch, *Conversations with God: Book 1* (New York: Penquin Books, 1996), 44.

Chapter 17

[1] Eknath Easawan, *Seeing with the Eyes of Love*, 14.

[2] Ibid., 153.

[3] Ernest Becker, *The Denial of Death* (New York: The Free Press, 1995), 261.

[4] Oriah Mountain Dreamer, *The Invitation*, 75.

[5] Jay Parini, *Jesus The Human Face of God*, 2.

6   Marcus Borg, *Meeting Jesus Again for the First Time*, 27.
7   Ibid., 27.
8   Jay Parini, *Jesus the Human Face of God*, 31.
9   Marcus Borg, *Meeting Jesus Again for the First Time*, 27.
10 Ibid., 27.
11 Deepak Chopra, *The Third Jesus*, 25.
12 Abraham Malow, *Motivation and Personality* (New York: Harper and Brothers, 1954).
13 Paramahansa Yogananda, *The Autobiography of a Yogi*, 262.
14 Joseph Campbell, *The Power of Myth*.
15 Paramahansa Yogananda, *The Autobiography of a Yogi*.
16 Jay Parini, *Jesus The Human Face of God*, 50.
17 Marcus Borg, *Meeting Jesus Again for the First Time*, 39.
18 Ibid., 9.
19 Mathew Kelly, *Rediscover Jesus* (Kentucky: Beacon Publishing, 2015), 50.
20 Marcus Borg, *Meeting Jesus Again for the First Time*, 123-124.
21 Joseph Campbell, *The Power of Myth*, 209.
22 Marcus Borg, *The Heart of Christianity*, 118.
23 Deepak Chopra, *The Third Jesus*, 43.
24 Philip Yancey, *The Jesus I Never Knew*, 98.
25 Joseph Campbell, *The Power of Myth*, 124.
26 Elizabeth Johnson, *Quest for the Living God*, 34.
27 Joseph Langford, *Mother Teresa's Secret Fire*, 142.
28 Ibid., 142.
29 Deepak Chopra, *The Third Jesus*, 78.

Chapter 18
1   Deepak Chopra, *The Third Jesus*, 40.
2   Ibid., 44.
3   Joseph Campbell, *The Power of Myth*, 57.
4   Jay Parini, *Jesus The Human Face of God*, ix.
5   Marcus Borg, *Meeting Jesus Again for the First Time*, 14.
6   Jay Parini, *Jesus The Human Face of God*, xix.
7   Eknath Easawan, *Seeing with the Eyes of Love*, 192.
8   Elizabeth Johnson, *Quest for the Living God*, 44.
9   Joseph Langford, *Mother Teresa's Secret Fire*, 121.
10 Joseph Campbell, *The Power of Myth*, 161.
11 Marcus Borg, *The Heart of Christianity*, 132-133.
12 Joseph Langford, *Mother Teresa's Secret Fire*, 179.
13 Ibid., 87–88.
14 Anthony Doerr, *All the Light We Cannot See* (New York: Scribner, 2010).
15 Joseph Langford, *Mother Teresa's Secret Fire*, 77.
16 Paramahansa Yogananda, *The Autobiography of a Yogi*, 143.

17 Marcus Borg, *The Heart of Christianity*, 233.
18 Henri Nouwen, *Life of the Beloved*, 133.
19 Joseph Campbell, *The Power of Myth*, 45.
20 Marcus Borg, *The Heart of Christianity*, 155.
21 Joseph Campbell, *The Power of Myth*, 53.
22 Henri Nouwen, *Life of the Beloved*, 123.
23 Marcus Borg, *The Heart of Christianity*, 178.
24 Joseph Langford, *Mother Teresa's Secret Fire* 71.
25 Ernest Becker, *The Denial of Death*, 90.
26 Joseph Campbell, *The Power of Myth*, 70.

ABOUT THE AUTHOR

DR. WILLIAM E. WARD, a licensed psychologist in private practice, specializes in individual, marital and family therapy. He has been a professor and counselor at Ramapo College, New Jersey and a consultant for the United Nations in New York City. Dr. Ward holds an MA from Seton Hall University and an Ed.D. from Rutgers University. He trained in psychotherapy at the Alfred Adler Institute in New York City. He attended, for four years, the Immaculate Conception Seminary, studying philosophy and theology courses. He is the author of The Good Enough Spouse: Resolve or Dissolve a Conflicted Marriage and a pending book, The Upside of Being Down. Dr. Ward is the father of four children and resides in Spring Lake Heights, NJ.

CPSIA information can be obtained
at www.ICGtesting.com
Printed in the USA
LVHW071925010719
622842LV00011B/273/P